DATE DUE

APR 0 9 2007

The Poetic Voices of COLERIDGE

THE POETIC VOICES OF
COLERIDGE

A Study of His Desire for Spontaneity and Passion for Order

MAX F. SCHULZ   University of Southern California

DETROIT 1964, WAYNE STATE UNIVERSITY PRESS

COPYRIGHT © 1963 BY WAYNE STATE UNIVERSITY PRESS

DETROIT, MICHIGAN 48202   ALL RIGHTS RESERVED

PUBLISHED SIMULTANEOUSLY IN CANADA BY AMBASSADOR BOOKS, LIMITED

TORONTO, ONTARIO, CANADA

LIBRARY OF CONGRESS CATALOG CARD NUMBER 62–16347

SECOND REVISED EDITION, DECEMBER 1964

The Press gratefully acknowledges the assistance of the Ford Foundation in the publication of this book

FOR MURIEL

CONTENTS

PREFACE 1

Chapter

I INTRODUCTION 5

II THE FARRAGO VOICE 11

III THE PROPHECY VOICE 27

IV THE VENTRILOQUISM VOICE 51

V THE CONVERSATION VOICE 73

VI THE DREAM VOICE 101

VII THE CONFESSION VOICE 131

VIII THE IMPROVISATION VOICE 153

IX THE SONG VOICE 171

X CONCLUSION 183

Appendix

I A SUBSPECIES OF THE FARRAGO POEM 197

II THE CONCLUSION TO "DEJECTION" 201

III GLYCINE'S SONG AND "HERBSTLIED" 207

TEXT REFERENCES 211

NOTES 213

PREFACE

Interest in Coleridge's poetry has increased considerably in recent years. The long critical neglect of his verse, brought on I suspect by the wrong turn Coleridgean studies took after John Livingston Lowes' remarkable book, seems to have ended. The new books, however, either concentrate on a single poem or, at most, on two or three, or approach all the poems from a restricted point of view such as politics. Since the last survey of the whole of Coleridge's poetic achievement occurred as long ago as the nineteenth century, a re-examination is long overdue. My study attempts to point out the direction that such a re-examination might profitably take, by analyzing the inventiveness with which Coleridge tackled the perennial problem of how to retain the spontaneity of the original experience while giving it the poetic order and form which would make that experience communicable.

I cannot recall exactly when this book took its present shape, principally, I suppose, because little of it sprang into being full-born. Its gestation was slow (and laborious), the cumulative growth as imperceptible as "fruit ripening in stillness." I remember, however, my surprise the first time I opened Ernest Hartley Coleridge's edition of his grandfather's poetical works to find that Coleridge was the author of more than "The Ancient Mariner," "Kubla Khan," and "Christabel." The revelation that he had written other poems, both good and indifferent, in a variety of daringly innovative as well as historically traditional styles, grew as I read through Ernest Hartley Coleridge's two volumes. My book, which attempts to correct the prevailing misconception that Coleridge is a narrow poet of several inexplicable successes, undoubtedly dates from my first reading of these volumes.

I also remember how struck I was, at an early stage in my study, by Coleridge's continual struggle to reproduce in his verse the natural ca-

I

dences of speech. Nor has my subsequent reading altered my belief that his poetry is an analog of his brilliant colloquial powers, that his favorite and most successful method of communication was in a sense simply elevated to esthetic form. Hence the title and my treatment of the kinds of poetry he wrote as modes of speech.

I have reluctantly kept my comments about Coleridge's life to a minimum, restricting myself to the biographical material which bears directly on the poems. Biographies of Coleridge are not wanting, for he has a perennial fascination for us; and the reader interested in this side of him can go to them. I do believe, however, that the wealth of new material recently made available, with more to come, calls for a re-examination of our accepted ideas about him, particularly about the transitional years 1800 to 1810, but this is a subject for a future study, on which I am now at work.

It is a pleasure to acknowledge the generous assistance I have had from both friends and strangers, especially from my former colleagues at Tulane University, Professor Richard Harter Fogle, whose knowledge of Coleridge was available to me at all times, and Professor Floyd Mc-Allister, who read each chapter and gave unstintingly of his advice on matters of style and content; from my former associates at Wayne State University, particularly Professors Robert F. Gleckner, Leslie L. Hanawalt, and A. Dayle Wallace, who read the book at varying stages of its development and offered many valuable suggestions and, equally important, much encouragement; from Miss Kathleen Coburn of Victoria College, and Mr. Donald W. Krummel of the Newberry Library, who verified for me items in the Coleridge canon; from Mrs. Robert C. Whittemore and Miss Betty Ann Mailhes, the reference librarians of the Howard-Tilton Memorial Library at Tulane University, and Miss Catherine Nelson of the Edwin Watts Chubb Library at Ohio University, who were forever getting me needed books; from Mrs. Sarah Kost, secretary of the English Department at Tulane University, who uncomplainingly typed the entire manuscript twice and with rare good humor retyped many pages a third and fourth time when my errant pen spoiled them with new revisions; and from Professor Alexander Brede, whose careful editing of the final manuscript for Wayne State University Press benefited it considerably.

I also wish to thank the Tulane University Council on Research for a grant during the summer of 1959 to work on the book.

My debt to both the old and the new waves of Coleridgeans is great.

To name them all would unfortunately produce a list longer than the Homeric roll-call of captains in the Greek army; so I must content myself with this general acknowledgment.

The last and greatest obligation I owe to my wife, who for years has heard me out on the subject of Coleridge with patience, interest, and even enthusiasm.

Portions of this book have appeared elsewhere, which I have been generously granted permission to reprint: several pages of Chapter VI, in another context, in *Tulane Studies in English,* IX (1959); and Chapter VIII, with some differences, in *Tulane Studies in English,* X (1960).

I am grateful to The Macmillan Company for permission to reprint six lines from William Butler Yeats' "Adam's Curse," which appeared in *Collected Poems,* 1949, and to A. D. Peters and Jonathan Cape Limited for permission to use C. Day Lewis' "A Carol," which appeared in *Collected Poems,* published by Jonathan Cape Limited, London, in 1954.

I should add a word about my documentation. To obviate extensive footnoting, I have used two methods. I refer to the standard editions of Coleridge's writings and to the most frequently cited secondary works by abbreviations in parentheses immediately after the quotation or citation. The abbreviations are amplified under the heading "Text References." All other sources are given in notes, in the usual manner, at the end of the book.

I have handled the mechanics of the quotations from Coleridge and others in two ways: in long passages I have kept the original capitalization, spelling, and punctuation, except for minor changes. Where their quaint caps and dots and dashes and spelling were likely to distract the reader, as in brief quotations or in quotations within my own sentences, I have normalized according to the usual modern style.

M. F. S.

Of criticism we may perhaps say that those divine poets, Homer, Aeschylus, and the two compeers, Dante, Shakespeare, Spenser, Milton, who deserve to have Critics, Κριταί, are placed above criticism in the vulgar sense, and move in the sphere of religion, while those who are not such scarcely deserve criticism in any sense. But speaking generally, it is far, far better to distinguish poetry into different classes; and, instead of fault-finding, to say this belongs to such or such a class—thus voting inferiority in the *sort* rather than censure on the particular poem or poet. We may *outgrow* certain *sorts* of poetry (Young's *Night-thoughts,* for instance) without arraigning their excellence *proprio genere*. In short, the wise is the genial; and the genial judgment is to distinguish accurately the character and characteristics of each poem, praising them according to their force and vivacity in their own kind—and to reserve reprehension for such as have no *character*—tho' the wisest reprehension would be not to speak of them at all.

—Marginalia in the flyleaves of Milton's
Poems Upon Several Occasions (London, 1791)

I

INTRODUCTION

*T*o suggest that Coleridge's poems are carefully wrought artifacts is still viewed in some quarters as presumptive. For over a century the tradition has been that they defy analysis because the best of them are enchanted records of unearthly realms peopled by Mongol warriors, old navigators, albatrosses, and Lamia witch-women, and the rest are artless cast-offs of a dreaming mind. Although this view has its roots in Victorian soil, most of its current foliage stems from Lowes' influential book, *The Road to Xanadu*. If we cannot "explain" a work of pure imagination, he suggests, perhaps we can describe how it comes into being and thus plumb a little the ultimately fathomless depths of its magic. Accordingly, he uses Coleridge's description of the imagination—"the true inward creatrix, [which] instantly out of the chaos of elements or shattered fragments of memory, puts together some form to fit it" (*AP,* p. 244)—as a key to the mysterious creative process which produced "The Ancient Mariner" and "Kubla Khan." The imaginative results (I use the term respectfully in the Coleridgean sense) of his scholarship cast a charmed shadow over our conception of Coleridge the poet in much the same way that the slack sails of the ancient mariner's ship throw a horror-tinted shade over his vision of the water snakes swimming in its becalmed shadow. His success in ferreting out the disparate origins of the images which form the matrix of these two poems—origins to be found primarily in Coleridge's reading in esoteric books and only infrequently in his daily experience—is like a siren's song in the ears of countless readers, luring them into the shallow waters of source hunting with the notion that the meaning of the poem lies in that direction. Nor is Lowes entirely immune from this hysteria. Although he occasionally reminds us that artistry had some hand in the final shaping of "The Ancient Mariner," when he confronts the miracle of "Kubla Khan" he disregards his own note of sanity, kneels, and praises the purity of its fusion of disparate ingredients, free of the stain of "content" and conscious craftsmanship. And his many disciples for a generation now have likewise abandoned common-sense and propriety in their headlong enthusiasm to follow the seductive trail leading from Coleridge's reading to his poems. Thus, Lowes' leviathan has spawned innumerable notes purporting to trace to its true source the "sacred river" of Coleridge's mind in its creative journey from the twilight realms of consciousness to the "romantic chasm" of poetic accomplishment.

The traffic along the byways of Coleridge's reading has consequently left the high road of his poetry relatively untraveled. The poems (except for the great triumvirate of "The Ancient Mariner," "Kubla Khan," and "Christabel") remain largely unexplored, and, like darkest Africa, shrouded in myths and taboos. The most persistent of these misconceptions, curiously, considering the admiration felt by this century for the catholicity and methodology of his thought, is that Coleridge is a poet limited to several unique visions rather than a versatile, self-critical artist learning from his predecessors and his own errors. As recently as 1940, Richard W. Armour and Raymond F. Howes, the editors of *Coleridge the Talker,* could say about him: "The careful reader of his poems quickly discovers that in general he tended, as in his prose, to be subjective and rambling rather than objective and methodical, and that much of his verse, even excluding the impromptu doggerel, lacks the touch of conscious artistry."[1]

A few critics are beginning to question this counterfeit portrait which has passed as currency for so long. R. C. Bald argued in 1940 that "Coleridge's reading was deliberately planned to store up in his mind materials that could be used in his poetry and that the conscious element in the composition of *The Ancient Mariner* must therefore be stressed more than it has been" (Bald, pp. 1-2). Humphry House in 1951 pleaded the case of Coleridge as a poet who selected appropriate poetic styles for expressing his different topics; who composed political odes in the manner of Gray/Mason, blank verse meditations à la Cowper, and ballad narratives after the fashion of folk-poems; whose poetic efforts thus embraced a variety of genres (House, pp. 70-86). Elisabeth Schneider in 1953 presented in *Coleridge, Opium, and Kubla Khan* a brief for "Kubla Khan," in which she suggests that Coleridge originally planned to write an oriental tale. Others more recently have followed the lead of Robert Penn Warren in his widely-known reading of "The Ancient Mariner" and assumed that Coleridge's poems—in this case the conversation poems—have a content and form which are analyzable.[2] And in 1957, as if designed to corroborate the new portrait of Coleridge as a self-conscious writer, was published the first volume of Kathleen Coburn's edition of the notebooks. The notations of ideas and images for future poems recorded in them reveal a mind knowing where it is going and moving purposefully toward that goal.

My contention is that Coleridge's poems are the work of an artist seeking definite ends, and that they are not an unvarying product of a "manual somnambulism"[3]—although Coleridge sometimes liked to pretend that they were—but richly varied artifacts. Viewed against the background of late eighteenth-century efforts to return poetry to a natural diction and form, they exhibit at least seven different resolutions of a major problem in poetry for him: how to give utterance to the unaffected response of his mind and heart so as to retain the original spontaneity of the experience. The problem is one which has plagued poets from Wordsworth to Frost. Yeats defines it in memorable lines in "Adam's Curse":

> We sat together at one summer's end,
> That beautiful mild woman, your close friend,
> And you and I, and talked of poetry.
> I said, 'A line will take us hours maybe;
> Yet if it does not seem a moment's thought,
> Our stitching and unstitching has been naught.'

Like most Romantic poets, Coleridge grapples with this "sullen art," which promises to transform his experience into communicable form but which also forever threatens to reduce the experience to a sequence of labored comments. At first he uses traditional genres, modifying them somewhat to fit his vision. These are his farrago, prophecy, and ventriloquism voices, which utilize respectively the poetic traditions of sensibility, sublimity, and balladry, habits of thought and expression popular with poets from Gray and Collins to Hood and Letitia Elizabeth Landon. Coleridge achieves magnificent results in the latter two voices; yet neither evolves into a style natural to him and his time, which is one of his avowed poetic aims. In the dream, the conversation, the confession, and the improvisation voices, however, he comes close to realizing this ideal of poetry, which he defined in 1812 in an outline for a projected lecture thus: To achieve "the spirit of poetry common to all ages—and to imitate the ancients wisely, we should do as they did, that is, embody that spirit in forms adapted to all the circumstances of time, state of society, &c" (*CL,* III, 419). Still relying initially on established forms, he evolves in these four voices new combinations of naturalness and artistry. Even in the dream voice, where he looks as much to the past as the present, illustrating his belief that poetry is the "recalling of passion in tranquillity" (*N,* I, 787), the poems are so organized as to suggest having been recorded coinstantaneously with the felt experience. In all seven voices, with varying degrees of success, Coleridge realizes "the balance, the perfect reconciliation, effected between [the] two conflicting principles of the *free life* and of the confining *form!*" (*BL,* II, 235). To effect this balance is a concern of all the English Romantic poets, but especially so of Coleridge, for whom a reconciliation of opposites, particularly of nature and art, is a ruling tenet of much of his thought.

I have tried in my discussion of these voices to steer a middle course between grouping the poems chronologically according to date of composition and categorically according to genre. Such a course has both defects and virtues. Besides beginning with relatively unsuccessful poems, it implies a neater sequence of development and autonomy of categories than is actually the case. Coleridge was obviously writing more than one kind of poem at a time. Still, each stage of his development coincides with a different genre sufficiently to warrant such an organization. And the advantages more than offset any distortion which may have occurred. This procedure has allowed me to examine each group of poems as a unique achievement; at the same time it has permitted me, in Keats's words,[4] to go the same steps as the author and thus see each group in relation to the others. Also, such a grouping illustrates how Coleridge, while simultaneously affirming genre and organic theories of literature in his criticism, moves steadily in his practice of poetry from an early reliance on traditional modes of expression toward modifications of them according to the inner demands of the creative experience shaping the poem—an evolution which influenced my decision to substitute for the traditional terms names descriptive of the new organic forms.

One final word. I have attempted no exhaustive treatment of Coleridge's poetry. Taking my cue from his idea of the critic's task, as advocated in the quotation preceding this introduction, I have confined myself to isolating the kinds of poems he wrote, defining the aims and limitations of their forms and placing them in their respective literary traditions, in the hope that such a re-evaluation will lead to a juster estimate of the nature and range of his achievement than those concentrating on the ballad narratives have hitherto offered. I readily admit that Coleridge may never have formulated his intentions as precisely as I have defined them. Lack of knowledge about an author's intentions is a critical difficulty that is with us always. To let criticism atrophy as a result, however, seems hardly a desirable solution. To insist, furthermore, upon such explicit formulations in every instance is sometimes to insist upon irrelevancies. The important thing is that Coleridge wrote poems capable of being categorized and arranged in such a way as to suggest the central vision which guided and shaped his achievement. To seek to comprehend this vision by whatever means at our disposal—in this instance, the kinds of poems he wrote—is a legitimate task of criticism.

One great distinction I appeared to myself to see plainly between even the characteristic faults of our elder poets and the false beauty of the moderns. In the former, from DONNE to COWLEY, we find the most fantastic out-of-the-way thoughts, but in the most pure and genuine mother English; in the latter, the most obvious thoughts in language the most fantastic and arbitrary. Our faulty elder poets sacrificed the passion and passionate flow of poetry to the subtleties of intellect and to the starts of wit; the moderns, to the glare and glitter of a perpetual, yet broken and heterogeneous, imagery, or rather to an amphibious something, made up half of image and half of abstract meaning. The one sacrificed the heart to the head; the other, both heart and head to point and drapery. . . .

It is true . . . that from diffidence in my own powers, I for a short time adopted a laborious and florid diction, which I myself deemed, if not absolutely vicious, yet of inferior worth. Gradually, however, my practice conformed to my better judgment. . . .

—*Biographia Literaria,* Chapter I

II

THE FARRAGO VOICE

Coleridge did not immediately perfect a style responsive to the quietly relaxed tones of his speaking voice. To achieve a verse capable of suggesting the nuances of spontaneity heard in his mature poetic voices, he had first to unlearn some false practices of the day. One was the habit of courting a free associational flow of ideas and emotions and then celebrating them poetically with rhetorical extravagance and amorphous loquacity—for example, the pleasing melancholy of "Lines Written at Shurton Bars . . . September 1795 in Answer to a Letter from Bristol." It is well known that many of the poems written prior to the *annus mirabilis* owe their "swell and glitter both of thought and diction" (*BL*, I, 3) to this practice. What has been almost overlooked by critics[1] is that Coleridge, while indulgently recording these tender sentiments in one set of poems, was satirizing the insipidity of such efforts in another group of poems.

Here is Coleridge on himself in November 1797 in "Sonnets Attempted in the Manner of Contemporary Writers":

> And this reft house is that the which he built,
> Lamented Jack! And here his malt he pil'd,
> Cautious in vain! These rats that squeak so wild,
> Squeak, not unconscious of their father's guilt.
> Did ye not see her gleaming thro' the glade?
> Belike, 'twas she, the maiden all forlorn.
> What though she milk no cow with crumpled horn,
> Yet *aye* she haunts the dale where *erst* she stray'd;
> And *aye* beside her stalks her amorous knight!
> Still on his thighs their wonted brogues are worn,
> And thro' those brogues, still tatter'd and betorn,
> His hindward charms gleam an unearthly white;
> As when thro' broken clouds at night's high noon
> Peeps in fair fragments forth the full-orb'd harvest-moon!

In this poetically slight, but satirically clever, sonnet, Coleridge is criticizing the "indiscriminate use of elaborate and swelling language and imagery" (*BL*, I, 17), exaggerated sentiments, and heterogeneous subject-matter of contemporary romantic verse.

As interesting as the object attacked is the means employed. A parody of the sticky, currently popular Della Cruscan mode, it uses the manner and method—false diction and amorphous design—of the object that it is criticizing. The first thing to note is its wayward handling of theme, or themes. The sonnet, entitled "On a Ruined House in a Romantic Country," occupies itself with the decayed house for two and one-half lines, or for four lines if we include the abrupt transition to the squeaking rats as somehow also developing the "ruin" theme. The second quatrain veers to a description of a phantom milkmaiden who forlornly haunts the abandoned farm. The third quatrain shifts to a portrait of her "amorous knight," whose white buttocks shining through tattered raiments are likened in the final couplet to a harvest moon peeping through broken clouds.

Who is to say where the emphasis lies in this diffuse vision of ruined house, forlorn maiden, amorous knight, and harvest moon? And what of "lamented Jack," whose home the poem purports to talk about but quickly drops for the "tale" of ghostly maid and swain? Coleridge referred jokingly to this exercise in contumely as "The House that Jack Built" (*BL*, I, 19); and the poem is certainly constructed in much the same haphazard fashion as was the house of nursery rhyme fame, piece added to piece in absent-minded afterthought.

The diction and syntax develop the same spasms. From a cultivation of late eighteenth-century sensibility, which attaches feelings of guilt to dumb rats and feebly ekes out the "ten low words" of the first line at the expense of syntax, Coleridge aspires, in the second and third quatrains, to a proud Spenserian diction which pictures rustic Rosalinds and boorish Hobbinols as fair Britomarts and gallant Artegals. But these inflated romantic sentiments collapse under the weight of his scorn when we read that the "hindward charms" of the yokel peep through tattered "brogues." To complete this withering dismissal of the contemporary poetic manner, the harvest moon image, beautiful in itself, acquires fantastic distortions of tone when likened to the ragtag knight.

The deliberate bathos of "The House that Jack Built" reveals a Coleridge who seldom figures in the textbooks or biographies: a man with a keen wit and an acid tongue. We sometimes forget that he grew up during the Silver Age of English satire. The satirical bent of the second half of the century—represented by the activity of Charles Churchill, "Peter Pindar," William Mason, and William Gifford—must inevitably have affected him. Certainly the man who can equate the intellectual qualifications of the literary reviewer with the physical prerequisites of the harem eunuch (*BL*, I, 42) has a talent for biting irony. And in his youth, Coleridge exercised this talent in a small group of poems which include "Sonnets Attempted in the Manner of Contemporary Writers," "Addressed to a Young Man of Fortune Who Abandoned Himself to an Indolent and Causeless Melancholy," "To a Friend Who Had Declared His Intention of Writing No More Poetry," "Lines Composed in a Concert-room," and "A Christmas Carol."

Rejecting the satire of the school of Pope, with its exhausted heroic couplets, he tried to fashion a satirical mode which imitates the romantic mannerisms of the poetry of sentiment then in vogue but distorts them for ironic effects. The chief characteristics of this poetry—incongruity and diffusion, akin to the unruddered associational flow of Mistress Quickly's chatter—have prompted me to call them Coleridge's farrago poems. In them, the affected simplicity of the contemporary poetasters becomes vulgarized, their lofty sentiments inflated, and their pretended spontaneity undisciplined. Like the conversation poems, most address close friends; unlike the conversation group, they offer kindly advice to the friend as a pretext for criticizing his shortcomings; in addition, the personal criticism frequently conceals a diatribe against poetic fashions or social wrongs. It is senseless to pretend that these poems have literary merit; the reasons for including them in this study are that they illustrate a little known side of Coleridge's personality and represent his first effort to find an idiom honestly his own.

The similarity of and difference between the sentiment of the Della Cruscan verse and the satire of the farrago poem may be clearer if we look at two poems illustrating these contrary points of view. "To a Young Friend [Charles Lloyd] on His Proposing to Domesticate with the Author" presents the romantic attitude:

> A MOUNT, not wearisome and bare and steep,
>   But a green mountain variously up-piled,
> Where o'er the jutting rocks soft mosses creep,
> Or colour'd lichens with slow oozing weep;
>   Where cypress and the darker yew start wild;

And, 'mid the summer torrent's gentle dash
Dance brighten'd the red clusters of the ash;
 Beneath whose boughs, by those still sounds beguil'd,
Calm Pensiveness might muse herself to sleep;
  Till haply startled by some fleecy dam,
The rustling on the bushy cliff above
With melancholy bleat of anxious love,
  Made meek enquiry for her wandering lamb:
 Such a green mountain 'twere most sweet to climb,
E'en while the bosom ach'd with loneliness—
How more than sweet, if some dear friend should bless
 The adventurous toil, and up the path sublime
Now lead, now follow: the glad landscape round,
Wide and more wide, increasing without bound!

 O then 'twere loveliest sympathy, to mark
The berries of the half-uprooted ash
Dripping and bright; and list the torrent's dash,—
 Beneath the cypress, or the yew more dark,
Seated at ease, on some smooth mossy rock;
In social silence now, and now to unlock
The treasur'd heart; arm linked in friendly arm,
Save if the one, his muse's witching charm
Muttering brow-bent, at unwatch'd distance lag;
 Till high o'er head his beckoning friend appears,
And from the forehead of the topmost crag
 Shouts eagerly: for haply *there* uprears
That shadowing Pine its old romantic limbs,
 Which latest shall detain the enamour'd sight
Seen from below, when eve the valley dims,
 Tinged yellow with the rich departing light;
 And haply, bason'd in some unsunn'd cleft,
A beauteous spring, the rock's collected tears,
Sleeps shelter'd there, scarce wrinkled by the gale!
 Together thus, the world's vain turmoil left,
Stretch'd on the crag, and shadow'd by the pine,
 And bending o'er the clear delicious fount,
Ah! dearest youth! it were a lot divine
To cheat our noons in moralizing mood,

While west-winds fann'd our temples toil-bedew'd:
    Then downwards slope, oft pausing, from the mount,
To some lone mansion, in some woody dale,
Where smiling with blue eye, Domestic Bliss
Gives *this* the Husband's, *that* the Brother's kiss!

We may bid farewell to Coleridge and his soul-mate at their cottage door. There is no need to climb with them another hill and gaze at still another green and sublime prospect for twenty-seven more lines. The digression, cultivation of melancholy, and association of nature with a tender feeling is sufficiently clear in the lines quoted. Details are daubed on with a profuse hand. Romantically, Coleridge envisions his friend vanishing to re-appear on a crag high overhead. This idle fancy diffuses to include a description of a pine tree standing shadowy and melancholy in the twilight. Then, without apparent reason he expatiates upon a spring basined among the rocks. The romantic seclusion of the "unsunn'd cleft" prompts him to muse sentimentally about the unruffled "sleep" of the water there. Details and sentiments are included because they interest the poet and develop a mood, not because they advance the thought of the poem. Ironically, on 17 December 1796, at the very time that he was indulging himself in these "'painted mists' that occasionally rise from the marshes at the foot of Parnassus" (*BL,* I, 12), Coleridge was damning Della Cruscanism and agreeing with Thelwall's strictures that "in some (indeed in many of my poems,) there is a garishness and swell of diction, which I hope, that my poems in future, if I write any, will be clear of"; for poetry, he pontificates, "ought not always to have its highest relish" (*CL,* I, 278–79).

Poetical extravagance betrays Coleridge into describing the spring as "the rock's collected tears." The themes of friendship and poesy lure him into stale and turgid sentiments which reveal the kinship of the poem with the even staler sentiments of Della Cruscanism as professed, for example, by Perdita Robinson in "Ode to the Muse":[2]

Or, when, at twilight's placid hour,
We stroll to some sequester'd bow'r;
And watch the haughty Sun retire
Beneath his canopy of fire;
While slow the dusky clouds enfold
Day's crimson curtains fring'd with gold;
And o'er the meadows faintly fly
Pale shadows of the purpling sky.

The foothills of Helicon tramped over by Mrs. Robinson are a part of the same slightly higher range clambered over by Coleridge and his prospective boarder. Both poets court the unfrequented byways; both with affected modesty seek "nooks untrod,"

> Where Inspiration, his diviner strains
> Low-murmuring, lay. ("To a Young Friend")

"To a Young Friend Who Had Declared His Intention of Writing No More Poetry" illustrates the farrago voice. Like the poem to Lloyd, it also addresses an acquaintance, Charles Lamb, and has poesy as its subject:

> Dear Charles! whilst yet thou wert a babe, I ween
> That Genius plung'd thee in that wizard fount
> Hight Castalie: and (sureties of thy faith)
> That Pity and Simplicity stood by,
> And promis'd for thee, that thou shouldst renounce
> The world's low cares and lying vanities,
> Steadfast and rooted in the heavenly Muse,
> And wash'd and sanctified to Poesy.
> Yes—thou wert plung'd, but with forgetful hand
> Held, as by Thetis erst her warrior son:
> And with those recreant unbaptizéd heels
> Thou'rt flying from thy bounden ministeries—
> So sore it seems and burdensome a task
> To weave unwithering flowers! But take thou heed:
> For thou art vulnerable, wild-eyed boy,
> And I have arrows mystically dipped
> Such as may stop thy speed. Is thy Burns dead?
> And shall he die unwept, and sink to earth
> 'Without the meed of one melodious tear'?
> Thy Burns, and Nature's own belovéd bard,
> Who to the 'Illustrious of his native Land
> So properly did look for patronage.'
> Ghost of Maecenas! hide thy blushing face!
> They snatch'd him from the sickle and the plough—
> To gauge ale-firkins.
>
> Oh! for shame return!
> On a bleak rock, midway the Aonian mount,

There stands a lone and melancholy tree,
Whose agéd branches to the midnight blast
Make solemn music: pluck its darkest bough,
Ere yet the unwholesome night-dew be exhaled
And weeping wreath it round thy Poet's tomb.
Then in the outskirts, where pollutions grow,
Pick the rank henbane and the dusky flowers
Of night-shade, or its red and tempting fruit,
These with stopped nostril and glove-guarded hand
Knit in nice intertexture, so to twine,
The illustrious brow of Scotch Nobility!

In this poem, Coleridge is as inflated in his rhetoric and as digressive in his thought as he is in the address to Lloyd; the difference between the two poems is one of intention and degree. Coleridge now uses a Spenserian diction and a fantastic conceit; but he uses it just grotesquely enough that we are uncertain of his intentions, whether serious or satirical, until toward the end of the first section when he mentions Burns and shifts to the colloquial syntax and low language of "They snatch'd him from the sickle and the plough—to gauge ale-firkins." Only then is it clear that the elevated diction is being contrasted with the drop in tone as a way of gaining satirical effect.[3]

A similar farrago of themes characterizes the poem. Said to have appeared originally in a Bristol newspaper in aid of a subscription for Burns' family, it ostensibly criticizes the shameful treatment which the Scotch poet received from his countrymen. Yet, the poem is addressed to Charles Lamb, and not until line 17 is Burns even mentioned. It is apparent that Coleridge is presuming upon his tender regard for Lamb—which gives him license to criticize that unsuspecting one's faults—to condemn the Scotch patrons of Burns. Through his scorn for Lamb's rejection of the unfading flowers of poesy, he also expresses his contempt for the Caledonian betrayers of the muse. The insolence of his familiar tone gives to the satire a withering, caustic tone that it would not otherwise have.

The farrago poem is then an unholy version of the contemporary Della Cruscan expression of friendship, and represents an early effort of Coleridge to escape the aesthetic limitations of the popular verse of the day. That these two kinds of poetry should originate in a single sensibility and mode of expression is not surprising, for both are outgrowths of eighteenth-century benevolism, which portrayed man as naturally good but corrupted by existing institutions. The sentiments of a young democrat of the 1790's frequently combined tender sensibility with revolutionary ardor. Coleridge, in his youth one of the young democrats, exhibits himself in the farrago poems as being simultaneously a man of feeling and of Godwinian rationalism. Influenced during his poetically formative years by the poetry of sentiment, he was trying, by the second half of 1796, to divert its vulgar colloquialism, garish language, meandering thought, and sentimental intention to didactic purposes. If we add to his preoccupation with the problem of style, his concern at this time with social reform, we have the two recurrent themes of the farrago poem.

Several are addressed to friends familiar with Coleridge's style and hence expected to recognize the satire of the farrago mannerisms—and such expectations were not ill founded. Thin-skinned Southey interpreted the sonnet "To Simplicity"—"written to ridicule infantine simplicity, vulgar colloquialisms, and ladylike friendships" (*CL,* I, 359)—as an attack on his poetry although Coleridge swore that Lamb was the target (*CL,* I, 357, 358n). And Lamb must have had the Burns poem in mind when, on 10 December 1796, in answer to a request from Coleridge for permission to publish it, he playfully responds: "With regard to my leaving off versifying, you have said so many pretty things, so many fine compliments, ingeniously decked out in the garb of sincerity, and undoubtedly springing from a present feeling somewhat like sincerity, that you might melt the most un-muse-ical soul." In the next paragraph, as a preamble to granting permission to publish the poem, he remarks, perhaps with an arch reference to its inflammatory nature, "You sent me some very sweet lines relative to Burns, but it was at a time when, in my highly agitated and perhaps distorted state of mind, I thought it a duty to read 'em hastily and burn 'em."[4] This, of course, refers to the first and most tragic instance of Mary Lamb's periodic bouts with insanity and the entire passage therefore may be meant seriously; but it may also refer to the heated attack in the poem on the aristocracy and, hence, meant playfully to reflect Lamb's pretended political timidity. Like coterie jokes, many of the farrago poems circulated among a Coleridge-Lamb-Southey clique able to recognize the double-edged comments in them about friends, poetry, and politics.

Thus, the farrago poem "Addressed to a Young Man of Fortune [Lloyd] Who Abandoned Himself to an Indolent and Causeless Melancholy" attacks economic injustice under the pretense of offering a cure for a friend's unwarranted depression. As if this were not enough indirection, Coleridge chooses to develop both themes in a "night-piece" which parodies the language and tone of the graveyard poets. Like them, he courts the mood of "Il Penseroso," but reverses the result of their gloomy allegiance. They retired to graveyards and dank tombs to induce causeless melancholy; he recommends the same environment to cure it. The derogation of the "Il Penseroso" theme provides him with the means of criticizing those who court false feelings (i.e., the graveyard poet when he seeks to be gloomy, and the friend when he prefers to be melancholy). The conception of the multiple levels here is subtle and sophisticated. Unfortunately, Coleridge's craftmanship at this time seems inadequate to fuse the many themes into one whole. The oblique development hinders us from realizing, until we read the final admonition,

What nature makes thee mourn, she bids thee heal!

(i.e., the world's evil as well as the friend's melancholy), that Coleridge's chief target is a populace callous to social injustices.

In the farrago poems just examined, the visage of Coleridge's poetical, social, and political criticism peers through a grinning mask of friendship. But in two poems, "Lines Composed in a Concert-room" and "A Christmas Carol," he dispenses with the friendship *persona*.

"Lines Composed in a Concert-room," as published in the *Morning Post* for 24 September 1799, numbered fifty-eight lines; when reprinted in *Sibylline Leaves*, lines 41–58 were omitted. It is with the original, or complete, version that we are concerned here. Read as a plea for liberty, the poem, for three-fourths of its length, contrasts the manufactured arias of a "harlot . . . breast" distended in "intricacies of laborious song," to the natural music of Scotch dance tunes, sad flute airs, and tragic ballads. Only when we reach line 48, with its "trump and timbrel clang, and popular shout," do we realize that the poem is not primarily extolling "nature's passion-warbled plaint" but is celebrating a victory over "freedom's latest foe."[5] Then we see that the long introduction deriding the "squalls" of a concert singer is also censuring the "heartless scene" of tyranny; that the *aristocratic* vanity of the music-room—with "my lady" sneering at "some maid of humbler estate," and "pert captain" and "primmer priest" engaging in scandalous prattle—is being contrasted unfavorably with the *republican* conviviality of dancing to Scottish tunes "By moonshine, on the balmy summer-night/ . . . amid the tedded hay." In terms of the impulse originally motivating the poem, music is merely the means by which Coleridge wins the reader's thoughts and emotions before disclosing to him that politics is the real sphere of operations of the poem. The music image also works, in an aesthetic side effect, to prevent the fragmentation of statement which usually afflicts the farrago voice.

"A Christmas Carol" is just as wayward a poem. For three stanzas it appears to be striving for the sublimity of Milton's "On the Morning of Christ's Nativity." The same motifs appear: the shepherds at the stable, the humility of the Virgin-Mother, and the angelic song of a new peace on earth. Stanza 4 initiates a new point of view; even with the reference to peace in stanza 3, the transition to the obscene suggestion that war is the sweet theme of song and noble office of youth and love is abrupt. But we realize, when the poem concludes with the Virgin-Mother shrilly condemning the "murderous fiend" war and humbly expressing joy over the birth of the Prince of Peace, that "A Christmas Carol" is no ordinary Yuletide poem heralding the Nativity, but one indicting Coleridge's contemporaries for complacently suspending their daily blood-letting to celebrate the advent of the kingdom of peace. By contrasting the "low estate" of peace and the courtly habitude of war, Coleridge emphasizes his point that the current Christmas celebration is an empty feast day. Also, by vulgarizing Mary's motherhood and ennobling war's lineage, he has not only increased the bitterness of tone but has indirectly underscored, as in "Lines Composed in a Concert-room," the evils of social inequality and political injustice.

Coleridge's utilization of one area of experience as a commentary on another area—a method refined to perfection by Eliot—indicates the maturity and modernity of his poetic sensibility. Unhappily, as we shall recognize in other of his voices, he is a restless innovator, who, like Ezra Pound, is content to leave to more patient men the task of consolidation. Whether for this reason or simply the shortcomings of the method, the farrago poem never quite comes off. The extent and object of its satire should be discernible if it is to be effective. Unfortunately, its indirect development works against eliciting a clear response from the reader. The farrago poem starts with one tone and changes midway to another which is usually the key to understanding the poem. Thus, one gropes uncertainly at the beginning for the right frame of reference. The degree of its failure is revealed by the success of such a poem as C. Day Lewis's "A Carol," which uses the same tactics of multiple reference but manages a unified tone nonetheless.

Oh hush thee, my baby,
Thy cradle's in pawn:
No blankets to cover thee
Cold and forlorn.
The stars in the bright sky
Look down and are dumb
At the heir of the ages
Asleep in a slum.

The hooters are blowing,
No heed let him take;
When baby is hungry
'Tis best not to wake.
Thy mother is crying,
Thy dad's on the dole:
Two shillings a week is
The price of a soul.

In Lewis's poem, we hear echoes almost immediately of the Christmas carol "Away in a Manger"; and the bitter moral condemnation implicit in the parody fuses with the angry social protest explicit in the poem. Because the farrago poem lacks this unity of tone, the satire is less instantly apparent and less sharply realized. Not until we reach the second half of "A Christmas Carol," for example, with its preposterous defense of war, do we realize that Coleridge's prosaic rendition of the Nativity is not a failure of poetic inspiration, and not another trite emulation of Milton's celebration of the birth of Christ, but a savagely ironic commentary on the Napoleonic era. A meaner description in the opening stanzas of Mary and the Babe or an obvious parody of Milton's poem might have clarified Coleridge's intention.

The lack of focus multiplies the possibilities of misinterpretation— always a danger in satire. Since the farrago poem resembles with embarrassing exactness the "shreds and patches" of Robert Merry and the Della Cruscan circle of poetesses, the reader can conceivably misinterpret it as a serious exercise in the picturesque, the grand, or the beautiful; he can mistake it for the kind of poem that it is exploiting for satirical purposes. Nor does wearing its coat of many colors with a satirical air insure it against the danger of being mistaken for a sincere but gauche hankering after the pretentious nonchalance of Perdita Robinson and Anna Matilda. Nor does Coleridge help us, either, when, in later years after his revolutionary zeal had waned, he reprints "Lines Composed in a Concert-room" minus the final eighteen lines containing the clue that the poem is attacking the enemies of freedom, not criticizing the unsociability of the music salon and the aridity of classical music. As a consequence, the "puny pathos" (*CL*, I, 357) of the farrago poem masquerades so convincingly in the finery of Wartonian sentiment that readers, more often than not, mistake its wry incongruity for artless pretension.

The possibility of mistaken identity raises the question of how certain we can be that these poems are meant as satires. Readers attempting to discern Coleridge's intentions have blundered in the past. One does not know, for example, whether Coleridge published "The Hour When We Shall Meet Again" in *The Watchman* on 9 March 1796 as a sincere expression or satirical parody of sentiment. Yet his editor reprinted it in *Literary Remains* (1836) "under 'the sportive title "Darwiniana," on the supposition that it was written' in half-mockery of Darwin's style with its *dulcia vitia*" (*CPW*, I, 96 n). A year earlier, Henry Nelson Coleridge in *Table Talk* had satirically affixed to the poem a contrary supposition: "A lady, who had read 'The Ancient Mariner' and 'Christabel,' told Mr. Coleridge, after reading the above lines, 'that *now* she did, indeed, see that he was a poet!'" (*TT*, II, 359 n). Here is a poem, then, conforming to the contemporary taste for the *dulcia vitia,* that was read as both an instance of the truly poetic and a satirical parody of a bad style.

Do we not similarly risk confusing Coleridge's intentions in the farrago poem? Certainly in better known poems, he evinces that he could write tumid, tasteless, or pointless lines (Della Cruscan or Bowlesian or whatever); an example is the incredible amalgam of prosaic description and bombastic sentiment comprising "Reflections on Having Left a Place of Retirement." Yet, in a poem like "Reflections," there is a predominant tone. Similarly in the farrago poems already analyzed, the satire, although diffuse, is unmistakable. We cannot always, however, be so certain. "The Picture," for example, is essentially a confessional poem; yet its amorphous development, heterogeneous tone, and mixed diction—turgid Miltonics cheek by jowl with the ingenuous strains of Gessner's pastoral idylls and the natural idiom of Coleridge's conversational voice—hint that he is using the farrago manner to chastise one of the sterile poetic traditions rife in the second half of the eighteenth century. "To the Author of Poems Published Anonymously at Bristol in September 1795" turns an erstwhile praise of Joseph Cottle's verse into a backhand dismissal of simplicity and a fervid embracing of sublimity as the medium of poesy and thus may be another Coleridgean attempt to transform a poem of friendship into a critique on poetics. If these two poems employ the satirical formula of the farrago voice, then the endemic fault of the voice, its lack of focus, involves both in meaningless ambiguity; for we do not know if their statements are made straight-faced or ironically.

Donald Davie argues that impure diction and amorphous structure were used by Coleridge to create an effect of spontaneity; and certainly the farrago poems do convey the impression of having been composed under the uncontrollable proddings of Orpheus. Viewed from the rather tidy perspective which pictures Coleridge as working sometimes blindly, sometimes consciously, toward a poetry embodying spontaneity and yet including the virtues of order, the farrago voice represents an unsuccessful, pre-*annus mirabilis* experiment. If he shows a youthful skill in irony and wit, still he lacks the satirist's single-mindedness and the poetic technique, or the will, to convert the contemporary romantic effusion into a satirical weapon. Perhaps, after all, the transformation was not possible; and the attempt reflects the misguided zeal of his immature judgment. At any rate, he failed to write good poems in the farrago voice; and our major interest in it lies in its illustrating his poetic growing pains. Inevitably, Coleridge became disenchanted with the voice, because basically the gods amorphous and incongruous offended his sensibility. "Similes, figures, etc.," he maintained, "will all find their place sooner or later, each as the luminary of a sphere of its own. There can be no galaxy in poetry" (*MC*, p. 343). His repeated definition of a poem as a whole composition in which the parts "mutually support and explain each other" (*BL*, II, 10), as well as his praise of Milton's general plan for *Paradise Lost*, his adulation of Shakespeare's organic unity, and his disquisition on the need for method, all testify to his abiding concern for the design of a thing. He was sensitive to the absence of method, more than once citing Mistress Quickly's speech as the quintessence of discursive wit, and condemnatory of its vagaries, as, for example, in 1811, when he "read passages from Jean Paul in illustration of his absurd accumulation of images and his unpicturesque and incongruous collection of features in one picture" (*MC*, p. 390).

Although the publication in November 1797 of "Sonnets Attempted in the Manner of Contemporary Writers" foreshadows the imminent rejection of the farrago voice, two full years passed before Coleridge abandoned serious use of the voice entirely. He does not seem to have written any additional farrago poems during the year of his association with the

Wordsworths at Nether Stowey or during the year of his sojourn in Germany; but upon his return to England he published at the end of 1799 in the *Morning Post* "Lines Composed in a Concert-room" (24 September)[6] and "A Christmas Carol" (25 December). The reversion to a voice essentially alien to the poems of 1797–98—the ballads and conversation pieces—which are probably his most successful, infers that he was still not certain of his true poetic voice. The return to the farrago voice also conforms to a characteristic pattern of action: when his poetic power flagged, he tended to revert to the modes of verse popular in his school days. This momentary lapse in self-criticism is apparent in his references to "A Christmas Carol"; he calls it not without pride "a quaint performance" and offers it to Southey for the *Annual Anthology* (*CL,* I, 552). These two poems are the last unmistakable instances of the farrago manner. On 10 January 1800 he published "Talleyrand to Lord Grenville," which uses diffusiveness for satirical purposes but otherwise does not develop the indirection and multiple themes of the farrago voice.[7] Interestingly, the political emphasis of it and the two farrago poems of 1799 suggests that Coleridge came to think of this poetic voice as particularly suitable for political satire —a natural association, considering the political themes implicit in the farrago poems of 1795–97.

In all probability what helped end the farrago experiment was the excitement of acquiring a ventriloquistic skill able to parody the naturalness of folk-literature and of perfecting a conversational manner able to create the illusion of discursiveness without literally duplicating its incongruities of tone, diction, and structure. With "This Lime-tree Bower" in June 1797 Coleridge reached poetic maturity. The emergence of these new poetic skills was not miraculous, but the inevitable result of changes taking place in his poetic style, which between 1796 and 1798 became increasingly natural in diction and organic in structure. This mastery of language and form is well illustrated by the evolution which his sublime, or prophetic, poetry underwent.

For me to discuss the *literary* merits of this hasty composition were idle and presumptuous. If it be found to possess that impetuosity of Transition, and that Precipitation of Fancy and Feeling, which are the *essential* excellencies of the sublimer Ode, its deficiency in less important respects will be easily pardoned by those from whom alone praise could give me pleasure. . . . I am more anxious lest the *moral* spirit of the Ode should be mistaken. You, I am sure, will not fail to recollect that among the Ancients, the Bard and the Prophet were one and the same character; and you *know* that although I prophesy curses, I pray fervently for blessings.

—Dedicatory Letter Prefacing
"Ode on the Departing Year, 1796"

III

THE PROPHECY VOICE

A Sunday service was not the only occasion when the preaching spirit descended on Coleridge. In "To the Author of Poems" (1795), he sermonizes on poetry, his text taken from the first book of Cottle's *Poems,* his lesson directed at the "unboastful bard" who courts with "smooth melody" and "modest verse" an unpretentious earthbound muse. Flap your wings and "soar, my friend," he exhorts;

> . . . Poesy demands th' impassion'd theme:
> Waked by Heaven's silent dews at Eve's mild gleam
> What balmy sweets Pomona breathes around!
> But if the vext air rush a stormy stream
> Or Autumn's shrill gust moan in plaintive sound,
> With fruits and flowers she loads the tempest-honor'd
> ground.

That Coleridge should call on Cottle for the "impassion'd theme" is not surprising, for he held the view of his century that poetry "presupposes a more continuous state of passion" than prose (*AP,* p. 229), with the corollary that the more passionate expression was also the more poetic.

The natural form of expression for this lyric fury was believed to be the ode, which had been associated from Cowley onward with Pindar, the supreme example of the poet-prophet through whom man speaks to God, and God to man. Hence, Coleridge is following poetic tradition when he connects, as in the quotation beginning this chapter, the impassioned outburst of the prophet with the prophetic utterance of the poet.

His poems which essay this prophetic voice are "Religious Musings," "Monody on the Death of Chatterton," "The Destiny of Nations," "Ode on the Departing Year, 1796," "France: An Ode," "Ode to Georgiana, Duchess of Devonshire," "Ode to Tranquillity," and "Hymn Before Sun-rise, in the Vale of Chamouni." In these poems, Coleridge ranges in tone from the thunderous accusations of an Elijah to the comforting accents of a Hosea to the ecstatic visions of an Ezekiel.

The Hebraic analogy is intentional because there is a note of Psalmist despondency in these poems, despite their being in the tradition of the prosopopoeia of the Pindarick ode.[1] In a letter to Thelwall of 17 December 1796, Coleridge compares the "impassioned eloquence" and thunderous sublimity of Old Testament poetry to the "disgustingly tame" "quarrels of Jupiter and Juno, the whimpering of wounded Venus, and the jokes of the celestials on the lameness of Vulcan" of Greek verse (CL, I, 281). The Hebraic note in the prophecy poems may reflect this preference for Hebrew poetry. Certainly his predilection for the Psalms is overt in the paean to nature sung in "Hymn Before Sun-rise."

In the prophecy poems, Coleridge sings of the illusoriness of liberty, man's inhumanity to man, and the sublimity of God; but, from first to last, he celebrates nature. He begins by viewing it as a melancholy retreat for the freedom-lover ("Monody" and "Ode on the Departing Year"); but he soon transfigures it into a metaphysical concept of liberty and hope ("France: An Ode"); and ends exaltedly worshipping in it the pervasive presence of God ("Hymn Before Sun-rise").

I have included "Dejection: An Ode" among the prophecy poems, but with some misgivings, for it might equally be considered a conversation or confession poem—as I have indicated in my discussion of the confession voice. Written originally as a "Verse Epistle to Sara [Hutchinson]," it reflects the transitional period between the Germany and the Malta trips when the round of Coleridge's life still turned in the old grooves; but the attitudes which characterize the next thirty years were already beginning to appear. Thus, it shares with the conversation poems of the Clevedon and Nether Stowey years a common imagery, a straightforward syntax and conversational tone, a return at the end to the situation or description opening the poem, and an emotional pattern which begins calmly, rises in fervor, and then sinks back into calmness. Contrariwise, the unresolved cry of despair heard in the poem heralds the backward glance, the lament for misused powers, and the introspection soon to be developed in the confession poem. But, because Coleridge carefully recast its rambling epistolary style into a formal ode, I have followed his direction and also grouped it with the sublime poems, even though the apocalyptic vision so arrogantly asserted in "Ode on the Departing Year" is here tempered by the humble realization that he is too humanly "near-sighted" after all for a poet-seer.

"Dejection," with its lament for the loss of prophetic vision, belongs to 1802. In the previous decade, Coleridge had known few misgivings of this sort. Then, he had characterized himself as pre-eminently a poet of either "tenderness or passion" (*CL,* I, 279). In agreement with the time, he had relegated his tender moods to his poems of friendship and reserved his passionate tones for the poems of apocalypse, on which he wished to secure his reputation (cf. *CL,* I, 205). Voicing these views to Thelwall in a letter of 17 December 1796, he expresses excitement over Collins' "Ode on the Poetical Character" because its impassioned tone whirls him along with great agitations of enthusiasm. Such poetry, he believes, gives "more general pleasure" than the "most impassioned scene in Schiller or Shakespere," and is therefore "more valuable" (*CL,* I, 279).

This is high praise for the ode, even for someone with the enthusiasm of Coleridge. Sufficiently subjective and impassioned for the most inspired poet, the ode in the eighteenth century epitomized poetic spontaneity. Speaking for his age, Herder characterizes it as the "first born child of emotion, the origin of poetry, the germ of life."[2] In support of this sentiment, Archibald Alison reiterates in his widely read *Principles of Taste* that sublime poetry is dependent on the image-making propensity of the imagination, which in turn is dependent on warmth of feeling. "When the passions are roused," he writes, quoting Whately's *Observations upon Modern Gardening,* "their course is unrestrained, when the fancy is on the wing, its flight is unbounded" (p. 44). From such theorizing stem Coleridge's exhortation to Cottle to let his view reflect the "rapid, fervent, flashing" light of "fancy's beam" ("To the Author of Poems") and the efforts of the Augustan poets to assail "the very top of the scale of sublimity" (*CL,* I, 224) by "poetizing" their song with flights of visionary fancy—which frequently included sight-seeing trips distant indeed from the scheduled line of flight. Some poetasters of the age went so far as to interpret this doctrine of "spontaneous" expression as a denunciation of revision. Even Coleridge, as a "young Jacobin" of literature, was not entirely guiltless of this heresy.

A passion, however, for giving meaningful unity to experience kept him from ever giving whole-hearted allegiance to the lawlessness of the Pindarick. Like Modigliani in our century, he seems to have compensated for the chaos and disintegration of his personal life by seeking serenity and wholeness in art. A major critical touchstone is his belief that a poem proposes "to itself such delight from the *whole,* as is compatible with a distinct gratification from each component *part*" (*BL,* II, 10). Instances abound in his practical criticism of applications of this touchstone long before he formulated it so magisterially in the *Biographia Literaria.* A neat use of it to define a defect in William Taylor's translation of *Lenore* occurs in a letter to Taylor of 25 January 1800. Paraphrasing a series of letters which had passed between him and Wordsworth while they were both in Germany, he writes:

> 'We [William and Dorothy Wordsworth] have read "Leonora" and a few little things of Bürger; but upon the whole we were disappointed, particularly in "Leonora," which we thought in several passages inferior to the English translation. *"Wie donnerten die Brücken,"*—how inferior to
> "The Bridges thunder as they pass,
> But earthly sound was none &c., &c." '
> I admitted in my reply, that there are more passages of poetry in your translation but affirmed that it wanted the *rapidity* and *oneness* of the original; and that in the beauty quoted the idea was so striking that it made me *pause, stand still* and *look,* when I ought to have been driving on with the horse. (*CL,* I, 565)

A zeal for oneness distinguishes Coleridge's mastery of the ode as a vehicle of orphic insight. The appearance at mid-century of "The Progress of Poesy" and "The Bard" and West's translation of Pindar indicated a trend away from the excesses of Cowley toward a control based on an understanding of the metrics of Pindar. The prophetic voice of Coleridge illustrates a similar evolution from "Ode on the Departing Year" to "Hymn Before Sun-rise." Each ode relies less than the previous one on an outward semblance of unity. Each increasingly takes its design from a central idea. As a consequence, the lifeless mask of external form is ultimately replaced in the prophecy poems by the vital presence of an inner unity (cf. *BL,* II, 258–59). This growing organic unity reflects the maturation of Coleridge's artistry between 1797 and 1802, a richly creative period which concludes with "Dejection" and "Hymn Before Sun-rise."

"Ode on the Departing Year," written in December 1796, shows close kinship with the "Greek Ode on Astronomy," which Coleridge wrote for the Browne Gold Medal in 1793—assuming that the English translation of Southey is faithful to the lost original.[3] The Cantabrigian Coleridge is somewhat more optimistic about his ability to soar at will into the empyrean than is the Bristolian Coleridge, whom the adversity of economics, retrenchment of politics, and humbling of marriage had somewhat depressed. He asserts with Platonic fervor in the early poem that "with pious madness wise," he can "expand [his] wings divine" and "roam the starry path of heaven," "a god the gods among." Three years of chastening experience, while not suppressing his faith in the "immortal mind," prompt him to reaffirm his prophetic vision in the second poem in a negative way:

> Starting from my silent sadness
> Then with *no unholy madness,*
> Ere yet the enter'd cloud foreclos'd my sight,
> I raised the impetuous song. (My italics)

Except for this sobering of his youthful idealism, the two poems conform to the same poetic conventions: personified abstractions, sublime diction, and diffuse structure. If anything, the sustained enthusiasm of the "Greek Ode on Astronomy" gives it a unity of tone lacking in the bewildering ambivalence of anger, despair, and hope characterizing "Ode on the Departing Year." In other words, at the end of 1796—when he is also formulating the farrago poems "Addressed to a Young Man of Fortune" and "To a Friend Who Had Declared His Intention of Writing No More Poetry"—Coleridge is still writing sublime poetry within the eighteenth-century tradition of the Pindarick ode.

"Ode on the Departing Year" casts Coleridge in the anomalous role of giving an outward semblance of form to an inward disorder. The poem consists of a series of strophes, antistrophes, and epodes, as if the external regularity of such tripartite Pindaric division were analogous to an internal order. The contrary is closer to the truth. Not strophe and antistrophe but prophetic transport—a euphemism for chaos—dictates the organization of the thought. The ode begins with the poet contemplating the heavens with "silent sadness." Suddenly seeing the train of the departing year, he is prompted to raise "the impetuous song, and solemnis[e] his flight." The "impetuous song" develops in successive fits such diverse themes as a plea for men to suspend their private joys and sorrows and devote themselves to the cause of suffering humanity; a denunciation of the "insatiate hag," Catherine of Russia; an inflammatory speech by the spirit of earth; a patriotic eulogy of pastoral England; and a shrill prophecy of England's destruction. Coleridge so enthusiastically loads his poem with "fulness and profusion of point in the parts" that he fails to stamp a "unity of impression upon the whole" (*TT,* II, 215).

"France: An Ode," written about a year and a half later, has gained in unity of thought and emotion. Coleridge has abandoned polystrophes for a simple monostrophic form. For unity, however, he relies heavily on the repetition of a complex metrical pattern. An elaborate rhyme scheme (abba/ cdcd/ ee/ fgfg/ hihjjij), many polysyllabic rhymes, and an intricate arrangement of line-lengths (10–10–10–10/ 11–11–11–11/ 8–8/ 9–10– 9–12/ 10–10–10–10–10–10–10) constitute each stanza.

Coleridge apparently constructed these stanzas with both the Shakespearean and the Petrarchan sonnets in mind. Each is like an inflated sonnet. Two quatrains and a couplet advance the first idea; then a third quatrain extends this thought and an Alexandrine brings the whole statement to a momentary conclusion. A seven-line coda functioning like a final sestet resolves the thought and concludes the stanza. In "France: An Ode," Coleridge has perfected a strophe which keeps the emotional versatility of the Pindarick and at the same time exploits the logical sequence and dramatic emphasis of the sonnet. His brilliance as a metrical innovator is as evident here as in "Christabel." Especially praiseworthy is his use of a tetrameter couplet after the first two quatrains to give variety to a long statement and to furnish either an anticlimax to the first movement of thought or transition to the third quatrain. Also, his resort to an Alexandrine in the fourteenth line to climax the first statement, followed by seven decasyllabic lines which conclude the second statement and the stanza, is metrical wizardry. It is only a step from Coleridge's baroque amplification of the sonnet in "France: An Ode" to Keats's graceful contraction of the same form in "Ode on a Grecian Urn"; and both adaptations result from the search of the English Romantic poets for new poetic forms.

Also contributing to the unity of "France: An Ode" are its opening and closing apostrophes to nature. They give a frame to the narrative of Coleridge's growing realization that only in the visible appearances of nature will man find the eternal laws of freedom operating. Especially artful as a consequence is the coalescence of image and theme in the conclusion.

"Ode to the Duchess of Devonshire," published in December 1799, twenty months after "France: An Ode," and "Ode to Tranquillity," published in December 1801, are also improvements on the amorphous "Ode on the Departing Year." Of interest in "Ode to the Duchess of Devonshire" is the use of a refrain to unite a triad of loosely related panegyrics; while in "Ode to Tranquillity" occur a regular stanza and moderate tone, which accord well with the theme.

Coleridge's search for a structure responsive to his vision comes close to realization in the great "Dejection" ode. In other respects, however, "Dejection" is an anomaly among the prophecy poems. Like "Ode on the Departing Year," "France: An Ode," and "Ode to Tranquillity," it is a song of disillusionment; but unlike them, it is reflective rather than didactic. It has no palpable design upon the reader, as Wordsworth's poetry (so Keats claims)[4] and Coleridge's early odes manifestly have. The year is 1802. Coleridge is no longer the confident prophet of the 1790's. Despair is leading him into a night of the spirit in which the sound of the wind fails to send his soul abroad to fuse with the spirit of nature.

The years, however, had enriched his perception of what constitutes the inner unity of a poem. The experience of writing the "diffuse" conversation poems had taught him how to organize his content around a key image or idea, in lieu of the external formalities of a genre, and thereby fuse form and content into a single entity. In "Dejection," the storm functions as a key image. With considerable viability, it concentrates into a unified statement Coleridge's complex and ambivalent feelings of listless dejection and aroused grief, and of hopeful anticipation and disappointing frustration. Vividly evocative of the tension resulting from these dual responses and fully integrated as a part of the storm imagery are the supplementary motifs of fertility-sterility and freedom-restriction. As a result, the poem, although outwardly formless, is inwardly a model of patterned statement. As in "France: An Ode," Coleridge opens and closes his introspective monologue with descriptions of nature but improves on the early poem by objectifying his state of mind with the natural setting of luminous sunset, rising and falling wind, dark rain-tossed night, and inharmonious draft of an aeolian harp, now dully sobbing, and now agonizingly screaming. There is no dislocation of diction, no two sets of terminology, as in "France: An Ode." Considered to be about the failure of imagination, the theme develops through a series of nature-poet equations: light stands to joy as dark to dejection, and calm stands to passivity of imagination as storm to activity of imagination.

At the outset, Coleridge notes the correspondence between the tranquil evening and his inactive imagination. In contrast to the inert grief with which he now faces the darkened sky is the creative joy he recalls having once felt in "a light, a glory, a fair luminous cloud." A "new-moon winter-bright" with the old moon in its lap, however, is a portent of a change in the weather. Perhaps this radiant moon, he hopes, also augurs the rebirth of his imagination. So he eagerly awaits the April shower which will re-awaken the earth and perhaps quicken his spirit.[5]

But his hope proves false. Instead of a gentle spring rain, the April storm is a wild onslaught of wind and water. Unlike the "noises, faintly wafted on the wind," to which he anticipated attuning his mind in "To a Young Friend," this squall raises a terrifying din, wringing shrieks of agony from the aeolian harp hung in the poet's window.

Such "tempest's swell" ("To the Rev. George Coleridge") is not necessarily destructive. In other poems, Coleridge clearly identifies a tumultuous wind with the sublime soaring of the creative imagination. In "To the Author of Poems," he admonishes Cottle for listening to the "sweet undersong" of nature's sounds, the "unceasing rill" and "soft wren or lark's descending trill," when instead Cottle should have been gathering from poesy's "tempest-honor'd ground" the "fruits and flowers" blown down by the "stormy stream" and the "shrill gust" of the impassioned muse. And in "To Matilda Betham from a Stranger," he exclaims:

> Poetic feelings, like the stretching boughs
> Of mighty oaks, pay homage to the gales,
> Toss in the strong winds, drive before the gust,
> Themselves one giddy storm of fluttering leaves.

These winds are not, however, comparable in every respect with the wind in "Dejection." The wind of "To the Author of Poems" is "a stormy stream" or "autumn's shrill gust." It is harvesting the "mellow fruitfulness" of summer. Contrariwise, the swelling gust of "Dejection" is an April wind. Regardless of how hard it blows, it will find little fruit or foliage to harvest from the "dark-brown gardens" and "peeping flowers" of this time of year. Nor is the comparable stagnancy of Coleridge's spirit exactly the horn of plenty. The "beautiful and beauty-making power" of joy, which allows man to envelop the earth with a "light, a glory, a fair luminous cloud," must issue forth from the soul; but, as he admits dejectedly, his soul is void of the "sweet and potent voice" of joy, and his sensibility deadened to the sights and sounds of earth. Furthermore, as Coleridge recognizes in "To Matilda Betham," the "giddy storm" of the fancy needs to be balanced by wise self-control. Let your emotions "toss in the strong winds, drive before the gust," he advises, while you, "self-limited," remain

> Equally near the fixed and solid trunk
> Of Truth and Nature in the howling storm,
> As in the calm that stills the aspen grove.
> Be bold, meek Woman! but be wisely bold!

No such judicious thought and feeling counteract the wind of "Dejection." Amid the budding promise of April, it makes a "devil's yule, with worse than wintry song." It is a "mad lutanist" whose "melancholy theme" ("To a Young Friend") parallels the poet's bleak mood. Consequently, we have little reason to believe that the "blank eye" of his heart and mind offers effective balance to its arbitrary fury. If the quickening force of the storm activates the sensibility of the poet, then it will in all probability, considering his abject despair, simply corroborate the "melancholy theme" of his thoughts. And this is exactly what happens. In the early evening, Coleridge's mood of "stifled, drowsy, unimpassioned grief" matches the lull of the air before the oncoming storm. As the evening progresses and the storm arrives, his spirit is aroused; but, like the turbulent wind which wrenches from the lute cheerless agonies, his despondency elicits from his mind "viper thoughts" about the sterility of his once creative imagination.

The reptilian image with which Coleridge expressly characterizes his state of mind conveys perfectly the continued constriction of his imagination. His "viper thoughts . . . coil around [his] mind" in a painful grip reminiscent of the snake's strangling embrace of the dove in Bracy's dream in "Christabel":

> "I saw that dove,
>
> . . . .
> Fluttering, and uttering fearful moan,
>
> . . . .
> I saw a bright green snake
> Coiled around its wings and neck.
>
> . . . .
> And with the dove it heaves and stirs,
> Swelling its neck as she swelled hers!"

The image—one of pain and contraction and confinement—is used by Coleridge again in "The Wanderings of Cain":

> Never morning lark had poised himself over this desert; but the huge serpent often hissed there beneath the talons of the vulture, and the vulture screamed, his wings imprisoned within the coils of the serpent.

Conversely, the soaring flight and song of a bird frequently appear in Coleridge's writing as emblematic of the giddy moment of visionary insight. A vivid instance occurs in a prose note of 10 September 1823 prefacing an early draft of "Youth and Age":

> I stopt to hear . . . [a] Sky-Lark that was a Song-Fountain, dashing up and sparkling to the Ear's eye, in full column, or ornamented Shaft of sound in the order of Gothic Extravaganza, out of Sight, over the Cornfields on the descent of the Mountain on the other side—out of sight, tho' twice I beheld its *mute* shoot downward in the sunshine like a falling star of silver. (*CPW*, II, 1084-85)

In the poem apparently inspired by this experience, he wryly recognizes that his once "mounting spirit," to use the words of Hopkins' "The Caged Skylark," now dwells songless "in his bone-house, mean house," like a "dare-gale skylark scanted in a dull cage." That Coleridge associated the reptile-bird image with the inhibition of his "mounting spirit" is substantiated by the coalescence of the two concepts in a notebook entry analyzing the causes of his opium taking:

> I have never loved Evil for its own sake; no! nor ever sought pleasure for its own sake, but only as the means of escaping from pains that coiled round my mental powers, as a serpent around the body & wings of an Eagle! My sole sensuality was *not* to be in pain![6] (*N*, II, 2368)

Essentially the same comment (that his train of thought is unable to break free of the restrictions of selfhood) obtains in the line which we have been considering in "Dejection." The "dull pain" which he feels in the early hours of the evening "startles" into life as the sunset fades and the wind rises. It moves and lives in the form of unhappy thoughts of an "inanimate cold world," in which the vivifying imagination is dead. Such "viper thoughts" coil around his mind and effectively continue the painful crippling of his aspiring imagination.

Most painful of all for Coleridge is the recognition that he is responsible for his "viper thoughts," that he is ironically both guilty perpetrator and innocent victim of his inactive imagination. The cross web of associations implicit in the "viper" image, which we have been tracing, also includes this idea. J. B. Beer comments that the imagery of *Zapolya*, "while marking no new departure, repeats many of the trends which have been noticed in Coleridge's earlier poetry" (Beer, p. 301). Nowhere is this acute observation more amply illustrated than in the snake symbolism which both "Dejection" and *Zapolya* share. Coleridge repeatedly uses the snake in the play as an emblem of treachery. "Chef" Ragozzi deplores the wiles of the usurper Emerick in terms of this image:

> O rare tune of a tyrant's promises
> That can enchant the serpent treachery
> From forth its lurking hole in the heart.
> (Part 1, 452–54)

And Laska, in reply to Glycine's suggestion that a serpent has stung him, angrily retorts,

> No, serpent! no; 'tis you that sting me; you!
> (Part 2, I, i, 183)

With these words he accuses her of betraying their betrothal and thus stinging him to the heart. In both instances the treachery afflicts the heart —or feelings. Even more specifically, the snake is associated in *Zapolya* with self-delusion. When Emerick attempts to justify his usurpation of the throne, Raab Kiuprili cries,

> Mark how the scorpion, falsehood,
> Coils round its own perplexity, and fixes
> Its sting in its own head! (Part 1, 348–50)

Earlier in the action, when Kiuprili first hears of Emerick's treacherous plans to kill the rightful king, he attempts to gain entrance to the palace. Balked in this action, he exclaims:

> Must I, hag-ridden, pant as in a dream?
> Or, like an eagle, whose strong wings press up
> Against a coiling serpent's folds, can I
> Strike but for mockery, and with a restless beak
> Gore my own breast? (Part 1, 88–92)

Unlike Kiuprili, who recognizes the mockery, self-delusion—and, above all, self-destruction—in an act of despair and hence poses, only to reject, a foolhardy defiance of Emerick as a possible course of action, Coleridge, in desperation to correct an intolerable situation, has acted to alleviate the pain of his thoughts and feelings and, in doing so, has betrayed his own sensibility. He has coached his mind "to be still and patient" and, worse yet, diverted it to "abstruse research" until

> that which suits a part infects the whole,
> And now is almost grown the habit of my soul.

37

The suspension of his "shaping spirit of imagination," which he intended in self-delusion to be a temporary measure, has treacherously become a permanent catastrophe. He has "gored his own breast" and now bemoans the self-inflicted wounds—his dead imagination and the attendant despair. It is these "viper thoughts" which sting him and perpetuate the constriction of his imagination.

Thus, the snake image "blends and harmonizes" (*BL,* II, 12) in its symbolism the nature and cause of Coleridge's dejection. Most important, it supports the symbolism of the developing storm, whose increasing fury parallels the intensification of Coleridge's dejection. In keeping with the dark stormy night of his despair, no moon at the edge of the rain cloud floods the night with joyous light, no brilliant colors from a hundred fire-flags light up the sky as if to herald the regeneration of his spirit as they do for the ancient mariner; over Coleridge's head rages a black midnight storm and in his heart a "dark dream" of dejection. The result is a symbolism responsive to every nuance of the poet's mind, and a "unity of impression upon the whole" unknown to the early odes.

Coleridge uses a similar structure of nature imagery in "Hymn Before Sun-rise." Written in the same year as "Dejection," it is the last in the manner of the prophecy voice—unless one includes the Indian summer flowering of "Youth and Age," in which Coleridge develops the theme of the ages of man (youth, middle age, and old age) in a tripartite structure consisting ostensibly of strophe, antistrophe, and epode; I have, however, included it among the confession poems. If the countless exclamations and questions of "Hymn Before Sun-rise" suggest a less than inspired Coleridge trying to whip up his flagging enthusiasm, still, the fusion of idea and image is a fitting climax to Coleridge's attempt to tame the cloud-pawing Pegasus that was the eighteenth-century ode, while retaining its appealing traits of spontaneity, impassioned thought, and divine insight. The poem describes a mountain growing visible in the spreading light of dawn; watching is the poet whose eyes sweep upward in a slow-traveling arc to its summit, as his voice with mounting spiritual exaltation, in the tradition of David and the Psalms rather than that of Pindar, rises with the gathering voices of nature in a thousand-voiced praise of God.

Both F. R. Leavis and, more recently, Harold Bloom have compared "Hymn Before Sun-rise" to Shelley's "Mont Blanc" and Wordsworth's famous description of the Simplon Pass in *The Prelude.* There is little need to go over the same ground a third time. No one would wish to deny that "the prime fault" of Coleridge's vision of the Alps "is probably its

high-pitched quality,"[7] especially when read against the intense excitement but stately articulation of Wordsworth's vision. Where both critics
err is in their neglect of the coherent use of relationships as a syntax (to use
Earl R. Wasserman's phrasing in a recent study of Shelley's "Mont
Blanc")[8] with which Coleridge creates the world of "Hymn Before Sun-
rise." Harold Bloom's resort to biography as an explanation of the quality
of desperation in the poem is a sympathetic attempt to understand the
forces prompting Coleridge to write the poem, but such an explanation
hardly furthers our understanding of the architectonics of the poem. His
error of omission, however, considering that Shelley rather than Coleridge
is his main concern, is venial in comparison to Leavis's sin of commission.
Leavis complains that "Hymn Before Sun-rise" expresses a conflicting attitude toward the mountain; he argues that Coleridge strives for sublimity
with words like *awful, rave, dread,* while incongruously responding to the
sweet beguiling sounds of the mountain.[9] Leavis is attacking Coleridge's
very conception of the poem; for it is this compound of "wildest" and
"softest and most beautiful" appearances (as Coleridge, following Friederike Brun's lead, characterizes the mountain in the preface to the poem in
the *Morning Post* for 11 September 1802) which Coleridge means to reconcile in the integrating act of the "Hymn."

More perceptive to the design of the poem than Leavis is Adrien Bonjour, who sees (Bonjour, pp. 72–81) the antithesis between strife and harmony, with its counterparts in the contrast between night and day, as an
instance of Coleridge's consummate ability to mould ideas and images
into a unified structure of thought. In the night, the mountain pierces the
ebon mass of the sky, "as with a wedge!" Like a mighty sovereign past
whose "awful form" marches an endless troop of stars, it struggles against
the dark, substantial black of the night. In the dawn, the mountain resides
in this same sky as if in its "habitation from eternity"; there, in its "own
calm home," it reflects the waxing light of day. Thus, the mount functions
as intermediary between earth and heaven; it rests on sunless pillars sunk
deep in the ground and rises into the sunlit brightness of the sky where it
battles night and welcomes day. And this motif (earth-night-strife versus
heaven-dawn-harmony) matches the poet's own exaltation before nature:
his awe and fear endured in the confining dark of night and his faith and
joy felt in the spreading light of day.

As Bonjour points out, Coleridge did not achieve this balance of opposites during the initial inspiration on Scafell 5 August 1802 when he "involuntarily poured forth a hymn in the manner of the *Psalms*" (*CL,* II,

864). Nor does he seem to have realized the thematic potentialities of this antithesis when afterward, as he tells Sotheby in a letter of 10 September 1802, he "thought the ideas etc. disproportionate to our humble mountains —and accidentally lighting on a short note in some swiss poems, concerning the Vale of Chamouni, and its mountain . . . transferred myself thither, in the spirit, and adapted my former feelings to these grander external objects" (*CL,* II, 865).[10] For when he published the poem in the *Morning Post,* 11 September 1802, he was still linking Mont Blanc, herald of light, with antithetical darkness in the line,

> O blacker than the darkness, all the night.

Not until October 1803 was this thematic ambiguity corrected. At that time, Coleridge changed the line in a manuscript version sent to Sir George Beaumont to read:

> Struggling with the darkness all the night!

With this revision, Coleridge clarifies the light-dark symbolism in conformity with the other parts of the poem and with the Platonic-Christian concept of darkness as contrary to, and brightness as analogous to, all that is positive. The light-dark symbolism of "Dejection" testifies that such consistency of imagery was not a fortuitous accident. Wordsworth's similar handling of light imagery in "Ode on Intimations of Immortality"—a poem closely associated in time, theme, and origin to "Dejection"—indicates that both poets, with the experience of the conversation poems and "Tintern Abbey" to support their efforts, were simultaneously exploring the possibilities of a key image as one means of giving internal order to the Pindarick ode.

Contributing to the unity and sublimity of "Hymn Before Sun-rise" are at least two thematic oppositions which underscore the argument of the light-dark antithesis that a struggle is being waged around the mountain by the forces of day and night. One is an animate-inanimate antithesis. Associated with light and life are the "living flowers that skirt the eternal frost," the "wild goats sporting round the eagle's nest," and the eagles, "play-mates of the mountain-storm." Opposed to them are the "motionless torrents," "silent cataracts," and "dark and icy caverns" of inanimate nature, in which night and death, explicitly equated in line 40, become one.

Another antithesis is that of silence and sound. In the Stygian pre-dawn, the "silent mount," surrounded by a "silent sea of pines," struggles silently against the engulfing night. As day breaks, however, the torrents, ice-falls, snow-line flowers, meadow streams, and pine groves of the mountain "utter forth God, and fill the hills with praise." The description of this ground swell of noise, of "the everlasting universe of things" (to use Shelley's apposite phrase in "Mont Blanc"), harmonizing with one voice in the waxing light to thunder "God," occupies the final three-fourths of the poem.

The comprehensiveness of the mountain reconciles these contraries of sight and sound through its eternal relationship with night and day and earth and sky. Coleridge has combined in his description of Mont Blanc two literary conventions of long standing: the tradition of the mountain as lordly monarch (cf. Denham's "Cooper's Hill") and the equation of sublimity and religious awe with immensity and height. Envisioned in the darkness as an earthbound, worldly sovereign, the mountain appears grandly spiritualized in the dawn light, residing at ethereal heights where clouds of incense veil its breast. Its "bald awful head" which had struggled all night against the "ebon mass" of the air loftily acknowledges the presence of God from its morning abode in the "pure serene." Its upward thrust and seeming immateriality lead the poet to contemplation of the divine. With this integrating act, the personification of the mountain becomes poetically functional. As "dread ambassador from earth to heaven," it greets the sun (God) with the "thousand voices" of nature—and the voice of the poet.

Harold Bloom errs in attributing to the poem "a Hebraic identification of the mountain with its Creator."[11] Nor is "anthropomorphic" the right descriptive word for what is poetically mere excessive personification. Furthermore, to define the poetic statement at first as pantheistic and then as conventionally Christian (which Bloom also claims for the poem) is to accuse the poet of philosophical confusion. Coleridge was a subtle enough metaphysician not to let himself be trapped by that error. Indeed, his horror of pantheism is sufficiently pervasive in his writings, as for example in his criticism of Schelling, that it needs no documentation. In "Hymn Before Sun-rise" he carefully keeps the mountain and God separate. With Wordsworthian concentration he gazes upon Mont Blanc until it reveals its spiritual significance. In this action, whereby subject and object unite to become reality, his soul projects outward and fuses with the mountain; together they soar upward into "the pure serene." The mountain cannot then be simultaneously the ambassador conveying the poet's worship from earth to heaven and God, the object of his worship. At the moment of his adoration of "the invisible alone," Coleridge carefully tells us, the mountain did "vanish from [his] thought." If, two lines later, he discloses that it was "blending with [his] thought," he is not contradicting himself, but describing the reality which obtains during the act of perception, when perceiver and thing perceived form a supplementary union; in such an action the sentient being knows itself in and derives its experience from the external object, while the external object acquires being as a subjective and hence living portion of the mind, nature becoming thought and thought nature (*BL*, II, 258). In its war against the evil and terror of the night and conversely in its adoration of the spirituality and joy of the day, the mountain functions as a surrogate of the poet's consciousness.

"Hymn Before Sun-rise" is a true Romantic poem in its creation of a world which structurally conforms to the logic of its material. Its interlocking series of oppositions, particularly the light-dark and silence-sound antitheses, conveys the impression that Coleridge is actually standing in the predawn spontaneously chanting each detail of the mountain as it becomes gradually discernible in the waxing light. In the first two stanzas, night still obliterates the valley of Chamouni; masses rather than particulars loom overhead. Mont Blanc is visible only in outline; the pines are an undifferentiated "sea" of darkness; even the two rivers raving at the base of the mountain, where the poet is standing, are heard, not seen. It is in this predawn stillness, broken only by the sound of the Arve and Arve-iron, that the poet blends the night of his soul with the black outline of the mountain and soars upward in wordless worship of the invisible. But with increasing light, the poet offers up vocal worship as well—his own and nature's. He enumerates the features of the mountain as they become visible. The peak is seen first. It appears like one of the stars in the sky, "earth's rosy star," as it catches the first rays of the unseen sun. Then, as the night gradually grays into light, five torrents flowing down Mont Blanc's slopes break into view. Then appear jagged black rocks which form a wild bed for the mountain streams; higher up, the ice-falls become visible sloping down from the brow of Mont Blanc. It is now light enough to discern colors and details other than the rosy glow of the sun glinting on the mountain top. Blue glacier flowers, small meadow streams, pine groves, piles of snow, even wild goats sporting around the upper reaches of the mountain become visible. Finally, the mountain is seen to have more than one peak. Such pictorial progression, with its impression of having been written on the spot, pleads the spontaneity of the divine afflatus.

It is apparent that poetic prophecy, unlike religious vision, cannot do without the aid of artistry, which makes all the more pathetic Coleridge's reluctance to disclose that a poem as well as a note had guided his imaginative journey from the English lake country to the Swiss Alps, especially when the organization of "Hymn Before Sun-rise" is so obviously superior to the Alpine verses of Friederike Brun, which are its poetic antecedent. A measure of the wholeness of concept distinguishing "Hymn Before Sun-rise" despite its literary borrowings may be gained by comparing it with early poems of Coleridge similarly derived, for example, "Monody on the Death of Chatterton," which is a pastiche of Miltonic and eighteenth-century elegiac sentiments. The structure of "Hymn Before Sun-rise" is then an index of Coleridge's mastery, after a decade of ode writing, of an individual prophetic voice capable of assimilating diverse influences. Its fully integrated vision of Mont Blanc is not too mean for comparison (if we overlook the frenetic tone of the rhetoric) with the paradoxes of motion and stasis, and of process and permanence, of Wordsworth's great description of the Simplon Pass and the dialectic of internal and external, and of mind and things, of Shelley's "Mont Blanc."

The dialectics of "Mont Blanc" and "Hymn Before Sun-rise," especially, assume similar forms while, paradoxically, pursuing dissimilar goals. Shelley, intent upon ascertaining how much the human imagination can know of the power which gives being to the things of this world, begins his poem (sections 1 and 2) with a description of the ravine of the Arve, which functions as an analog of the mind. Then he ranges upward (section 3) to contemplate the silent, frozen peak of Mont Blanc, analog of the unknown power in the universe; but inevitably he must turn to follow the metamorphosis of the mountain (section 4) from frozen peak and eternal snows to glacier to river and ravine, downward again to the mind of man. "Mont Blanc yet gleams on high:—the power is there," Shelley is forced to conclude in section 5, but the "secret strength of things," which inhabits it and governs thought, remains ultimately blank and faceless; what man knows of "the everlasting universe of things" is not the thing in itself but what "flows through the mind" and is given being by "the human mind's imaginings." Coleridge, on the other hand, assumes at the outset that the power which flows through all things is "invisible" and hence unknowable. His purpose is simply to praise this power. The argument of the poem, in conformity with such an intention, sweeps in worshipful awe upward from mountain base to mountain peak and concludes with the gaze fixed upon the "intense inane." The poem functions as an act of adoration of the invisible. In such an act the manifold things of nature, while "still present to the bodily sense," vanish from the enrapt con-

centration of the communicant's thought. As an emblem of the poet's consciousness, the mountain appropriately appears at the opening of the poem
as an indistinct "ebon mass," associated with the terror and awesomeness
of the predawn; and at the close, as a cloud-obscured peak, its bulk va-
porized by the poet's "dim eyes suffused with tears" of religious love. In
both poems, then, as in Wordsworth's, the external object is being made
to reveal the internal world of human experience.

Despite his mastery of the form, Coleridge evidently felt that he could
not rely on his own sensibility. The forced tone of "Hymn Before Sun-
rise" indicates that he had reason to distrust his poetic powers. Questionable, however, is the explanation that he repeatedly gives for its supposed
failure. In poem and letter he blames his scientific studies. "I have been,
during the last three months, undergoing a process of intellectual *exsic-
cation,*" he writes to Godwin, 25 March 1801:

> In my long Illness I had compelled into hours of Delight many a sleepless,
> painful hour of Darkness by chasing down metaphysical Game—and
> since then I have continued the Hunt, till I found myself unaware at the
> Root of Pure Mathematics—and up that tall smooth Tree, whose few poor
> Branches are all at its very summit, am I climbing by pure adhesive
> strength of arms and thighs—still slipping down, still renewing my ascent.
> —You would not know me—! all sounds of similitude keep at such a
> distance from each other in my mind, that I have *forgotten* how to make
> a rhyme—I look at the Mountains (that visible God Almighty that looks
> in at all my windows) I look at the Mountains only for the Curves of
> their outlines; the Stars, as I behold them, form themselves into Triangles
> —and my hands are scarred with scratches from a Cat, whose back I was
> rubbing in the Dark in order to see whether the sparks from it were
> refrangible by a Prism. The Poet is dead in me—my imagination (or rather
> the Somewhat that had been imaginative) lies, like a Cold Snuff on the
> circular Rim of a Brass Candle-stick, without even a stink of Tallow to
> remind you that it was once cloathed & mitred with Flame. That is past
> by!—I was once a Volume of Gold Leaf, rising & riding on every breath
> of Fancy—but I have beaten myself back into weight & density, & now I
> sink in quicksilver, yea, remain squat and square on the earth amid the
> hurricane, that makes Oaks and Straws join in one Dance, fifty yards high
> in the Element. (*CL,* II, 713–14)

His scientific studies may be partly responsible for his unpoetic mood, but
they certainly are not the whole answer. In fact, the imaginativeness of this
passage makes us wonder if his imagination was as quiescent as he feared.
There is the suggestion that it functioned perfectly well when the material

and manner of presentation were congenial. Such a hypothesis gains weight when we remember that he had been voicing the theme of "Hymn Before Sun-rise" for almost three years in letters extolling the sublime beauty of the Westmorland and Cumberland mountains. Why then should he resort to Friederike Brun's poem for inspiration and accept so perfunctorily the hackneyed attitude of his day toward the mountain? The answer, perhaps, lies in the curious fact that his need to draw on other poetry to inspire in him the "lofty strain" is greater with the prophecy voice than with the other voices. Such a fact hints at the basic uncongeniality for him of the sublime voice. Unfortunately, he started writing poetry at an unpropitious time (for him) in literary history when the poetic climate called for sublimity. Dutifully, Coleridge conformed to this climate of opinion. In 1790 in the Christ's Hospital version of "Monody," he entreated seraphic Chatterton:

> Grant me, like thee, the lyre to sound,
> Like thee, with fire divine to glow.

But a high-pitched tone of "fire divine" was not his normal poetic voice. And when he succeeded in drawing such sound from his lyre, as in "Dejection," the certainty of language stemmed from the poem having been originally conceived in the low-keyed statement of a versified letter. Without the wisdom of hindsight to guide his choice of poetic form, Coleridge began in 1790 a twelve-year struggle to write viable poetry within the enervated tradition of neo-classical verse. This struggle terminated with the uniquely sublime analysis of his state of mind in "Dejection" and the aspiring vision of God in "Hymn Before Sun-rise." After these two poems, he virtually stopped trying to soar aloft on "meditation's heaven-ward wing," resigned for the last thirty years of his life to treading the earth on mortal feet. By this time it must have been apparent to him, as it is to us, that his success with some of the other voices was more consistent and individual.

Both Coleridge and Wordsworth worked to institute the rhythms and diction of contemporary speech as the verbal medium of the ode. And the effective blend of "natural notes" ("To William Wordsworth") and the urbane tone of "Dejection" and "Ode on Intimations of Immortality" testify to their success. For passionate language they substituted "a song divine of high and passionate thoughts" (to use Coleridge's characteriza-

tion of *The Prelude* in "To William Wordsworth"). They also worked to
tighten the form of the ode; and the configurations of these two poems
and of "Hymn Before Sun-rise" are equally indicative of their success. The
configuration of references into a coherent poetic syntax in Coleridge's
two odes is especially impressive and reflects his mastery of the art of con-
necting "parts to a whole, so that each part is at once end and means" (*SC,*
I, 223).

In his criticism Coleridge attempted to keep the Augustan distinction
between means and ends (parts and whole) while also accepting the Romantic concept of organicism which sees parts and whole as one.[12] A similar effort marks his poetry. He starts usually with a traditional form (as,
for example, in the prophecy voice) but modifies it to fit his predilection
for seeing life not as a mechanical progression from means to an end but
as an organic growth of parts so suggestive in miniature of the whole that
the distinction between parts and whole tends to blur. Architectonically,
"Hymn Before Sun-rise" is a whole in which the successive instants of
Coleridge's experience are subsumed by the single image of the mountain: both man and mountain are mutual aspirants toward the light of
heaven, and as night gives way to dawn and his eyes sweep from base to
summit, following the soaring outline of the mountain, his soul fuses with
its spirit and swells "vast to heaven." In a like way, in "Dejection," the successive instants of Coleridge's despondency are subsumed by the storm
image. Not only in his criticism, then, but also in his poetry, Coleridge effectively unites the Neo-Classical and Romantic points of view.

In their metaphoric fusions of the objects of nature and the sensibility
of the poet (in which the images copied from nature are modified by a
predominant passion transferred from the poet's own spirit, *BL,* II, 16),
"Hymn Before Sun-rise" and "Dejection" approach the ideal of organic
form that Coleridge was fond of defining: "The organic form . . . is in-
nate; it shapes as it develops itself from within, and the fullness of its development is one and the same with the perfection of its outward form.
Such is the life, such the form. Nature, the prime genial artist, inexhaustible in diverse powers, is equally inexhaustible in forms. Each exterior is
the physiognomy of the being within" (*SC,* I, 224). The convention of
prosopopoeia is still invoked, but how much more naturally than the apostrophes to abstract terms—caricatured by Coleridge in the line, "INNOCU-
LATION, heavenly maid! descend!" (*BL,* II, 66)—which graced the pages
of Dodsley's collection and charmed the circle of the Wartons. A critic
such as George Shuster may dislike "Hymn Before Sun-rise" because it

uses the "pathetic fallacy" too lavishly;[13] yet undeniably this personification leads logically and irrevocably to the climactic presentation of the
mountain as ambassador to the court of God and, to this extent, vindicates
the lesson that James Bowyer, Head Master of Christ's Hospital, drove
home to his small charges: "Poetry, even that of the loftiest and, seemingly, that of the wildest odes, had a logic of its own, as severe as that of
science; and more difficult, because more subtle, more complex, and dependent on more, and more fugitive causes" (*BL,* I, 4).

The high tribute paid in *Biographia Literaria* to the imaginative
power of Wordsworth can apply equally as well to Coleridge in his best
poetic moments. In the attempt to give dramatic propriety to metaphors,
which had been "stripped of their justifying reasons and converted into
mere artifices of connection or ornament" by the false poetic style of their
contemporaries (*BL,* II, 28), both poets developed along parallel courses.
Both strove to make language reveal the sympathetic relationship existent
between man and the world external to him. To estimate the degree of influence one had on the other seems a pointless—ultimately fruitless—task
now; for any judicious estimate must recognize that each was obviously a
catalyst for the other. Despite this close association the forms taken by
their poetic organizations of the "one life within us and abroad" ("The
Eolian Harp")—in short, part of what constitutes their poetic signatures—
differ perceptibly. Wordsworth, paradoxically, with at once great looseness
of form and great intensity of effect, hangs his sudden perceptions that the
outer world reflects his inner experience onto a narrative frame, as, for example, his memory of "spots of time" in *The Prelude* and his vision of the
leech gatherer as stone and sea beast in "Resolution and Independence."
The structure of the Coleridgean poem derives more uncompromisingly
from the inner organization and being of the poetic material, as, for example, his use of the storm in "Dejection" and the mountain in "Hymn
Before Sun-rise." These odes acquire a logic of structure from a concentration upon nature so intense that the natural object acquires the mood and
feeling of the poet, while imparting to that mood a natural form.

Coleridge's vision of the oneness of life is not unique with the prophecy poem. To see simultaneously the individual form of a thing and the
multitudinous relation of it with a greater whole is idiosyncratic with him,
particularly during the years immediately preceding and following the
Germany trip of 1798–99. In a letter to his wife dated 17 May 1799 from
Germany, he describes the dark pine forests, leaping and foaming water-
falls, and snow patches of a mountain scene so strikingly similar to the one

pictured in "Hymn Before Sun-rise" that his memory of it, especially the sound of the fir trees, may have contributed to the imaginative vision of Mont Blanc: "Now again is nothing but pines and firs, above, below, around us!—How awful is [the] deep unison of their undividable murmur—What a *one* thing it is [—it is a sound] that [im]presses the dim notion of the Omnipresent" (*CL*, I, 502). To see that life is multiple and yet one, however, was not enough for Coleridge; how to give external design to this impression so that others could perceive it was an artistic problem with which he struggled endlessly. In 1804, in a Malta notebook, he confesses the difficulty of conveying his perception of the unity in variety of the hollows and swells of the ocean: "O said I as I looked at the blue, yellow, green, & purple green Sea, with all its hollows & swells, & cut-glass surfaces—O what an Ocean of lovely forms!—and I was vexed, teazed, that the sentence sounded like a play of Words. But it was not, the mind within me was struggling to express the marvellous distinctness & unconfounded personality of each of the million millions of forms, & yet the undivided Unity in which they subsisted" (*N*, II, 2344). Like this passage, Coleridge's poetic voices are not plays on words but serious efforts to circumvent the imprecision of language. With the ventriloquism poems, he still relies on the forms of literary convention; but with the conversation, dream, confession, and improvisation poems, he boldly creates poetic configurations which give "individual unity" to his experience in forms natural to that experience.

There is a pretty little Ballad-song ["Sleep you, or wake you, Lady bright?"] introduced [into *The Castle Spectre,* II, iii]—and Lewis, I think, has great & peculiar excellence in these compositions. The simplicity & naturalness is his own, & not imitated; for it is made to subsist in congruity with a language perfectly modern—the language of his own times, in the same way that the language of the writer of "Sir Cauline" was the language of *his* times. This, I think, a rare merit: at least, I find, *I* cannot attain this innocent nakedness, except by *assumption*—I resemble the Duchess of Kingston, who masqueraded in the character of "Eve before the Fall," in flesh-coloured Silk.

—Letter to William Wordsworth, 23 January 1798

THE VENTRILOQUISM VOICE

In his farrago and his prophecy poems, Coleridge follows the sensibility and the sublime schools of versifying. In them he apes the rhetoric of the eighteenth century. In another group of poems, which include two of his most popular works, "The Ancient Mariner" and "Christabel," and several of his less frequently read endeavors, "The Three Graves," Parts III and IV, "The Ballad of the Dark Ladié," "Love,"[1] "Alice du Clos; or, the Forked Tongue," and "Baron Guelph of Adelstan," he follows the vogue for ballad narratives. Imitating their colloquial diction and stark action helped him to prune from his writing an "indiscriminate use of elaborate and swelling language and imagery" (*BL*, I, 17) and achieve a poetry suggestive of spontaneous simplicity.

Probably as early as the autumn of 1795 and the first draft of "The Eolian Harp," Coleridge had tried to perfect a simple and natural style characteristic of his person and of the language of his time. Certainly by 1797 he was striving (as he explains in the Preface to the second edition of *Poems*) "to tame the swell and glitter both of thought and diction" (*CPW*, II, 1145) which mars such poems as "To a Young Friend on His Proposing to Domesticate with the Author," "Monody on the Death of Chatterton," and "Religious Musings." The conversation poem "Frost at Midnight" (written in February 1798) is one of the supreme results of his effort to simplify his style; but in the conversation voice he attains this naturalness at the expense of strong emotion. Its natural style derives in part from its low-keyed tone; when Coleridge pitches the tone to a higher key, as in "Reflections on Having Left a Place of Retirement," bombastic Miltonisms recur. In contrast to such descriptive-meditative verse, the ballad manages frequently to combine simplicity of diction with intensity of thought. But not until his close association with Wordsworth does Coleridge attempt to realize this poetic ideal through the ballad form. By January 1798, however, this intention is explicit in his confession to Wordsworth that he had not yet attained in his style to an "innocent nakedness, except by assumption" (*CL,* I, 379). In this same month he was hard at work on "The Ancient Mariner"; and his note to Wordsworth indicates his suspicion that its simplicity derives not from his style but from his assumption of the ballad mode.

The ballad, functioning as "a species of ventriloquism" (*BL,* II, 109), made it possible for him to affect simplicity and naturalness. Its ruthless excision of everything but the essential action, supplied him with a model of objectivity and brevity and, therefore with a corrective to his habit, learned from an apprenticeship to the orphic and sentimental muses, of stringing together loosely connected series of subjective and descriptive phrases. Though a sophisticated product of one poet rather than the accretions of numerous minstrels, "The Ancient Mariner," like the ballad or folk-song, tells a story with the stress on a crucial situation—the consequences of killing an albatross on a sea voyage—which is presented in a series of clearly marked stages, either of little scenes or of their equivalent in dialog.

To accelerate the narrative, Coleridge employs conventionalized description, parallelism, and cumulative iteration, so characteristic of the curiously effective simplicity of the ballad. The classic use of these devices, pointed out by Lowes, narrates the progress of the ship as it sails south:

> The Sun came up upon the left,
> Out of the sea came he!
> And he shone bright, and on the right
> Went down into the sea;

crosses the line:

> Higher and higher every day,
> Till over the mast at noon—

rounds the Horn:

> And now there came both mist and snow,
> And it grew wondrous cold:
> And ice, mast-high, came floating by,
> As green as emerald;

and beats its way north again:

> The Sun now rose upon the right:
> Out of the sea came he,

Still hid in mist, and on the left
Went down into the sea.

Even closer to a set formula are these lines describing the ship under full
sail:

The fair breeze blew, the white foam flew,
The furrow followed free;
We were the first that ever burst
Into that silent sea.

Such stylized description not only helped Coleridge to simplify his
language but also to create richly textured poetry. Not the least of the
beauties here is the union of sense and sound. The alliterated explosives *b*
and continuants *f* support the descriptions of the wind pushing against the
sails and of the keel surging through the water. Equally impressive is the
way Coleridge uses the two halves of the stanza to suggest the surprise felt
by the mariners at finding themselves on an unknown sea. The familiar
details of sailing described in the first two lines contrast startlingly with the
unfamiliar world depicted in the next two lines. And the further contrast
drawn between the disrupting headway of the ship and the pristine silence
of the unexplored sea—between activity and stillness—contributes to the
shock of surprise which the swift transition of these lines from the known
to the unknown communicates.

Freed from the artificial inhibitions of eighteenth-century poetic diction, Coleridge employs the unencumbered syntax and concrete language
of general usage with ease. He resists, for example, the temptation to call a
breeze by its beloved pseudonym "gale"—a weakness of diction shared
by half the conversation poems. Only once does he backslide, when the
breeze blowing on the mariner's cheek as the ship approaches home reminds him of the zephyrs blowing across Quantock meadows, and the fatal proximity of Georgian parks and bucolic vistas sets the scene for a brief
fall from grace in the line, "Like a meadow-gale of spring."

For all the brilliance of "The Ancient Mariner," however, the achievement of simplicity in the ballad mode remains a recognizable trick; it does
not—except for "The Ancient Mariner"—have the true inflection of his
naked voice. For this reason, Coleridge's ballad narratives may appropriately, I think, be called his ventriloquism poems. Distinguished from
the corpus of his poetry by their singularity and by a high percentage of
fragments, they are the products of a brilliant but short-lived, because ultimately unnatural, voice.

Because of its rich texture, recurrent imagery, and patterned action, "The Ancient Mariner" begs an allegorical reading; and readers have not been shy about offering one. Hugh I'A. Fausset sees the poem as an allegory of the strange terrors and endless monologs of Coleridge's life;[2] George Whalley, as a projection of Coleridge's early sufferings and a vivid prophecy of the sufferings to come;[3] Maud Bodkin, as an expression of the rebirth archetype;[4] E. M. W. Tillyard, as a mental and spiritual voyage into the unknown;[5] Robert Penn Warren, as a dual allegory of the workings of the creative imagination and the sacramental vision;[6] and both Gertrude Garrigues and J. B. Beer—fittingly as one of the earliest and one of the most recent to attempt to fit all the parts of the voyage into a coherent, systematic allegory—as "an image of the fall of mankind."[7]

There is an element of truth in all these readings and much agreement, as the likeness of Warren's, Garrigues', and Beer's readings suggests. Most readers admit into their interpretation the basic actions of a crime committed against self, laws of hospitality, nature, and God; the consequent death of the spirit, isolation from living beings, and dryness of heart;[8] the act of redemption through expression of love for external living things; and the partial recovery of creative vitality, rebirth of spontaneous feeling, and reintegration of being with the external world. Most recognize the blessing of the water snakes as a reversal of the consequences of the killing of the albatross and the return of the mariner to the living community of man and nature. Most sense some correlation between the action and the symbolism of wind and sun and moon.

Yet, none of these interpretations satisfactorily explains all the details and actions of the poem. None subsumes its rich suggestiveness of language and narrative. Both the biographical and the Jungian critical *aperçus* used by Fausset, Whalley, and Bodkin are forever leading the reader away from the poem into non-poetic areas of thought. As spiritual adventurers (so Tillyard would have them), the mariners are shockingly imperceptive: they mistakenly identify the albatross with the "good south wind" and then, when the wind continues to blow after the bird's death, they reverse themselves and see it as an ill-omen "that brought the fog and mist." As symbols of the understanding and imagination, and of punishment and redemption, in a world of natural and spiritual order (so Warren formulates them), the sun and moon are provokingly inconsistent, being associated with both malevolent and beneficent actions. And while Beer's use of the Osiris and Isis myth allows him to explain the good-bad ambiguity of the sun associations with considerable success,[9] he does this only by transforming Coleridge into a turn-of-the-century Blake. Coleridge may have bragged to Thelwall that he was "deep in all out of the way books" and that "accounts of all the strange phantasms that ever possessed your philosophy-dreamers from Tauth [Thoth], the Egyptian, to Taylor, the English pagan," were his "darling studies" (*CL,* I, 260); still, he was no visionary and occultist but an eminently sane heir of English rationalism and German metaphysics.

Indeed, the truth is that the narrative of the poem is frequently working at cross purposes to the concatenation of meanings suggested by the lyrical, or descriptive, passages. In our effort to formulate "a coherent and convincing explanation of the miscellaneous detail in the difficult parts of the poem" (House, p. 107), we tend to forget that "The Ancient Mariner" (as E. E. Stoll and Newell F. Ford somewhat crankily remind us[10]) is "a literary fairy-tale" and "a supernatural ballad"—in short, initially and primarily a sea tale! Much in the poem is structurally functional without necessarily having symbolical significance. The presence of the wedding-guest, for example, works to give credence to the mariner's story. Like Kate Leslie's slackening resistance to Cipriano and the Quetzalcoatl movement in Lawrence's *The Plumed Serpent,* the wedding-guest's incredulity is slowly overcome by the insistence of the mariner and the events of the voyage. Both literary structures contain within them an antagonistic view; and the dramatic action of winning over this opposition asserts the validity of the central statement. There is also the ever present possibility, to cite a second example, that the superstitious mariner's belief in a causative relation between human actions and natural events is the result of his searing experience of being becalmed, and faced with isolation and death, on strange equatorial seas. That is, "The Ancient Mariner" may be read as a dramatic study in abnormal psychology rather than as a symbolical presentation of the natural and spiritual oneness of the universe.

Although such a reading is not my intention, it has much in its favor historically. "The Ancient Mariner" was written in 1797–98, a time when Coleridge and Wordsworth were exploring the poetic possibilities of psychological subject-matter. "The Three Graves"—"a common ballad-tale" worked on by both poets during the Nether Stowey days but never finished—was conceived, Coleridge writes in the Preface, as "illustrating the mode in which the mind is affected . . . [by witchcraft], and the progress and symptoms of the morbid action on the fancy" (*CPW,* I, 268–69). "The Wanderings of Cain"—another joint enterprise of the two poets during the same period—projects a psychological analysis of the effect of guilt on Cain. It is perhaps no accident, then, that "The Ancient Mariner" first appears in the 1798 volume of *Lyrical Ballads,* along with such studies of the abnormalities of the human mind as "The Mad Mother," "The Idiot Boy," "Goody Blake and Harry Gill," and "The Thorn."

If my comments about the psychological realism of "The Ancient Mariner" are somewhat gratuitous, my reference to its appearance in the *Lyrical Ballads* is very much to the point. Its inclusion in a volume of verse whose title indicates an attempt of the authors to combine two kinds of poetry (the balladic and the lyrical) was probably no accident. F. W. Bateson's analysis of Wordsworth's style into two voices, Augustan and Romantic,[11] may be helpful here. But the analogy should not be pushed. Bateson's definition of the Romantic manner as subjective, sentimental, and egocentric also defines one part of the Augustan temperament at the end of the eighteenth century. For this reason, his distinction is an artificial one and not finally applicable to "The Ancient Mariner." The ballad and the lyric actually represent two ways of looking at things (animistic and moral, impersonal and social). The union—and divergence—of these two points of view in "The Ancient Mariner" produces the occasional disjunction between narrative and descriptive facts, which strains symbolic readings of the poem.

The circumstances surrounding the mariner's killing of the albatross and his blessing of the water snakes illustrate this dualism. The simple seamen interpret the entrance and exit of the bird as responsible for natural events. They believe that it "made the breeze to blow" and, contrariwise, when the sun appears later, that it "[brought] the fog and mist." The seamen respond to its killing with righteousness or abhorrence, depending on the weather they consider the act to have provoked. There is little reaction to the deed in terms of a moral code (unless the seamen's characterization of it as a "hellish thing" implies one). They punish the mariner because they think that the killing has affected the wind, not because they think that the killing is bad. The growling, roaring, howling ice and the storm blast with its "o'ertaking wings" underscore this stern, animistic world, in which each thing has a life of its own and the law of an eye for an eye prevails. The air is peopled with supernatural agents of vengeance and mercy. Across an austere seascape blows a capricious wind. Temptation masquerades as an albatross and a water snake; Nemesis, as a polar spirit; guardian spirits, as an angelic host. A simple acceptance of fate pervades the world of "The Ancient Mariner," as it does the world of

"Edward," "The Three Ravens," and "The Ancient Ballad of Chevy Chase."

At the same time, Coleridge transcends the ballad form. He adds to its severely limited narrative the lyricism and idealism of a regency Englishman. As most readers have testified, a strong moral tone does pervade the poem. Significantly this tone, as defined in the gloss, takes the form of indignation over the betrayal of one admitted, so to speak, to share the rights and obligations of the family circle. The albatross is "hailed . . . in God's name" "as if it had been a Christian soul." It eats the seamen's food and attends their vesper services. As the gloss puts it, the seamen receive the bird "with great joy and hospitality." The killing of the bird is then a betrayal of trust; and the seamen subsequently punish the mariner for his act of inhospitality. In a sense we are reminded of the pagan world of the epic, where an act of violence against one who has shared our drink and food is an unforgivable crime. In another sense, we partake of the moral and social climate of the Coleridges, Wordsworths, and Pooles in Nether Stowey at the end of the eighteenth century. The community of men pictured here is similar to that celebrated by Wordsworth in "The Old Cumberland Beggar" and "Tintern Abbey"; the indignation expressed at the treatment of the albatross, akin to that voiced by Coleridge at the imagined violation of wife, babe, and friends in "Fears in Solitude."

In effect, the poem offers two explanations of the seamen's response to the incidents of the voyage: one balladic and supported by the narrative events, the other lyrical and supported by the Christian references, descriptive details, and prose commentary. Sometimes only the primary viewpoint is operating. Thus, the dying of the seamen under the aegis of "the star-dogged moon" conforms only to the superstitious, animistic world of the ballad. At other times the details in the poem combine to assert both views simultaneously as in the incident of the albatross or in the action of the mariner blessing the water snakes swimming in the moonlight—which we shall shortly consider. In these unified portions of the poem, with their evocation of a world in which moral order and reverence for life obtain, we hear most faithfully the sound of Coleridge's real, rather than his ventriloquism, voice.

When Coleridge wrote the gloss in 1815–16, in which he spells out for us the nature of the mariner's guilt, the close ties of love and friendship connected with Nether Stowey and the composition of "The Ancient Mariner" had been severed for five or six years. Since November 1810, he had been drifting from house to house, dependent on the hospitality of others. He must have looked back to that early glorious time with considerable nostalgia as he composed the prose gloss, for it glows with moving tribute to hospitality and family solidarity. In 1828, when he prepared "The Wanderings of Cain" for the press, he similarly looked back, through even more years than when he had written the gloss to "The Ancient Mariner," and exclaimed fervently in the Preface, "Nether Stowey . . . *sanctum et amabile nomen!* rich by so many associations and recollections." This climate of tender regard for others informs a variety of Coleridge's poems written during the first halcyon years of his marriage and association with Wordsworth. "The Ancient Mariner" and the conversation and friendship poems clearly share a common response to the social scene. It is not strange then that "The Ancient Mariner" should also share in the lyrical impulse which produced these other poems. Not only its moral tone but also its descriptions of nature (some of which are hardly appropriate to a seaman) testify to this common origin. Frequently admired is the description of the ice met by the ship; less frequently mentioned but just as lyrically inspired is the description of the sounds made by the angelic spirits:

> Around, around, flew each sweet sound,
> Then darted to the Sun;
> Slowly the sounds came back again,
> Now mixed, now one by one.

> Sometimes a-dropping from the sky
> I heard the sky-lark sing;
> Sometimes all little birds that are,
> How they seemed to fill the sea and air
> With their sweet jargoning!

> And now 'twas like all instruments,
> Now like a lonely flute;
> And now it is an angel's song,
> That makes the heavens be mute.

> It ceased; yet still the sails made on
> A pleasant noise till noon,
> A noise like of a hidden brook
> In the leafy month of June,

That to the sleeping woods all night
Singeth a quiet tune.

And his harking back in 1815–16 to the time when "The Ancient Mariner" was conceived produced the haunting nostalgia of the much admired description of the mariner longing for surcease of his misery:

> In his loneliness and fixedness he yearneth towards the journeying Moon, and the stars that still sojourn yet still move onward; and every where the blue sky belongs to them, and is their appointed rest, and their native country and their own natural homes, which they enter unannounced, as lords that are certainly expected, and yet there is a silent joy at their arrival.

In this passage, as in the lines of verse accompanying them, Coleridge combines a cultivation of sentiment and regard for home with an attribution of being to all things. The fusion of these lyrical and balladic ingredients gives to "The Ancient Mariner" an intensity and atmosphere unknown to the poetry of the decade.

Miraculously, the poem does not read like a pastiche. Its union of public and private worlds purifies Coleridge's style, letting his naked voice come through to assert two concepts which he believed to be conditions of reality: (1) the interrelation of subject and object, whole and parts, unity and variety, and (2) the expression of love. Reality, he writes in *The Friend,* derives from the mental act of perception—"The intelligence in the one tend[ing] to *objectize* itself, and in the other to *know* itself in the object" (*BL,* I, 188)—whereby a balance of unity *with* variety ideally obtains:

> In a self-conscious and thence reflecting being, no instinct can exist without engendering the belief of an object corresponding to it, either present or future, real or capable of being realized; much less the instinct, in which humanity itself is grounded—that by which, in every act of conscious perception, we at once identify our being with that of the world without us, and yet place ourselves in contra-distinction to that world.[12]

Coleridge believed that love most effectively united one man's thought and being with another's. The souls of lovers become one, he writes in 1804, adapting Adam's punning praise of Eve (*Paradise Lost,* IX, 227–28) to express his feeling for Sara Hutchinson:

> Sole Maid, associate sole, to me beyond
> Compare all living creatures dear. (*N,* II, 1946)

With Sara Hutchinson probably again in mind, he exclaims in "Love's Sanctuary,"

> This yearning heart (Love! witness what I say)
> Enshrines thy form as purely as it may.

Since he considered love as productive of a "union absolute" of two beings (Fragment 31), he quite logically defined its opposite, hatred, as a denial of the existence of externalities. In an analysis of hatred in the "Apologetic Preface to 'Fire, Famine, and Slaughter,'" probably written in 1815, he comments that "the more intense and insane the passion is, the fewer and the more fixed are the correspondent forms and notions. A rooted hatred . . . eddies round its favorite object, and exercises as it were a perpetual tautology of mind in thoughts and words which admit of no adequate substitutes. Like a fish in a globe of glass, it moves restlessly round and round the scanty circumference, which it cannot leave without losing its vital element" (*CPW,* II, 1099).

This definition of hatred describes the state of mind of the ancient mariner after his slaying of the albatross. He frees himself from his "tautology of mind in thoughts and words" by projecting his thoughts outward to remind himself of the "endless compositions of nature" in which, as in him, flow "the germinal causes" of joyous life (*BL,* II, 258–59). In the sojourning yet traveling moon and stars the mariner perceives the fixed unity with continuous progression which, in his fixedness, he desires. His longing for home reaches out to participate in the lordly welcome accorded to the journeying stars by the night sky, and the happiness which he attaches to such a situation suffuses his spirit. His thought, once subjective, now objectifies and combines with the calm disposition of nature. As the prose gloss tells us, from "despis[ing] the creatures of the calm and env[ying] that *they* should live," he beholds "by the light of the moon . . . God's creatures of the great calm. Their beauty and their happiness. He blesseth them in his heart. The spell begins to break." Coincident with his renewed wholeness of spirit and sense of oneness with nature, the albatross, emblem of his physical, spiritual, and imaginative isolation, drops from his neck.

In the total statement of "The Ancient Mariner," we recognize a poetic signature which transcends the anonymity of the ballad and declares itself, had we met it "running wild in the deserts of Arabia" (*CL,* I, 453), to be Coleridge![13] But his achievement in the ballad was short-lived. His judgment of "The Ancient Mariner" indicates, like a bird of ill omen, the direction subsequently taken by his ventriloquism voice. "[I] was preparing among other poems, 'The Dark Ladie' and the 'Christabel,'" he writes in retrospect, "in which I should have more nearly realized my ideal than I had done in my first attempt" (*BL,* II, 6). He, of course, is thinking primarily of his success in giving a semblance of poetic truth to the supernatural. Not without significance, however, are the two poems that he believes represent an advance over "The Ancient Mariner"; in both he reverts to the usual ballad narrative of his day. Allegiance to *The Faerie Queene* had prompted eighteenth-century poets to modify the concept of the ballad to fit the Spenserian vision of knights and ladies and medieval tournaments. The sea-setting of "The Ancient Mariner" kept Coleridge momentarily free of Spenserian romance and allowed him to reconcile, with great narrative tension, the realism and terseness of the folk-ballad and the sentiment and lyricism of Georgian verse. But with "The Dark Ladié" and "Christabel," Part I, he turns to the castellated landscape of medieval romances imitated by Scott and other contemporary balladeers.

This reversion to the literary tastes and sensibilities of the Burneys and Gillmans is foreshadowed in "The Ancient Mariner." One has only to read "Sir Patrick Spens" to perceive a basic difference between its terse narrative and the didactic and pictorial elaborateness of "The Ancient Mariner." The anonymous singer of "Sir Patrick Spens" tells his tale with stark economy; transition and explanation are omitted; all is situation. The king asks for a sailor. A knight recommends Sir Patrick. The king sends him an order to put to sea. The loyal liegeman laughs at the insane command, then weeps at the thought of certain death, and wonders who has plotted this against him. But he informs his crew that they will sail in the morning. One of them protests, foreseeing a storm. Still, they sail as scheduled. The ship sinks, leaving their hats floating on the water. The final scene shifts to the ladies ashore who will now await forever the return of their lords who lie in fifty fathoms of water. Only the essence of the story is given, the origin of the order sending Spens to sea and the consequences. The actual storm and the sinking remain implied in the silences.

When we turn to "The Ancient Mariner," we see instantly that Coleridge has modified the folk-ballad emphasis on men in action to include the contemporary taste for nature painting, atmosphere and mood, moral messages, and supernatural hugger-mugger. Fused with, and subsidiary to, the narrative at first, these ingredients assume increased importance in the second half of the poem. And weakened narrative control accompanies the change. In the first four sections, the realistically told narrative manages by the coincidence of occurrences in nature and events of the voyage to suggest the mysterious moral order of the world. The blowing of the good south wind and the becalming of the vessel follow the shooting of the albatross. The tropical rain storm concurs with the remorse of the mariner. The appearance of the sun coincides with the punishment of the seamen, the moon with salvation for the mariner. But Coleridge is unable to maintain this superb ordering of events with its evocation of cosmic order. With all but one of the sailors dead, he resorts to a *deus ex machina* to explain the return of the mariner. He summons a troop of angelic spirits to his aid. Significantly, as Lowes has noted (pp. 222–24), the angelic intervention was the only one of the six determining factors of the action—the other five are the killing of the albatross, the spectral persecution, the reanimation of the dead seamen, the skeleton ship, and the old navigator—not mentioned by either Coleridge or Wordsworth (so far as the records tell us) on the walking tour in November 1797, when the plan of the poem was first formulated. Could Coleridge have introduced the angelic troop at a later date as an expedient to get the vessel home?

The introduction of the angels may indicate that Coleridge is either shifting his interest to the moral import of his tale or losing control of the narrative. A good case can be made for each possibility. The last three sections devote a large percentage of the tale to recording the conversation of the polar spirit's fellow daemons, the actions of the seraph band, and the life and sentiments of the hermit and of the mariner. In all three instances, exposition, Gothic claptrap, and moral edification replace narrative progression. The polar daemons discuss the motive power of the ship and the penance of the mariner. The seraphs, after working the ship home and signaling ashore of its arrival, terrorize the mariner by departing in a lurid glow of red light from the bodies of the dead seamen. And the mariner, in the accents of the hermit, lectures the wedding-guest—and the reader—on the joys of church attendance and communal prayer. The story-telling impulse in Coleridge—never strong at any time—has succumbed to the tendentious ethical and didactic streak in him, which clearly monopolizes the final portions of the poem. Perhaps his famous comment to Mrs. Barbauld about the excessive and obtrusive moral of "The Ancient Mariner" does not require the subtle analysis or—worse yet—the skepticism to which critics have subjected it. Perhaps Coleridge meant exactly what he said, for the chief fault of "The Ancient Mariner" is that "the moral sentiment" does obtrude too "openly on the reader as a principle or cause of action in a work of such pure imagination" (*TT*, II, 155-56). As Kathleen Coburn remarks, apropos of her role as editor of his notebooks, "Coleridge makes better sense than we sometimes make of him" (*N*, I, xxxi). He recognized that moral sentiment pervades the second half of the poem, not just in the maxim about kindness to all living things, but also in the conception, motivation, and narration of the tale.

The ambiguous course of the ship from Part V onwards also reflects a weakening of narrative invention. It had been sailing north in the Pacific (gloss to line 105) before it was becalmed in the doldrums at the equator. When the spirit from the South Pole propels it—for a half day—no direction is given. Apparently with good reason! For the ship traverses the South Pacific and the South Atlantic—retracing its voyage out, from line to line around the Horn, which had taken months—traverses these vast stretches of water in twelve hours! There can be no other explanation. We are told in the gloss to line 105 that the ship reaches the equator in the Pacific before it is becalmed. In the gloss to line 380, we are told that "the lonesome spirit from the south-pole carries the ship as far as the line"— which must be the equator in the Atlantic, for the ship was already at the line in the Pacific when the polar spirit began moving it. The ship must be in the Atlantic or no sense can be made of the gloss to line 425, which relates that angelic spirits take over at the equator and "cause the vessel to drive northward." If the ship were still in the Pacific, Puget Sound, not the mariner's own country, would soon have hove over the horizon. But nothing of the kind occurs; shortly after the angelic spirits assume command, the vessel drifts across the harbor bar into its home port.

Once the central action of the sin, punishment, and redemption of the mariner is enacted to its conclusion, Coleridge has no reason for prolonging the journey; and the celestial machinery allows him with breathtaking efficiency to fling the mariner into a swound and rush the ship home at superhuman speed. Viewed thus, the poem illustrates an admirable skill in narrative proportion: the voyage out takes months and more than 300 lines; the return trip transpires in a twinkling of time and with angelic power. Unfortunately, Coleridge is unable to cope adequately with problems inherent in the narrative. Besides the ambiguous movements of the ship, the aura of mystery so richly permeating the drama of the outgoing voyage paradoxically vanishes with the appearance of the heavenly spirits. From relying upon a semblance of narrative realism to make believable the shadows of his imagination, Coleridge shifts midway in the poem to employing the supernatural to explain the narrative. He has sacrificed to the exigencies of the plot his avowed intention of transferring "from our inward nature a human interest and a semblance of truth sufficient to procure" for "persons and characters supernatural, or at least romantic, . . . that willing suspension of disbelief for the moment, which constitutes poetic faith" (*BL,* II, 6). No wonder the poem confused the reviewers and caused Coleridge to believe that "Christabel," Part I, which successfully transfers to romantic and supernatural beings a set of human characteristics and probable circumstances, more nearly realized his intentions.

One, however, should not make too much of these shortcomings. Despite its eighteenth-century orientation and obfuscated narrative, "The Ancient Mariner" remains vital and full-blooded and supremely expressive of Coleridge's naked voice. It balances balladic simplicity of narrative and diction with the Coleridgean voice of ratiocination and idealism (the fervid Coleridgean search for oneness underlying the "multeity" of experience) which we hear so clearly in the best of his other poetry and prose. But anemia in the form of Spenserian knights and ladies and Georgian sentiment and decorum soon weakens the ventriloquism voice. The ballad quickly becomes for Coleridge the mutated and imitable form that it was always for Scott. To see the gross possibilities of this transformation one need read no further than Bishop Percy's "The Hermit of Warkworth."

In "Christabel," Part I, Coleridge uses the scenic, medieval setting of the Spenserian epic. To be sure, he continues to suggest the supernatural through action: Geraldine swoons at the threshold of the courtyard; the mastiff bitch groans angrily; and the dying brands in the fireplace emit a tongue of flame when she passes. But now he also evokes a supernatural atmosphere with description: the picture of the chilly night sky (14–22), the comment on the stillness of the wind (43–52), the portrait of Geraldine (58–65), and the appearance of Christabel's room at night (175–83). In spite of relying increasingly upon such non-balladic elements, however, Coleridge maintains the perilous balance of incongruous ingredients which characterize "The Ancient Mariner." His awareness of good and evil and man's oneness with the external world adds moral and metaphysical dimensions to an otherwise stark recital of fearful occurrences.

But in Part II the narrative loses much of its suggestiveness. Henry Nelson Coleridge's epithet for the poem, "witchery by daylight,"[14] is misleading. Part I *bewitches* us with midnight moonshine; Part II awakes us to daylight and a *witch.* Geraldine's misfortunes, so mysterious in the half shadows of the night before, are now explicit in the light of the morning after as the unnatural natural history of a snake woman. After relying upon incident and setting to procure for Geraldine an aura of the uncanny, Coleridge accepts preternatural aid, in Part II, when his imagination fails him. Just as he had resorted in "The Ancient Mariner" to supernatural machinery to return the ship to home port, so in the second part of "Christabel," he turns to Lamia witchcraft to motivate the actions of Geraldine, Christabel, and Sir Leoline. And the effect is the same: a dissolution of mystery.

These preternatural events can be defended in theory. As if he were writing with his own poem in mind, Coleridge approves, in a letter to John Murray of 10 September 1814, of a comparable expediency used by Goethe in *Faust,* and these words may serve effectively in his own defense.

> I think the "Faust" a work of genius. . . . The Scenes in the Cathedral and in the Prison must delight and affect all Readers not pre-determined to dislike. But the Scenes of Witchery and that astonishing Witch-Gallop up the Brocken will be denounced as *fantastic* and absurd. Fantastic they *are,* and were meant to be; but I need not tell you, how many will detect the supposed fault for one, who can enter into the philosophy of that imaginative Superstition, which justifies it. (*CL,* III, 528)

More than thirteen years earlier, in a letter to Wordsworth of 30 January 1801, Lamb had lodged such a complaint against "The Ancient Mariner": "I dislike all the miraculous part of it, but the feelings of the man under the operation of such scenery dragged me along like Tom Piper's magic whistle." Coleridge knew the contents of this letter (cf. Lamb's letter of 15 February 1801 to Thomas Manning); and may have remembered this objection to the use of supernatural agents when he hypothesized the reaction of readers to *Faust.* Ever insistent upon principles in his myriad-mindedness, Coleridge answers such objections with the argument that a work of art has its own rules and creates its own standards of judgment; yet no explanation can alter the consequences for both "The Ancient Mariner" and "Christabel" of spelling out the marvelous in the broad daylight of cause and effect.

In the second halves of both poems, Coleridge caricatures a rich concatenation of mystery into a bald exposition of superstition. To compensate for the failure of narrative invention in "Christabel," he substitutes elaborately detailed landscapes. The daylight setting becomes explicitly topographical. From merely sketching the generalized outline of a medieval castle near a wood in Part I, Coleridge proceeds in Part II to specifying Lake Country names (Wyndermere, Brotha Head, and Langdale Pike) and to recounting local legends (the three sinful sextons' ghosts). In the tradition of the old romances, he introduces two hostile knights and fore-shadows the journey of a bard with a message from one of the knights to the other. That the change in emphasis is conscious, at least in after-thought, Coleridge makes clear in a letter to Allsop: "If I should finish 'Christabel,' I shall certainly extend it, and give new characters, and a greater number of incidents. This the 'reading public' require, and this is the reason that Sir Walter Scott's poems, tho so loosely written, are pleas-ing, and interest us by their picturesqueness" (Allsop, I, 64). To another person he is said to have confided his intention of devoting additional length and details to the description of scenery attending Bard Bracy's journey.[15] Coleridge's explanation of the reason for these additions differs from mine. He pleads the expediency of public demand. Whether a failure of narrative invention or a compromise with economic necessity, unques-tionably such picturesque prospects remove us from the harsh domain of the ballad and transport us to the landscaped vistas of William Gilpin and Georgian England.

Besides satisfying the eighteenth-century taste for scenery, the second part of "Christabel" also appeases the appetite of the age for well-expressed sentiments. The action dwells on Sir Leoline's sensitivity to a breach of hospitality, accompanied ironically by his insensitivity to the needs of his daughter. It also marks time while Coleridge reflects poignantly on the sadness of sundered friends, in the lovely lines beginning, "They had been friends in youth." Similarly, he contemplates in "The Conclusion to Part II" the paradoxical course that a father's love for his child takes when

> . . . pleasures flow in so thick and fast
> Upon his heart, that he at last
> Must needs express his love's excess
> With words of unmeant bitterness.

With such sentiments we approach the hearth of domesticity and warm ourselves at the fire of friendship and family felicity celebrated in the con-versation poems. Although the moral is not as obtrusive as in "The An-cient Mariner," obviously, such feelings are at variance with the unadorned action and impersonal point of view of the ballad. And most critics testify to the falling off in Part II of "Christabel" of the forceful effect of terseness, the narrative slowed down by description and exposition, its forward flow almost imperceptible, as feelings and thoughts are now tediously re-counted, not vividly evoked through events.

The failure of narrative in "The Ancient Mariner" and "Christabel" may also be, in part, the natural consequence of Coleridge's low opinion of plot. The parts of fiction which engaged his attention were language and character (cf. *SC,* I, 205–06). In his Shakespearean lectures, plot is usually ignored or dismissed as "a mere vehicle" for the author's thoughts (*SC,* II, 192). He expresses fear, in a famous letter to Cottle of April 1797 that Southey "will begin to rely too much on story and event in his poems, to the neglect of those lofty imaginings that are peculiar to, and definitive of, the poet" (*CL,* I, 320). With great consistency, Coleridge reflects this scorn for story when he prematurely discloses at the end of Part I that Christabel will eventually win salvation and marriage through her aptitude for prayer.

When we turn from "Christabel" to "The Ballad of the Dark Ladié," "Love," "Alice du Clos," and "Baron Guelph of Adelstan," we see that Coleridge accepts as had Collins and Chatterton the view of the century that the ballad is a tale of knights and ladies cavorting sometimes tragically but always romantically in forest glades. In these ballad tales, he enthrones the theme of romantic love, its sweetness and its tribulation. Tears flow copiously from the eyes of the "dark ladie." Fair Genevieve, in "Love," listens "with a fitting blush," thrilling in grief and weeping with pity and delight at the doleful tale her minstrel lover sings. Her sentiment is a far cry from the real tear wrung from the eye of Sir Patrick Spens when he realizes that his death is prearranged. We have obviously departed from the real, if frequently cruel, environment of the folk-ballad and stepped into the leafy world of hill and bower which Coleridge had visited in sentimental anticipation with his friend Lloyd.

If the subject-matter is sentimentalized, the artistic handling of the stanza as the unit of thought remains as superb in "The Dark Ladié" and "Love" as it is in "The Ancient Mariner." But the stanza of "Alice du Clos," probably written in the late 1820's, clearly reflects the enchantment cast over the eighteenth and early nineteenth centuries by Spenser. The stanzaic sentence of "The Ancient Mariner," designed for swiftly told action, has lengthened into a tapestry of color and sound and of details and digressions—notice the leisurely effort to enlist the reader's imagination and sympathy in favor of the beauty and innocence of Alice:

> Thus spake Sir Hugh the vassal knight
> 　To Alice, child of old Du Clos,
> As spotless fair, as any light
> 　As that moon-shiny doe,

The gold star on its brow, her sire's ancestral crest!
For ere the lark had left his nest,
    She in the garden bower below
Sate loosely wrapt in maiden white,
Her face half drooping from the sight,
    A snow-drop on a tuft of snow!

O close your eyes, and strive to see
The studious maid, with book on knee,—
    Ah! earliest-open'd flower;
While yet with keen unblunted light
The morning star shone opposite
    The lattice of her bower—
Alone of all the starry host,
    As if in prideful scorn
Of flight and fear he stay'd behind,
    To brave th' advancing morn.

Coleridge's emulation of Spenser produces an extended simile which might have come from *The Faerie Queene:*

    . . . and with a baleful smile
        The vassal knight reel'd off—
    Like a huge billow from a bark
        Toil'd in the deep sea-trough,
    That shouldering sideways in mid plunge,
        Is travers'd by a flash.
    And staggering onward, leaves the ear
        With dull and distant crash.

A similar shift marks the language. The concrete objects and primary colors celebrated in "The Ancient Mariner"—*mast high ice, emerald green, bloody sun, hot and copper sky, blue, glossy green,* and *velvet black water snakes flashing in the burning water*—blur in "Love," "The Dark Ladié," and "Alice du Clos" to a shadowy world of muted colors—*silver bark, moonshine blending with the lights of eve, soft and doleful airs, veiling mist,* and *twilight shade of a leafy screen.* The wedding-guest beating his breast and the eyes of the dead seamen cursing the mariner are emasculated to the "dark ladie" dropping a silent tear and Genevieve weeping with timorous plaint. The basic emotions of *hate, fear, love,* soften to the cultivated feelings of *pity, shame, meekness.* Activity—*cracked, growled, roared, howled*—subsides into quiescence—*sitting, drooping, wishing.*

The ballad seemed at first to offer Coleridge an alternative to the Miltonic diction and syntax of the farrago and prophecy poems. To the unadorned ballad tale of action, he added his vision of the immediacy of nature and his belief in the ethics of human conduct, effecting, as R. H. Fogle remarks, "a reconciliation between opposite satisfactions of recognition and surprise," whereby we "find more meaning than was bargained for" (Fogle, *AM,* p. 117). The fusion achieved one resounding success in "The Ancient Mariner." But the ballad was malleable in other hands as well as in Coleridge's—Spenser's, for example; and this lyrically sentient and richly pictorial model assumes increasing importance in Coleridge's poetic narratives. In his zeal to reproduce the simplicity of the folk-ballad, he passes from Miltonic sublimity to Spenserian decorativeness, two literary influences which initially quickened but ultimately stultified the sensibilities of many eighteenth-century poets.

Coleridge was unable, despite a life-long effort, to repeat the unique fusion of balladic and lyrical impulses that he had achieved in "The Ancient Mariner." In no other of his voices is found proportionally so many unfinished starts. Nor can this failure of poetic inspiration be blamed entirely upon lack of encouragement—as at a later date Coleridge was to excuse his unproductivity, charging Wordsworth with uncharitableness in decrying "The Ancient Mariner" and of deflecting him from that "distinctive current" of his own (*L,* II, 696). Wordsworth also entreated Coleridge to stop his concentrated studies in abstruse philosophy (*CL,* II, 707) but was sublimely unsuccessful, the mercurial Coleridge showing in his metaphysical pursuits a surprising pertinacity. The making of poetry, however, requires more than resolution; it needs a poetic style congenial to one's sensibility. In the long run, the ventriloquism voice offered Coleridge no such congeniality. The facts show that his inability to complete "Christabel" was not due to paralysis of his muse. During the years he fretted over it, he completed "Dejection," "Hymn Before Sun-rise," "A Daydream," and "To William Wordsworth"—to name only a few of the best in the other voices. Even the creation of "The Ancient Mariner," in comparison to the relative ease with which the poems of the other voices were composed, is a famous case history of literary birth pains. The poem went through five printings (1798, 1800, 1802, 1805, and 1817) and at least two major revisions (1800 and 1817) before reaching its final form. Archaic spelling and diction were tried and discarded. Much charnelhouse horror in the explicit mode of the Gothicists (cf. 1798 version, 181–85 and 481–98) had to be deleted, ambiguous narrative clarified. Not until the 1800 version, for example, does one learn that the wind accompanying the tropical storm "never reached the ship." Many such ambiguous parts of the narrative were eventually clarified by the prose gloss. We first learn from the gloss that the seamen "make themselves accomplices in the crime" of the mariner when they justify his murder of the albatross, and that "Death and Life-in-Death have diced for the ship's crew, and she (the latter) winneth the ancient mariner."[16] Although he came closest of any poet in English literature to mastering the deceptive simplicity of the ballad, Coleridge found it increasingly alien to his point of view and that of the age of sensibility in which he lived.

The qualified success of "The Introduction to the Tale of the Dark Ladie" epitomizes the pattern of compromise, substitution, and frustration governing his effort to write in the ballad mode. Subsequently entitled "Love" and offered as a substitute for the unfinished "Ballad," it finally struggled to a conclusion, at the end of 1799, as a sentiment-ridden tale of modern love. To be sure, the melodic achievement of the poem reminds us of "The Ancient Mariner" and "Christabel"—and the metrical gift of Coleridge. And the narrative asserts Coleridge's faith in love as the supreme value:

> All thoughts, all passions, all delights,
> Whatever stirs this mortal frame,
> All are but ministers of Love,
>   And feed his sacred flame.

But what are we to make of a girl who loves her betrothed best when he sings "the songs that make her grieve"? Such courting of doleful feelings is ultimately damaging to the tone of the poem.

When his narrative ingenuity or poetic imagination falters in the ventriloquism voice, Coleridge relies upon one or more expediencies: (1) he exploits supernatural devices ("The Three Graves," "The Ancient Mariner," and "Christabel"); (2) he resorts to clichés of sentiment ("Love" and "Alice du Clos"); or (3) he abandons the poem ("Ballad of the Dark Ladié," "The Three Graves," "Baron Guelph," and "Christabel"). Thus, Coleridge's failure in "Christabel" reflects the ultimate failure of the ventriloquism voice.

Ironically, not in the alien and severely limited simplicity of the ballad but in the natural and flexible accents of his own speaking voice was Coleridge finally to find a measure effectively modifying his Miltonic numbers into an innocently naked and spontaneously modern tongue. Unlike the conversation voice which we shall look at next, the simplicity of the ballad remained to the end of Coleridge's life a ventriloquistic medium. He was unable to transform it—except for a few glorious months—into a living voice responsive to his everyday thought as well as his midnight visions.

There are not a few poems . . . replete with every excellence of thought, image, and passion, which we expect or desire in the poetry of the milder muse, and yet so worded, that the reader sees no one reason either in the selection or the order of the words, why he might not have said the very same in an appropriate conversation, and cannot conceive how indeed he could have expressed such thoughts otherwise, without loss or injury to his meaning.

—*Biographia Literaria,* Chapter XIX

V

THE CONVERSATION VOICE

What Coleridge says about *Osorio* to William Lisle Bowles in a letter of 16 October 1797 may also be said about his conversation poems: "If there be any thing with which I am at all satisfied, it is—the style. I have endeavoured to have few sentences which *might not* be spoken in conversation, avoiding those that are *commonly* used in conversation" (*CL,* I, 356). In the conversation poems—"The Eolian Harp," "Reflections on Having Left a Place of Retirement," "This Lime-tree Bower My Prison," "Frost at Midnight," "Fears in Solitude," "The Nightingale," and "To William Wordsworth"—Coleridge creates a style at once spontaneous and formal, in whose inflection is heard his most characteristic—perhaps most mature—voice.

Like the farrago, prophecy, and ventriloquism voices, his conversation voice combines the old and the new. It derives from the descriptive-meditative poem; but he has given to the formal, stylized elements of this genre a new informality and spontaneity. His response to a short-lived domestic happiness and his philosophical belief in the oneness of life helped him to transform the topographical poem, with its apostrophe to nature, narrative and didactic digression, and stiff Thomsonian blank verse, into a record of friendly discourse or silent musing which is both spontaneous and whole.

The innovation in the address machinery is particularly happy. An intimate friend or a member of Coleridge's family replaces the conventional muse or green-robed nymph of the descriptive poem. In "The Eolian Harp," Coleridge speaks to his wife. "Reflections" opens with a similar address. But lecturing was a vice of the landscape poem not quickly outgrown; and Coleridge did not always resist the temptation to preach. In "Reflections," when he relates how he toiled to the top of a hill to survey the countryside, he forgets momentarily to whom he has been talking and delivers a sermon to the world. The same bad practice mars the otherwise excellent opening and closing of "Fears in Solitude." "This Lime-tree

Bower" and "Frost at Midnight," however, retain their good manners; each begins as a soliloquy but shifts gracefully to address an absent confidant: in the former, Charles Lamb, who is physically absent but spiritually present; and in the latter, Hartley Coleridge, who is physically present but asleep and spiritually absent. "The Nightingale" utilizes perfectly the impromptu nature of a chat. One hears in it the voice of the poet as he approaches with friends, as he moves away, and "all the interval," to quote Keats's impression of his chance meeting and two-mile stroll with the Highgate sage in 1819.[1] By the expedient of addressing wife, child, or friend, Coleridge insures an impression of conversation.

Their discursiveness also contributes to the naturalness of these poems. The descriptive poem was usually long—often book-length. It included diverse ingredients organized loosely in terms of the seasons of the year or hours of the day. The conversation poem is short; therefore it offers little opportunity for digression. Yet Coleridge has not forfeited the impression of unpremeditated talk inherent in a lack of method—as conveyed, for example, by Mistress Quickly's ramblings. He is boldly discursive in the conversation poems. "The Eolian Harp" comprises two scenes: evening in front of the cottage and afternoon on the hillside. "Reflections" moves successively through the following episodes: a description of the cottage, an encounter with a Bristol passerby, a view of the countryside from a hill, a disquisition on brotherly love, and again a reference to the cottage. "The Nightingale" consists of the roadside scene in which Coleridge says farewell to the Wordsworths, the castle-grove scene in which the gentle maid listens to the nightingales, and the garden scene in which Hartley is shown the moon. Each of the conversation poems is a collage of descriptions and episodes, which the autobiographical theme prevents from becoming, as in Erasmus Darwin's verses, "a succession of landscapes or paintings" (*N*, I, 132).

Equally suggestive of spontaneity is the conversational tone of the blank verse, which owes much to the "colloquial" style of Cowper's *The Task* (*MC*, p. 251) and "the *neutral ground*" of Daniel and Massinger's diction and meter (*BL*, II, 61).[2] From Cowper, Coleridge learned to fit the tense condensation of the Miltonic parenthesis to the relaxed ebb and flow of friendly talk, as in these lines from "Reflections":

> Once I saw
> (Hallowing his Sabbath-day by quietness)
> A wealthy son of Commerce saunter by,
> Bristowa's citizen: methought, it calm'd

His thirst of idle gold, and made him muse
With wiser feelings: for he paus'd, and look'd
With a pleas'd sadness, and gaz'd all around,
Then eyed our Cottage, and gaz'd round again,
And sigh'd, and said, it was a Blessèd Place.
And we *were* bless'd. Oft with patient ear
Long-listening to the viewless sky-lark's note
(Viewless, or haply for a moment seen
Gleaming on sunny wings) in whisper'd tones
I've said to my Belovèd. . . .

There is little question that Coleridge's mind was addicted to parenthetical expression, as anyone reading his prose is painfully aware; but parenthesis had meaning for him—and consequently for the conversation poems: they are "the drama of reason—and present the thought growing, instead of a mere hortus siccus" (*CL,* III, 282). And a realization of thought (whether internal dialog or talk) in process of formulation is part of his objective in the conversation poems.

Under the tutelage of Cowper's "divine chit-chat" (*CL,* I, 279), Coleridge learned to adapt the Miltonic measure, so obtrusive in his early verse, to the domestic contents of the conversation poem. At the same time, he did not succumb to the temptation of imitating Cowper's burlesque of Milton. He followed Cowper's movement toward a low-keyed naturalness, but added his own serious note, as the following quotations from Milton, Cowper, and Coleridge illustrate:

Sweet is the breath of morn, her rising sweet,
With charm of earliest Birds; pleasant the Sun
When first on this delightful Land he spreads
His orient Beams, on herb, tree, fruit, and floure,
Glistring with dew; fragrant the fertil earth
After soft showers; and sweet the coming on
Of grateful Eevning milde, then silent Night
With this her solemn Bird and this fair Moon,
And these the Gemms of Heav'n, her starrie train:
But neither breath of Morn when she ascends
With charm of earliest Birds, nor rising Sun
On this delightful land, nor herb, fruit, floure,
Glistring with dew, nor fragrance after showers,
Nor grateful Eevning milde, nor silent Night

With this her solemn Bird, nor walk by Moon,
Or glittering Starr-light without thee is sweet.
But wherefore all night long shine these, for whom
This glorious sight, when sleep hath shut all eyes?

(*Paradise Lost,* IV, 641–659)

The nurse sleeps sweetly, hired to watch the sick
Whom snoring she disturbs. As sweetly he
Who quits the coach-box at the midnight hour
To sleep within the carriage more secure,
His legs depending at the open door.
Sweet sleep enjoys the Curate in his desk,
The tedious Rector drawling o'er his head,
And sweet the Clerk below: but neither sleep
Of lazy nurse, who snores the sick man dead,
Nor his wife who quits the box at midnight hour
To slumber in the carriage more secure,
Nor sleep enjoy'd by Curate in his desk,
Nor yet the dozings of the Clerk are sweet,
Compared with the repose the Sofa yields.

(*The Task,* I, 89–102)

Pale beneath the blaze
Hung the transparent foliage; and I watch'd
Some broad and sunny leaf and lov'd to see
The shadow of the leaf and stem above
Dappling its sunshine! And that walnut-tree
Was richly ting'd, and a deep radiance lay
Full on the ancient ivy, which usurps
Those fronting elms, and now, with blackest mass
Makes their dark branches gleam a lighter hue
Through the late twilight: and though now the bat
Wheels silent by and not a swallow twitters,
Yet still the solitary humble-bee
Sings in the bean-flower! Henceforth I shall know
That Nature ne'er deserts the wise and pure;
No plot so narrow, be but Nature there,
No waste so vacant, but may well employ

> Each faculty of sense, and keep the heart
> Awake to Love and Beauty! ("This Lime-tree Bower")

Coleridge has improved upon Cowper to the extent that he dares be natural without the subterfuge of satire. Cowper, more at ease with the coy periphrasis "prickly and green-coated gourd" than with the household term "cucumber," will ordinarily hedge his use of a common or coarse word with mock-heroic levity. Before describing how to make a garden, for example, he feels the need to apologize mockingly to the "critic appetite" for the "sordid fare" that he is about to feed it. But his nerve fails before a word like "manure," which becomes "a stercorarious heap," its effluvium "A pestilent and most corrosive steam,/ Like a gross fog Boeotian." Compare Cowper's euphemisms with Coleridge's prosaic description in "Reflections" of the honeymoon cottage:

> In the open air
> Our Myrtles blossom'd; and across the porch
> Thick Jasmins twined: the little landscape round
> Was green and woody, and refresh'd the eye.
> It was a spot which you might aptly call
> The Valley of Seclusion!

and intrepid informality in the opening lines of "This Lime-tree Bower":

> Well, they are gone, and here must I remain,
> This lime-tree bower my prison!

Aided by natural diction and syntax and the repetition of key words, ideas, or phrases, Coleridge's blank verse suggests the stops and starts of impromptu speech, and to that extent, is a suppler, more idiomatic instrument than Cowper's narrative and descriptive measure.

We can watch Coleridge from poem to poem developing this conversational ease. In "The Eolian Harp" (August 1795), his effort metrically to emphasize intensity of feeling does not wholly succeed. The resort to italics tacitly admits failure:

> How exquisite the scents
> Snatch'd from yon bean-field! and the world *so* hush'd!

Failure also marks the demand that the meter support exclamations:

> And that simplest Lute,
> Placed length-ways in the clasping casement, hark!

> But thy more serious eye a mild reproof
> Darts, O belovéd Woman!

"Reflections" (published October 1796) reveals a growing ability to handle the dramatic possibilities of blank verse:

> I therefore go, and join head, heart, and hand,
> Active and firm, to fight the bloodless fight
> Of Science, Freedom, and the Truth in Christ.

If we overlook the sententiousness, we can recognize in these lines a skill-ful use of alliteration, spondee, and inverted foot to convey the mounting fervor of Coleridge's resolve to enter active life. Similarly, caesura and spondee combine in the first of the following two lines to support the idea of the steepness of the hill and the physical effort required to climb it:

> From that low Dell, steep up the stony Mount
> I climb'd with perilous toil and reach'd the top.

But in other instances, Coleridge still depends on italics, in lieu of the skill-ful deploy of syntax and metrics, to guide the reader:

> *Here* the bleak mount,
> The bare bleak mountain speckled thin with sheep;
> Grey clouds, that shadowing spot the sunny fields;
> And river, now with bushy rocks o'er-brow'd,
> Now winding bright and full, with naked banks;
> And seats, and lawns, the Abbey and the wood,
> And cots, and hamlets, and faint city-spire;
> The Channel *there,* the Islands and white sails,
> Dim coasts, and cloud-like hills, and shoreless Ocean—
> It seem'd like Omnipresence! God, methought,
> Had built him there a Temple: the whole World
> Seem'd *imag'd* in its vast circumference:
> No *wish* profan'd my overwhelmed heart.

By the middle of the following year, however, beginning with "This Lime-tree Bower" (June 1797) and followed by "Frost at Midnight" (February 1798), Coleridge shows that he has mastered a blank verse which follows his shifting thoughts and emotions with ease. And in "The Nightingale" (April 1798), particularly, he duplicates the inexhaustible and varied flow of his talk with startling fidelity. The meter underscores each pause and shift of thought in his description of the silent evening, including the interruption of his reflections to note the nightingale's song and to ask and answer a question:

> No cloud, no relique of the sunken day
> Distinguishes the West, no long thin slip
> Of sullen light, no obscure trembling hues.
> Come, we will rest on this old mossy bridge!
> You see the glimmer of the stream beneath,
> But hear no murmuring: it flows silently,
> O'er its soft bed of verdure. All is still,
> A balmy night! and though the stars be dim,
> Yet let us think upon the vernal showers
> That gladden the green earth, and we shall find
> A pleasure in the dimness of the stars.
> And hark! the Nightingale begins its song,
> "Most musical, most melancholy" bird!
> A melancholy bird? Oh! idle thought!
> In Nature there is nothing melancholy.

With dramatic effect, a caesura supports the reference to the silence of the birds; and enjambment, the narration of their ensuing outburst of song:

> . . . she knows all their notes,
> That gentle Maid! and oft, a moment's space,
> What time the moon was lost behind a cloud,
> Hath heard a pause of silence; till the moon
> Emerging, hath awakened earth and sky
> With one sensation, and those wakeful birds
> Have all burst forth in choral minstrelsy.

The blank verse reproduces the shifting accents of his farewell to the nightingale, which he repeats to the Wordsworths before breaking off to note the recurring song of the bird:

> Farewell, O Warbler! till to-morrow eve,
> And you, my friends, farewell, a short farewell!
> We have been loitering long and pleasantly,
> And now for our dear homes.—That strain again!
> Full fain it would delay me!

And it dramatically reproduces, with caesural and end-line pauses, the drop in Coleridge's voice as he apologizes for the tale about his son:

Well!—
It is a father's tale.

The natural rhythms of speech characterizing the blank verse of the conversation poems are probably no accident. Besides Cowper, Coleridge was also studying the Elizabethan dramatists—especially Massinger—during the years that he was writing the conversation poems. In later years, he repeatedly praises Massinger as unrivaled "in the art of reconciling metre with the natural rhythm of conversation" (*MC*, p. 77) and thus achieving a "middle style" which is a "happy imitation of the rhythm of animated talk in real life" (*MC*, p. 72) and the "nearest approach to the language of real life at all compatible with a fixed metre." Massinger became for him the representative of a poetic achievement contrary to that of Pope and subsequent writers in whom "it is the mechanical metre which determines the sense" (*MC*, p. 94). Although Coleridge was reading G. Colman's four-volume edition of Massinger in the summer of 1797 and again in the summer of 1798,[3] one cannot fix the degree of his indebtedness with certainty. One can only note that in the lectures of 1818 he praises Massinger's verse because it "may be more successfully adopted by writers in the present day" than Shakespeare's (*MC*, p. 94) and that he was reading this most colloquial of the Jacobean dramatists at a time when he first habitually pitched his own verse near the rhythms of speech.

The extent of Wordsworth's influence on the diction and metrics of Coleridge's poetry is also uncertain. There is some coincidence between the first outburst of this natural vein in "The Eolian Harp" and "Reflections" and the probable meeting of Coleridge and Wordsworth in Bristol in late August or early September 1795.[4] And certainly by 13 May 1796, when Coleridge writes to Thelwall that Wordsworth is "a very dear friend of mine, who is in my opinion the best poet of the age" (*CL*, I, 215), both poets seem to have been in regular communication with each other, Wordsworth even dropping his habitual reserve and dislike of criticism to let Coleridge sometime in March 1796 read and criticize *Salisbury Plain*.[5] If Wordsworth did not influence Coleridge's desire to write simply and colloquially, still the older poet's similar efforts probably confirmed Coleridge in his from late 1795 onwards. And their close association after June 1797 undoubtedly contributed to the sureness of diction of "This Lime-tree Bower" and "Frost at Midnight."

Yet, at no time does Coleridge seem to have subscribed wholeheartedly to Wordsworth's penchant for "matter-of-factness" (*BL*, II, 101). The subtitle which he added to "Reflections" ("A Poem which affects not to be Poetry") when it was published in the *Monthly Magazine*, October 1796, and the motto ("sermoni propriora") which he prefixed to the poem when it appeared in *Poems,* 1797, reflect his uneasiness at using in his poetry language "which is only proper in prose" (*BL,* II, 97). And his disagreement with Wordsworth's "poetic creed" as outlined in the Preface to the 1800 *Lyrical Ballads*—although it was "half a child of my own brain," he admits to Southey in a letter of 29 July 1802, "and the f[irst pass]ages were indeed partly taken from notes of mine" (*CL,* II, 830–31)—signifies his growing dissatisfaction with the prosaic "dead-colour" (*BL,* I, 16) of the spoken word as the medium of poetry. Wordsworth, he continues in the same letter,

> has written lately a number of Poems . . . the greater number of these to my feelings very excellent Compositions/ but here & there a daring Humbleness of Language & Versification, and a strict adherence to matter of fact, even to prolixity, that startled me/ his alterations likewise in Ruth perplexed me/ and I have thought & thought again/ & have not had my doubts solved by Wordsworth/ On the contrary, I rather suspect that some where or other there is a radical Difference in our theoretical opinions respecting Poetry. (*CL,* II, 830)

Coleridge was right in his suspicions. Basically he and Wordsworth disagreed in theory and practice about the constituents of poetry. As Coleridge puts it in a letter of 13 July 1802 to William Sotheby, "Poetry justifies, as poetry independent of any other passion, some new combinations of language, and commands the omission of many others allowable in other compositions." This truth about poetry, he continues, is not entirely understood by Wordsworth, who does not admit in his theory the possibility of different poems comprising different combinations of language, and who sometimes admits in his practice combinations more appropriate to prose (*CL,* II, 812). The difference between the two poets, as formulated here, is a real one. Coleridge characterizes poetry as being traditionally more artificial than prose. At the same time, he is linking this definition to the essentially organic view that subject-matter determines the language of a poem. Wordsworth, Coleridge laments, says "No" to both propositions. A few years later Coleridge was to point out in the *Biographia Literaria* that when Wordsworth errs in his poetry, he is usually writing according to his poetic theories. The same comment is applicable to Coleridge. Each poet tends to err in poetic practice in the direction of his theoretical predilections: Coleridge toward poetic bombast, and Wordsworth toward prosaic flatness. For a few years, approximately from 1795 to 1800, the development of their poetic paths, however, converged to pursue parallel courses. Since Coleridge's taste for high-flown words was ever present, Wordsworth's influence during these years was undoubtedly salutary.

By way of summary, then, we can say that the naturalness of the conversation poem derives in part from a low-keyed blank verse and a short, ruminative structure in which a close friend or relative appears as an unheard conversant. At the same time, the conversation poem has a unity which, in George McLean Harper's words, is "as exquisitely artistic as the most complicated sonnet."[6] This unity depends upon (1) a curving pattern of emotion, (2) a circular progression of thought, (3) a philosophy based on a concept of "the one life within us and abroad," and (4) an imagery expressive of this sense of the totality of experience.

The conversation poem traces two calm-exaltation-calm parabolas.[7] In each poem Coleridge starts conversationally in the hushed air of a momentarily silenced earth. Moved by a sudden thought or incident, his mood rises to a climax of exalted philosophical or ethical meditation and then sinks from this impassioned tone through quiet talk to the silence that had reigned in the beginning—only to repeat the sequence again. For example, "The Eolian Harp" begins on a note of evening quiet, broken only by the murmur of the distant sea, and Coleridge's voice. The "long sequacious notes" of a wind harp prompt him, with mounting fervor, to exclaim:

> O! the one Life within us and abroad,
> Which meets all motion and becomes its soul,
> A light in sound, a sound-like power in light,
> Rhythm in all thought, and joyance every where.

What can be more spontaneous than such a flight of exalted meditation prompted by a chance occurrence—the "warbles" of a wind harp ("The Eolian Harp"), the intrusion of a Sunday afternoon stroller ("Reflections"), the song of a nightingale ("The Nightingale"), or the flicker of a hearth flame ("Frost at Midnight")?

After reaching this philosophical height, Coleridge's fervor subsides to the ethical consideration that "it should have been impossible/ Not to love all things in a world so fill'd." And the meditation ends, as it began, with the one difference, that the opening references to the stillness of the evening and to the aeolian harp are now fused in one beautiful image:

> Where the breeze warbles, and the mute still air
> Is Music slumbering on her instrument

—an image which Keats must have remembered when he characterized poesy in "Sleep and Poetry" as "might half slumb'ring on its own right arm."

Although the scene shifts in the second half of the poem to a sunny hillside, the same sequence obtains: first the note of tranquillity, then the sudden sound of the wind harp breaking into the poet's reverie, finally the mounting exaltation of his thought, which terminates in his wondering

> if all of animated nature
> Be but organic Harps diversely fram'd,
> That tremble into thought, as o'er them sweeps
> Plastic and vast, one intellectual breeze,
> At once the Soul of each, and God of all.

This time, his wife's reproving eye prompts Coleridge to stop his philosophical daydreaming and reassert his belief in Christian love. And the poem ends, as it began, on the note of "peace, and this cot."

With one qualification! At the end Coleridge guiltily repudiates his metaphysical conjectures. He calls them

> shapings of the unregenerate mind;
> Bubbles that glitter as they rise and break
> On vain Philosophy's aye-babbling spring

and characterizes himself as "a sinful and most miserable man, wilder'd and dark." The same note of guilt occurs in "Reflections," although it is better integrated into the total statement of the poem. In "The Eolian Harp," feelings of guilt cause Coleridge to deny the "intellectual breeze" metaphysic—which is his central theme. Contrariwise, in "Reflections," his feelings of guilt motivate the central action; his belief that he should not enjoy his pastoral retreat while "unnumber'd brethren" toil and bleed moves him to renounce his life of retirement for one of humanitarian activity.[8]

A further indication that Coleridge was feeling his way toward a new poetic form in these two early conversation poems is the absence of the first calm-exaltation curve in the early versions of "The Eolian Harp." Although subsequent conversation poems conform to a dual rise and fall of statement, "The Eolian Harp" did not acquire such a form until its fourth printing, in *Sibylline Leaves,* in 1817. Then, for the first time, the initial curve of thought reaches a climax with the inclusion—in the errata at that —of the "one life within us and abroad" passage. It is as if Coleridge, when preparing his poems for *Sibylline Leaves,* had analyzed the structure of the conversation poems and then revised "The Eolian Harp" to bring it into conformity with the others. His attention, also, to unity is apparent in his adding material which complements thematically the second climax—even though he had begun by 1802 to deny the concept of the harp and "intellectual breeze" in favor of the projectivist belief that "we receive but what we give, and in our life alone does nature live" ("Dejection").

The conversation poem is circular in thought as well as in mood. Harper[9] may have had this characteristic in mind when he remarked that one of the beauties of these poems is a "return." "Reflections" opens and closes with a reference to the flowers about the cottage and the sound and smell of the nearby sea. "Fears in Solitude" begins and ends with paragraphs dwelling upon the beauty of the "green and silent dell" in which the poet has passed a few solemn hours. "Frost at Midnight" presents initially and finally a picture of frost and icicles on a windless winter night. Each poem is framed by Coleridge's joyous response to nature. Many critics have noted a similar convention in poems written by Wordsworth during the latter half of 1790. A famous instance is the return at the end of "Tintern Abbey" to the woods and cliffs and pastoral landscape described in the beginning. Even in "The Old Cumberland Beggar," which is not explicitly in the descriptive-meditative mode, Wordsworth concludes with a reference to the opening scene which depicts the old beggar at the side of the road sharing his meager repast with the birds.

The circular movement of the thought, however, is more complex than is apparent in such a simple "return." The center of each poem, as Humphry House (p. 79) remarks, is the ego, the "I." The conversation poem is organized around the seeing, remembering, projecting mind of the poet as he sits beside his cottage, reclines on a hillside under the afternoon sun, muses in a cottage room at night, or sits in an arbor of trees.

Both Albert Gérard and I have discussed elsewhere the systolic-diastolic,[10] or centrifugal-centripetal,[11] action of the mind which provides the basic pattern of the conversation poem. Coleridge, like the other Romantic poets, starts with his own thoughts. Lockian psychology had left little alternative. Since an objective knowledge of external reality is denied the Romantic poet, the ego (to quote Gérard) becomes for him "the basic certainty in which all else is rooted." It is important to note, however, that he is concerned "with the ego not in and for itself, but as an element in a complex and wide network of relationships which also embraced the fundamentals of human thought and experience: nature, man and God."[12]

"This Lime-tree Bower," for example, consists of a series of oscillations between the poet's mind and the panorama of nature. With each projection of his thought outward to engage the endless compositions of nature, he advances his understanding of the relationship existing between himself and the world beyond his self. The poem opens with Coleridge despondent. Because of an injured foot he is restricted to the lime-tree grove, while his house guests, Charles Lamb and the Wordsworths, ramble over the neighboring countryside on a sight-seeing tour. In the first action of the poem, Coleridge's thoughts expand to imagine the ramble of his friends from a secluded dell to a hill-top view of the ocean. Remembering how he once gazed "Silent with swimming sense . . . round/ On the wide landscape," he imagines how Lamb "struck with deep joy may stand" watching the sun set into the sea. The vision ends with the intellectual speculation that all nature pulsates with the same germinal causes of joyous life that flow through him. His thoughts then contract in the familiar return to consider the "delight" which he suddenly feels. Since he has progressed from melancholy to joy, he is now able to dispense with the memory of striking scenes and take delight, in a characteristically Wordsworthian manner, in the humble forms of nature which are all about him in the gathering dusk. His cognizance expands in the second action of the poem to include the patterns of light and shadow cast by the trees and of activity and sound caused by a bat wheeling noisily by, a swallow twittering, and a solitary bee singing in the bean flowers. This new vision ends with an assertion of faith in the healing presence of nature and loving influence of God.

> Henceforth I shall know
> That Nature ne'er deserts the wise and pure;
> No plot so narrow, be but Nature there,
> No waste so vacant, but may well employ
> Each faculty of sense, and keep the heart
> Awake to Love and Beauty! and sometimes
> 'Tis well to be bereft of promis'd good,
> That we may lift the soul, and contemplate
> With lively joy the joys we cannot share.

As if to illustrate this newly won insight, the poem ends with Coleridge expressing gladness in Lamb's happiness and in his own ability now to bless an ordinary rook which flies "creaking" overhead.

In "This Lime-tree Bower," the oscillation of thought coincides perfectly with the curve of emotion to form a controlled and unified pattern of alternating meditation and description. The poetic statement progresses with ease and clarity from the poet's concern with his ego, to his apprehension of the external thing, back to his ego. The poem comprises two of these cycles, each beginning and ending in references to the changing attitude of the writer toward his lime-tree prison. One of the shortcomings of "The Eolian Harp" is that Coleridge's guilt-ridden frame of mind at the end of the poem does not follow from his excited conjecture that all life is animated by "one intellectual breeze." His abject assertion of faith in Christ denies this joyous vision of cosmic unity. "Reflections" is equally unsuccessful because Coleridge never clearly establishes his state of mind.[13] He both reminisces about the bucolic quiet of his "place of retirement" and anticipates the "active life" of a social reformer. This ambivalence—reflected by the successive titles, "Reflections on Entering into Active Life" and "Reflections on Having Left a Place of Retirement"—remains pervasive throughout the poem, unresolved by the systolic movement of the poet's thoughts.

At the very core of the conversation poem is the belief that one force breathes through all, animate and inanimate alike; for, although man in his essence is distinct from nature, he co-exists with and is a part of its totality. "Wherever you be," as Plotinus has written, "you have only to range over against this omnipresent Being that in you which is capable of drawing from It, and you have your share in it: imagine a voice sounding over a vast waste of land, and not only over the emptiness above but over human beings; wherever you be in that great space you have but to listen and you take the voice entire—entire though yet with a difference."[14] And Coleridge restates this idea of the oneness of life when he exclaims to Thomas Wedgewood in a letter of 14 January 1803: "In simple earnest, I never find myself alone within the embracement of rocks and hills, a traveller up an Alpine road, but my spirit courses, drives, and eddies like a leaf in autumn. . . . The farther I ascend from animated nature, from men, and cattle, and the common birds of the woods, and fields, the greater becomes in me the intensity of the feeling of life; life seems to me then a universal spirit, that neither has, nor can have, an opposite. God is every where, I have exclaimed, and works every where" (CL, II, 916). Earlier, on 10 March 1798 in a letter to his brother George, he had asserted: "I devote myself to such works as encroach not on the anti-social passions—in poetry, to elevate the imagination and set the affections in right tune by the beauty of the inanimate impregnated, as with a living soul, by the presence of life. . . . I love fields and woods and mounta[ins] with almost a visionary fondness" (CL, I, 397). Explicit statement of this "theistic metaphysic of nature" (House, p. 80) occurs in each poem, from the often quoted lines in "The Eolian Harp" (44–48), "This Lime-tree Bower" (35–43), and "Frost at Midnight" (54–64), to the usually overlooked but similarly oriented lines in "Reflections" (36–40), "Fears in Solitude" (17–24), "The Nightingale" (24–34), and "To William Wordsworth" (11–26).

But Coleridge demands of nature more than a sense of kinship with the cosmos. He looks to it for his God-given knowledge of right and wrong. As he puts it in "Fears in Solitude," man finds "religious meanings in the forms of nature." Wordsworth defines this sublime concept of nature the teacher in memorable lines in "Tintern Abbey":

> And I have felt
> A presence that disturbs me with the joy
> Of elevated thoughts; a sense sublime
> Of something far more deeply interfused,
> Whose dwelling is the light of setting suns,
> And the round ocean and the living air,
> And the blue sky, and in the mind of man;
> A motion and a spirit, that impels
> All thinking things, all objects of all thought,
> And rolls through all things. Therefore am I still
> A lover of the meadows and the woods,
> And mountains; and of all that we behold
> From this green earth; of all the mighty world
> Of eye, and ear,—both what they half create,
> And what perceive; well pleased to recognise
> In nature and the language of the sense,
> The anchor of my purest thoughts, the nurse,
> The guide, the guardian of my heart, and soul
> Of all my moral being.

Like Wordsworth, Coleridge asserts that contemplation of the beauty of nature contributes to man's ethical and moral education. The rook which flies "creaking" over his head, a "dim speck" crossing "the mighty orb's dilated glory," reminds him that "no sound is dissonant which tells of life." The kestrel hawk in Hopkins' "The Windhover," diving out of the sun like a messenger from God, brings the poet's heart out of hiding and into communion with Christ; the rook in "This Lime-tree Bower," vanishing in the light of the setting sun ("nor dim, nor red, like God's own head"), similarly moves Coleridge's heart to loving communion with his fellow man and God. Remembering his childhood "in the great city, pent 'mid cloisters dim," Coleridge derives gladness from the thought that his child "shall learn far other lore." "Thou, my babe!" he promises in "Frost at Midnight,"

> shalt wander like a breeze
> By lakes and sandy shores, beneath the crags
> Of ancient mountain, and beneath the clouds,
> Which image in their bulk both lakes and shores
> And mountain crags: so shalt thou see and hear
> The lovely shapes and sounds intelligible
> Of that eternal language, which thy God
> Utters, who from eternity doth teach
> Himself in all, and all things in himself.
> Great universal Teacher! he shall mould
> Thy spirit, and by giving make it ask.

Notice that these lines are a forerunner of Wordsworth's explanation in "There Was a Boy" of the manner in which beautiful natural scenery influences the mind:

> . . . the visible scene
> Would enter unawares into his mind
> With its solemn imagery, its rocks,
> Its woods, and that uncertain heaven received
> Into the bosom of the steady lake.

The same spatial parallels obtain: the mind receives into its consciousness the visible scene of mountains, clouds, and lakes as the lake receives in its depths the image of sky and encircling hills.

Written during a period of domestic harmony, the conversation poem proclaims philosophically and religiously the joyous oneness of man and nature and of man and man. This metaphysic of the centrality of experience supplies it with the "body of thought" (*CL*, I, 137) which Coleridge believed indispensable for organizing the disparate elements of a poem into a whole. The conversation poem does not just clothe an idea in poetic dress; it derives part of its unity from that idea.

"The Nightingale," for example, is the least overtly unified of the conversation group. As such it testifies to Coleridge's success in writing poetry that suggests the random associative flow of spontaneous speech while remaining a carefully wrought artifact. Each of its three sections derives from the belief that through "the influxes/ Of shapes and sounds and shifting elements" of nature streams the "vernal" note of joy. Thus, in the first (1–49) section, Coleridge finds pleasure in the dark night, overcast sky, and dim stars, because "the vernal showers/ . . . gladden the green earth." He recognizes that the nightingale's song is one of "Nature's sweet voices, always full of love/ And joyance," not one of the melancholy sounds of night. He also recognizes that those who do not surrender their whole spirit to nature will not share in its harmony. For this reason, the self-centered man, unable to surrender himself to an external force, finds in nature his own distemper rather than the universal spirit permeating all. The second (49–86) and third (87–110) parts of the poem dramatize this message of joy. A lady "vowed and dedicate/ To something more than nature in the grove" perceives in the song of the nightingale an expression of the one force animating all nature. The birds also react to this force, refraining from song in the hushed and darkened interval when "the moon was lost behind a cloud," and greeting its reappearance with a "choral minstrelsy" that "like tipsy joy" "hath awakened earth and sky." Likewise, Hartley "suspends his sobs" when he sees the moon and "laughs most silently." Coleridge, the lady, the birds, and Hartley all hear "the voice of vernal hours" and respond rapturously. It is this substantiation of the idea that "in nature there is nothing melancholy" which gives oneness to the multiplicity of their experiences and unity to the diverse episodes of the poem.

In "The Nightingale," then, Coleridge joyously affirms the totality of life by combining his response to nature (in this instance, the nightingale's song, which is the immediate catalyst of his thoughts) with his memory of the similar joyful experiences of Hartley and the lady. And if Coleridge in a doggerel verse-letter to Wordsworth facetiously decried the subject as hackneyed and the Hartley episode as a digression, still he believed sufficiently in the harmony of the poem to ask for Wordsworth's criticism:

> In stale blank verse a subject stale
> I send *per post* my *Nightingale;*

And like an honest bard, dear Wordsworth,
You'll tell me what you think, my Bird's worth.
My opinion's briefly this—
His *bill* he opens not amiss;
And when he has sung a stave or so,
His breast, & some small space below,
So throbs & swells, that you might swear
No vulgar music's working there.
So far, so good; but then, 'od rot him!
There's something falls off at his bottom.
Yet, sure, no wonder it should breed,
That my Bird's Tail's a tail indeed
And makes its own inglorious harmony
Æolio crepitû, non carmine. (*CL,* I, 406)

What Wordsworth answered can only be conjectured; but apparently he agreed with Coleridge's better opinion of the poem, for it was included in the *Lyrical Ballads.* Nor did Wordsworth err if he approved of "The Nightingale"; for harmony—and not the inglorious noise that Coleridge jokingly had in mind—clearly distinguishes its structure of thought. If the scenes differ in setting and incident—still, they share a psychological experience and metaphysical conceit (the aeolian harp) which unify the otherwise desultory subject-matter of this descriptive-meditative poem. "The Nightingale" embodies Coleridge's concept of the bi-centrality of part and whole. Each scene has its own centrality of thought, while also uniting with the others to form the greater whole of the poem. Although poetic apostrophes to nightingales clutter the journals of the day,[15] Coleridge's treatment of the subject is fresh and artful.

Also giving unity to each poem is a master image—the harp in "The Eolian Harp," Christian innocence in "Reflections," birds in "The Nightingale," the silent processes of nature in "Frost at Midnight," peace in "Fears in Solitude," and the ocean tides obedient to an ever recurring life force in much of "To William Wordsworth"—which concentrates the verbal movement of each poem into a richer concatenation of meaning than might a simple series of statements.

In addition to a master image, most of the conversation poems share a cluster of images expressive of the oneness of life. The principal images include the *harp* (usually conceived of as a human or bird) on which the spiritual tones of the universe are sounded; the *wind* as the intellectual, creative breeze; *joy* as the concomitant of the wind music; *sun* or *moon* as the source of Godlike force which pulsates through nature; and *reflected sunlight* or *moonlight,* especially from a cloud, as the spiritual emanation.[16]

Plotinus may have suggested to Coleridge some of the imagery with such a statement as the following: "Into that heaven, all at rest, let the great soul be conceived to roll inward at every point, penetrating, permeating, from all sides pouring in its light. As the rays of the sun throwing their brilliance upon a lowering cloud make it gleam all gold, so the soul entering the material expanse of the heavens has given life, has given immortality."[17] The Claudian landscape flooded with the golden, cloud-reflected light of a sunset or sunrise may also have contributed something to the cluster. But the imagery could as easily have coalesced out of Coleridge's own keen response to nature. As early as 22 June 1796, in a postscript to Thelwall, he voices such a visionary (and vaguely Pantheistic) thought: "We have an hundred lovely scenes about Bristol, which would make you exclaim—O admirable *Nature!* and me, O gracious *God!*" (*CL,* I, 222).

One cannot say how consciously Coleridge manipulated the image cluster, but certainly it is one of the distinguishing marks of the conversation poems. In each instance the motif appears when his response to nature becomes so intense that he believes his spirit to have united with its great appearances by means of a visionary power which reflects upon his sight the bright reality of the Almighty Spirit. (Cf. "This Lime-tree Bower," 37–43; and "To William Wordsworth," 6–26.) The cluster, however, does not appear in entirety in any one poem; for example, the wind and harp predominate in "The Eolian Harp" and the reflecting cloud in "This Lime-tree Bower." In "The Nightingale" occurs the most complete clustering of the images:

> A most gentle Maid,
> Who dwelleth in her hospitable home
> Hard by the castle, and at latest eve
> (Even like a Lady vowed and dedicate
> To something more than Nature in the grove)
> Glides through the pathways; she knows all their notes,
> That gentle Maid! and oft, a moment's space,
> What time the moon was lost behind a cloud,
> Hath heard a pause of silence; till the moon
> Emerging, hath awakened earth and sky

With one sensation, and those wakeful birds
Have all burst forth in choral minstrelsy,
As if some sudden gale had swept at once
A hundred airy harps! And she hath watched
Many a nightingale perch giddily
On blossomy twig still swinging from the breeze
And to that motion tune his wanton song
Like tipsy Joy that reels with tossing head.

But even here the reflecting cloud is absent. By keeping the image cluster flexible, Coleridge retains the descriptive meaning of the words, while adding to them a plane of symbolic suggestiveness.

Thus, through multiple means, Coleridge conveys the spontaneity of conversation and yet retains the satisfaction of ordered experience. Prompted by his sensitivity to the appearances of nature, and by his joy in the friendship and love of the Clevedon and Nether Stowey sojourns, he renovated the exhausted descriptive genre of the eighteenth century, extending its range to include new matter and a new form. Under his poetic eye, the dead and empty husk of nature (*natura naturata*) copied by the eighteenth-century landscape poet becomes a living thing (*natura naturans*) expressive alike of its and the poet's inner being.

"This Lime-tree Bower" and "Frost at Midnight" are the most successful of the conversation poems. Of these two, "Frost at Midnight," readers agree, most completely realizes a fusion of form and content in a complex, but controlled, statement about the act of cognition. In the course of the poem the projecting mind of the poet engages with objects external to it, returning after each expansion of thought with more intense awareness of the processes of life and its relationship to them than it had when the poem began. In the following discussion of "Frost at Midnight," I have drawn freely on the readings of Humphry House and Robert Langbaum.[18] The point of view and ultimately the interpretation are, however, mine. Indeed, the full significance of the silence-sound imagery, and its concatenation with the poetic statement, are here explored, to my knowledge, for the first time.

The poem opens with a description of the weather, time, and setting. The poet's mind moves outward in space, taking cognizance of the winter cold and the night sounds, then of the village, and finally of "all the numberless goings-on of life." But his understanding of them remains limited. Hence, the calm night "disturbs and vexes" his meditation "with its

strange and extreme silentness." The life of the "populous village" and of
the "sea, hill, and wood" has no meaning for him; it is as strange and "in-
audible as dreams!" His thoughts turn from the outside world to the fire in
his room, only to move outward again, this time backward in time, his initial identification with the processes of life now narrowing to a consideration of the loneliness of his childhood. There are three scenes in the poem,
one laid in the present, one in the past, and one in the future: the poet as
grown man in the cottage, the poet as boy at school, and the poet's son as
"nature's priest" in the English lake district. The first two scenes give
somewhat the effect of a double exposure, one superimposed on the other,
with the details of the second only slightly altered by the difference in time
from those of the first. The poet's loneliness and sense of isolation from the
rest of the world as he sits in his silent cottage and watches a film of flame
flutter on the grate appear again in the scene in which the poet as lonely
schoolboy stares at the fluttering flame on the grate and dreams of being
visited by friend or relative. The scene describing Coleridge's childhood
climaxes the first movement of the poem. The mind of the poet then returns to contemplate the fate of his child sleeping near him, for his reminiscence of childhood (a projection of mind outward to engage the world
of experience, similar to the first movement of thought in "This Lime-tree
Bower") brings to mind his hopes for his son Hartley's childhood. After
once more remarking about the "deep calm" of the night, his mind expands again, this time to imagine the trees, lakes, and mountains which
will be Hartley's companions and mentors. The poetic statement is evolving in a snake-like fashion. It proceeds from a description of the poet's
childhood to a consideration of Hartley's childhood by means of the association in time and the contrast between what one saw, and the other will
see, of nature. Coleridge as a London schoolboy saw "nought lovely but the
sky and stars"; Hartley shall see everything that nature has to offer. The
description of nature produced by the conjecture about Hartley's future returns the poem in a beautiful transition to the opening context of seasons,
weather, and sounds. In this famous ending is fused the actual and the con-
jectural: the wintry midnight setting whose silence vexes the poet, with
which the poem opens, and the imagined cycle of seasons whose sights and
sounds (and silences) will nurture Hartley, with which the poem closes.
Most pertinently, the poet has progressed from an unhappy rejection of the
"deep calm" of midnight, in which the "goings-on of life" remain as imperceptible to him as the slow accumulation of frost, to an imaginative
communion with "the lovely shapes and sounds intelligible" of the "eter-

ᘰ

nal language" of nature with which God speaks to man. The silence is as
profound in the final description of nature as in the first, but it is now understood by the poet and will be heard and understood by Hartley. In this
poetic reconciliation of the actual and the imagined, Coleridge asserts the
oneness of the mind of man and the objects of nature, of the union of the
one and the many, and of subject and object. *Schulz 93*

On the level of the imagery, the poem is working toward the same
statement. Look at the image of silence. The deep calm of the room makes
Coleridge aware of the quiet breathing of Hartley and of the silent working of the frost outside. At this point in the poem, however, the two processes of life are distinct; Coleridge does not seem aware of their oneness.
The contrast between the still world and the moving flame—with the parallel between, even identification of, himself and the flame, as the "sole un-
quiet thing[s]"—leads the poet to consider his lonely childhood. These
memories cause him to think with selfless, loving concern of Hartley. With
this return of his thoughts to his child, after the engagement of his mind
with the world of experience, he recognizes that the beneficent and awe-
some processes of life taking place outside in nature and inside the cottage
in Hartley are identical. The "gentle breathings" of Hartley heard in the
"deep calm" of the room and in the "interspersèd vacancies" and "momentary pauses" of Coleridge's thought are analogous to the fall of snow from
the eaves and the "secret ministry" of the frost heard in the "trances of the
blast." The silence no longer vexes Coleridge's meditation. He understands
now that it is a part of the growth of his thought as it is of the eternal becoming of nature, indeed, that his musings, Hartley's breathing, and the
"secret ministry of frost" are all parts of the same process of nature.

The phrase "secret ministry" occurs twice, at the beginning and at the
end of the poem. The increased significance that the phrase has in its second occurrence underscores the increase in the poet's awareness which has
obtained through the action of the poem. In line 1, "secret ministry" calls
attention to the silent and imperceptible ways of frost. In its second occurrence, it has this meaning, plus the new meaning which the poetic statement has contributed to the growing, expanding image of silence. "The
secret ministry of frost" is no longer merely descriptive of the processes of
winter cold, but represents to the poet the silent, spiritual forces at work in
both man and nature; the silent formation of icicles has become an emblem of the eternal processes of life in man and in nature. *(94)*

Coleridge frequently associates sound and light imagery with the eternal becoming of nature, as he has here in "Frost at Midnight." The cease-

less "poetry of earth" and the changing effulgence of moon and sun remind him simultaneously of the passage of time and of the continuity of
life. The processes of nature signify the change of things but also paradoxically the permanence of being. The conjunction of these images and ideas
occurs in one of the moonscapes Coleridge jotted down in his notebooks in
the autumn of 1803:

> Wednesday Morning, 20 minutes past 2 o'clock. November 2nd. 1803.
> The Voice of the Greta, and the Cock-crowing: the Voice seems to
> grow, like a Flower on or about the water beyond the Bridge, while the
> Cock crowing is nowhere particular, it is at any place I imagine & do not
> distinctly see. A most remarkable Sky! The Moon, now waned to a perfect
> Ostrich's Egg, hangs over our House almost. . . . [Then follows a lengthy
> description of the sky as clouds slowly blot out moon and stars] . . . &
> now . . . the Moon is gone. The Cock-crowing too has ceased. The
> Greta sounds on, for ever. But I hear only the Ticking of my Watch, in
> the Pen-place of my Writing Desk, & the far lower note of the noise of
> the Fire—perpetual, yet seeming uncertain/ it is the low voice of quiet
> change, of Destruction doing its work by little & little. (N, I, 1635)

A recurrent theme of the conversation poems is that the sounds and sights
of nature combine to teach us of the changing separateness, yet constant
oneness, of life. As Coleridge puts it in a famous statement to Sotheby of
10 September 1802:

> . . . never to see or describe any interesting appearance in nature, without
> connecting it by dim analogies with the moral world, proves faintness of
> Impression. Nature has her proper interest; & he will know what it is, who
> believes & feels, that every Thing has a Life of its own, & that we are all
> one Life. A Poet's Heart & Intellect should be combined, intimately com-
> bined & unified, with the great appearances in Nature—& not merely held
> in solution & loose mixture with them, in the shape of formal Similes.
> (CL, II, 864)

But one must listen with soul as well as ear if one wishes to hear this joyous message of love:

> Oft with patient ear
> Long-listening to the viewless sky-lark's note
> (Viewless, or haply for a moment seen
> Gleaming on sunny wings) in whisper'd tones
> I've said to my Belovéd, 'Such, sweet Girl!
> The inobtrusive song of Happiness,

Unearthly minstrelsy! then only heard
When the Soul seeks to hear; when all is hush'd,
And the Heart listens!' ("Reflections")

Light and sound coalesce with the one life theme most explicitly in the
famous lines added to "The Eolian Harp" in 1817:

O! the one Life within us and abroad,
Which meets all motion and becomes its soul,
A light in sound, a sound-like power in light,
Rhythm in all thought, and joyance every where.

But the final lines of "Frost at Midnight" most beautifully realize—without uneasy resort to pantheism as in "The Eolian Harp"—the eternal oneness of being and infinite variety of becoming which comprise nature:

Therefore all seasons shall be sweet to thee,
Whether the summer clothe the general earth
With greenness, or the redbreast sit and sing
Betwixt the tufts of snow on the bare branch
Of mossy apple-tree, while the nigh thatch
Smokes in the sun-thaw; whether the eave-drops fall
Heard only in the trances of the blast,
Or if the secret ministry of frost
Shall hang them up in silent icicles,
Quietly shining to the quiet Moon.

Here the contraries of change and permanence become one through the in-
terpenetration of the seasons of the year and the fusion of sound (and silence) and light. If the processes of nature remind us of the passage of
time, they also reassure us, through the cycle of nature and the generations
of man, of the permanence of life. What Coleridge has just learned about
life from the "eternal language" of nature, Hartley will in his turn also
learn. And the reconciling act of the poem gives being to the otherwise
fragmentary apprehensions of the eye and ear and the cogitations of the
mind. "Frost at Midnight" is a perfect expression of the imagination as
Coleridge defined it in *The Statesman's Manual*: finished

. . . that reconciling and mediatory power, which incorporating the reason
in images of the sense, and organizing (as it were) the flux of the senses
by the permanence and self-circling energies of the reason, gives birth to a
system of symbols, harmonious in themselves, and consubstantial with the
truths of which they are conductors.[19]

Some variant readings of "Frost at Midnight" substantiate my belief that Coleridge was intent upon dramatizing this interplay between thing and mind. In versions published in the quarto pamphlet of 1798 and in the *Poetical Register* of 1808–09, he had directed the reader's attention to the activity of his "self-watching mind," which "loves not to behold a lifeless thing" and therefore "transfuses" to the thing "its own pleasures, its own will." Eventually he rejected this explicit description of what is transpiring in the poem as unnecessary, rightly leaving this interplay of mind and thing to be suggested by the relationships which comprise the dramatic structure of the poem.

"Frost at Midnight"—as well as the other conversation poems—is identical, not in semblance (*natura naturata*), but in essence (*natura naturans*), to the world of nature. The symbolic action of the poem in a real way illustrates Coleridge's contention that the act of perception is "a repetition in the finite mind of the eternal act of creation in the infinite *I am*" (*BL*, I, 202). In the organization of the poetic statement, the same reconciliation of mind and thing is occurring that obtains in the apprehension of reality. The movement of the mind is simultaneously the subject of the poem, as Humphry House states (p. 83), and the means by which the subject is given form.

Not the least of the beauties in the conversation poem is the delicate perception of humble forms of nature. In keeping with a philosophy of totality which attaches significance to everything, the commonplace is transformed by the poet's emotions into a new and strangely exciting sight, as a "corn-field, or the unripe flax," is transformed for us

> When, through its half-transparent stalks, at eve,
> The level sunshine glimmers with green light.
> ("Fears in Solitude")

This unique point of view transfigures the winter scene depicted in the much loved and often quoted final lines of "Frost at Midnight." Another instance of "the modifying colors of [Coleridge's] imagination" (*BL*, II, 3) is his description in "The Nightingale" of the "tipsy" birds swaying giddily on wind-tossed boughs. In "This Lime-tree Bower," the same poetic alchemy evokes with almost tactile vividness the chiaroscuro of leaf and noonday sun and the mysterious hush and half-light of evening:

> Pale beneath the blaze
> Hung the transparent foliage; and I watch'd

Some broad and sunny leaf, and lov'd to see
The shadow of the leaf and stem above
Dappling its sunshine! And that walnut-tree
Was richly ting'd, and a deep radiance lay
Full on the ancient ivy, which usurps
Those fronting elms, and now, with blackest mass
Makes their dark branches gleam a lighter hue
Through the late twilight: and though now the bat
Wheels silent by, and not a swallow twitters,
Yet still the solitary humble-bee
Sings in the bean-flower!

The quiet lyricism united with the close observation of nature found in these poems frequently reminds us of the silk-screen paintings of the Chinese calligraphers; and as in those, so in these, the incongruous occasionally rears its head. That is, Coleridge does stumble at times as he gropes toward a new conversational idiom. Now and then he forgets that he is not writing an impassioned ode. At such times, in his effort to emulate "the solemn lordliness of Milton" (*CL*, I, 279), he mars the otherwise neutral style of the conversation poem. Both "Reflections" and "Fears in Solitude" exhibit this incongruous mixture of styles. They are interesting examples of the plight of the transitional poem. Low-keyed in tone but occasionally high-pitched in execution, they have outgrown the prophetic voice but not yet wholly matured into the conversational.

The history of the conversation poems suggests that much trial and error went into Coleridge's achievement of a controlled informality of statement. Humphry House (pp. 81–82) has shown that the original ending of "Frost at Midnight" emulated the relaxed playfulness and domestic shapelessness of Cowper. Coleridge arrived at the concentrated form of the final non-Cowperian version only after multiple revisions which continued as late as 1828. A comparison of the first draft of "The Eolian Harp" with the received version similarly reveals Coleridge's constant struggle to tighten his line without sacrificing his informal tone. The well-known reference to the bean-field initially read:

What snatches of perfume
The noiseless gale from yonder bean-field wafts!

In the final version, he has concentrated this line and a half into one line, eliminated the ornate locution "noiseless gale," naturalized the Latinate syntax, and transformed the weak noun "snatches" into a verb which effectively carries the weight of meaning:

> How exquisite the scents
> Snatch'd from yon bean-field!

Unfortunately, the history of a Cowperian diffuseness and preciosity in "The Nightingale" did not end as happily. Lines 64–69 are comparable to the "low, creeping language and thoughts, under the pretence of simplicity" (*BL*, I, 17) satirized in "Sonnets Attempted in the Manner of Contemporary Writers." They contribute nothing new to the preceding description of the nightingales singing in the grove. Additionally unfortunate is the prosaic repetition—one might almost say Wordsworthian ring —of the phrase "their bright, bright eyes, their eyes both bright and full," and the stale sweetness of the lines

> Glistening, while many a glow-worm in the shade
> Lights up her love-torch.

Coleridge seems to have been undecided about the passage. He included it when the poem was printed in the *Lyrical Ballads* of 1798, but deleted it from the printing of 1800. In subsequent printings of the poem, he reinserted it, choosing to retain at least in this passage the loose form and tender mood of Cowper.

Such lapses of taste are infrequent in the conversation poems. Because their subject-matter and low-keyed tone most nearly reflect his mind as well as his preoccupation with the problem of form and content, they proceed in an orderly, if sometimes round about, manner to a conclusion. They do not just stop as does the 1798 quarto version of "Frost at Midnight," in which the original last six lines suggest a new beginning rather than a conclusion, but terminate with ringing finality. Emotionally and intellectually, each poem traverses a circle. Each has a philosophical center and an imagery organic to this centrality of belief. By such means Coleridge gives artful order to the conversation poem. At the same time, he conceals this artfulness by a relaxed, conversational blank verse, a random association of ideas such as might occur in a conversation between friends or members of a family, an initiation of the central thought or feeling by a chance action or occurrence, and an artless beginning and ending, which, like quiet converse, rises out of silence and sinks back into silence.

. . . as I first sink on the pillow, as if Sleep had indeed a material *realm,* as if when I sank on my pillow, I was entering that region & realized Faery Land of Sleep—O then what visions have I had, what dreams —the Bark, the Sea, all the shapes & sounds & adventures made up of the Stuff of Sleep and Dreams, & yet my Reason at the Rudder/ O what visions . . . & I sink down the waters, thro' Seas & Seas—yet warm, yet a Spirit—/

—Notebook XVI, 6–13 December 1803

It mingles with the pleasures of convalescence, with the breeze that trembles on my nerves, the thought how glad you will be to hear that I am striding back to my former health with such manful paces. . . . I have begun to take Bark, and I hope, that shortly I shall look back on my long & painful Illness only as a Storehouse of wild Dreams for Poems.

—Letter to Thomas Poole, 1 February 1801

VI

THE DREAM VOICE

*I*t is a truism among critics and biographers that "in the life and art of Coleridge the hours of sleep seem to have been almost more important than the waking hours" (Symons, p. 138). Certainly, as a psychological phenomenon, dreams figure frequently in the experience of Coleridge the man, a fact which Hugh I'Anson Fausset implies with the chapter titles of his biography of Coleridge: "The Child of Illusion," "The Pantisocratic Dream," "The Domestic Dream," "The Poetic Dream," "The Poetic Nightmare."[1] As an imaginative experience, dreams also represented a storehouse of shapes and sounds for Coleridge the poet (cf. *CL,* II, 668; and *N, I,* 1718). And Arthur Symons, as long ago as 1909, acutely remarked that Coleridge's poetic "technique is the transposition into his waking hours of the unconscious technique of dreams" (p. 139).

Symons' sweeping statement can lead to the injudicious assumption that Coleridge was no artist but an automatic writer jotting down words dictated to him by the lower depths of his psyche. Keeping this pitfall carefully in mind, we can see that Symons' critical pronouncement, while heady commentary in its comprehensive verve, is applicable, not so much to "The Ancient Mariner" and "Christabel" (two of the poems he had primarily in mind), as to a definable group of dream poems. Just as the conversation poems suggest the accents of friendly converse, so these dream poems reproduce in form and content the streamy nature of the reverie. Although their low-keyed tone and retrospective mood remind us of the conversation poems, they belong to a later period in Coleridge's life —to the years after 1800. He used his farrago, prophecy, ventriloquism, and conversation voices most extensively from 1795 to 1798; and all four voices reflect his effort during these years to correct the bad habits of bombast, Latinisms, and effusiveness. This struggle for a natural voice is no longer perceptible in the dream poems. By the end of 1798, he had mastered a simple poetic style responsive to the melancholy, contemplative muse which became with the passing of the years his habitual manner. Flexible to every bend of his pensive spirit, the dream poems indicate that his poetic achievement, like his intellectual curiosity, is many-sided, and includes more than "The Ancient Mariner," "Christabel," "Dejection," and the conversation poems.

Except for "Kubla Khan," the dream structure is first used by Coleridge about 1802 in "A Day-dream" ("My eyes make pictures, when they are shut") and "The Day-dream" ("If thou wert here, these tears were tears of light"). These poems reflect his interest at the time in the appearance and reality of the colors and shapes, the "eye-spectre," which haunted his opium nightmares and his phantom memories of Sara Hutchinson. He used it again a few years later in "Recollections of Love" and returned to it in the final decade of his life in "The Garden of Boccaccio," "Phantom or Fact," and "Love's Apparition and Evanishment." In these poems of his Indian summer, he dreams again "the fair promise of [his] spring" ("Monody").

In daydreams the mind, with varying degrees of passivity, surrenders itself to a series of "shapes and sounds and adventures" (*N,* I, 1718), heterogeneous and disconnected forms which combine in a kaleidoscopic succession. Intense or prolonged thought prior to the reverie may influence the nature of these images, and the reason may control somewhat the rudder of their direction; but in contrast to the full steerage of the mind during moments of normal mental activity, the images of the daydream, like the sacred river Alph, rise unsummoned, meander through a succession of self-evolving, ever-dissolving views, only to elude us finally by vanishing unbidden before our entranced eyes.

Coleridge's dream poem incorporates this mercurial world of images as part of its form and content. In "The Garden of Boccaccio," for example, the poet tells us that he has been wearily conning his memory for thoughts of glee or grief in an effort to escape from the numbing spell of the present. But all his faculties are slumbering. Suddenly a plate depicting an idyllic scene from Boccaccio materializes on his desk, placed there by the half-seen hands of a friend. The picture serves as a catalyst. From he "knows not whence" tumbles a miscellany of happy scenes which steal upon his "inward sight"

> Like flocks adown a newly bathéd steep
>> Emerging from a mist: or like a stream
> Of music soft that not dispels the sleep,
>> But casts in happier moulds the slumberer's dream.

The dream frame is unmistakable. One by one the visions which had stirred him as a boy—visions which his conscious thought had tried vainly to recall—unfold before his "idle eye with silent might": chants of scalds; lays of minstrels; rhymes of city pomp; verses of monk, priest, judge, mayor, and guildsman; and the songs of elfin nature, of bird and flower and stone. Coleridge awakes briefly from his reverie and views with "mastering" eyes the garden of Boccaccio illustrated in the print. He soon, however, nods over it, and the mental images recur, this time picturing Boccaccio's Tuscany with its cities, castles, boars, palaces, and gardens. The reverie ceases with a glimpse of Boccaccio sitting crosslegged, absorbed in Homer and Ovid. In much the same way might begin and end the sequences of images fabricating our daydreams.

We do not know how consciously Coleridge patterned this poem after the dream phenomenon. There is reason to believe, however, that the dream voice is an artful translation into poetic form of the involuntary, fragmentary, and hallucinatory features of his reveries. We know that he was alive to the manifold activities of the mind, even when it was supposedly in repose. "How much lies below [man's] own consciousness," he exclaims in 1803 apropos of a comment on the possibility of uniting in himself the powers of poetry, draftsmanship, and music (*N,* I, 1554). Familiarity with his own mental processes instructed him in the importance of the involuntary in a thought. Here is an instance, taken from many dealing with Sara Hutchinson, of his noting the uncontrollable activity of the mind: "By thinking of different parts of her dress I can at times recall her face—but not so vividly *as when it comes of itself*—and therefore I have ceased to try it" (*N,* I, 986; my italics). Two years later, in September 1803, he likens a transitory upwelling of images from the depths of his memory to what takes place in a dream:

> . . . overpowéred with the . . . Phaenomena I arose, lit my Candle, & wrote—of figures, even with open eyes/ of squares, . . . of various colours, & I know not what/ How in a few minutes I forgot such an Assemblage of distinct Impressions, ebullitions & piles of golden colour & thence to think of the Nature of Memory. So intense/ & yet in one Minute forgotten! the same is in Dreams/ (*N,* I, 1750)

The rich variety and intensity of Coleridge's mental life would have led him inevitably to explore this shadowy, but in his eyes nonetheless real, world through the imaginative realization of it in poetic form. But associationist psychology undoubtedly helped confirm his inclinations in this direction, for it gave eminent respectability to the writing of dream poems. Hartley ascribed the power of awakening a flow of images or ideas in the mind equally to imaginations, reveries, and dreams. The only difference between imaginations and reveries, he believed, was that in a reverie "the person being more attentive to his own thoughts, and less disturbed by foreign objects, more of his ideas are deducible from association, and fewer from new impressions." Dreams differed from both only in degree: "I say then, that dreams are nothing but the imaginations, fancies, or reveries of a sleeping man" (Hartley, I, 396, 397). Since the imagination was thought to be the poetry-making faculty, and recall of images or ideas its method of operation, then a reverie or dream represented an ideal poetic situation. Alison repeatedly asserts that this passive state of mind is the most favorable for producing an unobstructed train of mental images. When "the attention is so little occupied by any private or particular object of thought, as to leave us open to all the impressions, which the objects that are before us, can create" (p. 6), then, he claims,

> every man of sensibility will be conscious of a variety of great or pleasing images passing with rapidity in his imagination, beyond what the scene or description immediately before him can of themselves excite. They seem often, indeed, to have but a very distant relation to the object that at first excited them; and the object itself appears only to serve as a hint, to awaken the imagination, and to lead it through every analogous idea that has place in the memory. It is then, indeed, in this powerless state of reverie, when we are carried on by our conceptions, not guiding them, that the deepest emotions of beauty or sublimity are felt. . . . (Alison, pp. 41–42)

To write poems based on one's daydreams was therefore psychologically respectable and almost certainly imaginatively fruitful.

The artist in Coleridge, however, would have agreed with Lamb's stricture in an essay on the "Sanity of True Genius" that "the true poet dreams being awake. He is not possessed by his subject, but has dominion over it." Coleridge's respect for the creative imagination militated against his considering a random flow of images as the high point of a poem; these images must be resolved into a unity as well. He could not disregard the frequent illogicality of the shifting associations of the mind and claim as did some of his German contemporaries that dreaming is involuntary poetry.

Here, the psychology of his day—which he confirmed with his own experience—also came to his aid. According to the laws of association, bodily sensation affects the nature of one's reverie. Hartley had written categorically:

> It is to be observed . . . that in all the cases of imagination and reverie, the thoughts depend, in part, upon the then state of body or mind. A pleasurable or painful state of the stomach or brain, joy or grief, will make all the thoughts warp their own way, little or much. . . . Thus a person who has taken opium, sees either gay scenes, or ghastly ones, according as the opium excites pleasant or painful vibrations in the stomach. Hence it will follow that ideas will rise successively in dreams, which have no such connection as takes place in nature, in actual impressions, nor any such as is deducible from association. (Hartley, I, 397–98)

Coleridge records innumerable instances of the relation between the condition of his body and the images in his dream. Here is one from a letter to Poole written 9 October 1797: "Frequently have I, half-awake and half-asleep, my body diseased and fevered by my imagination, seen armies of ugly things bursting in upon me" (CL, I, 348). On 13 December 1803, he notes that a "slight pain in my side produced [in my dream] a fellow knuckling me there" (N, I, 1726). Another experience, recorded in a letter to Southey early in 1807, is interesting because of its similarity to the press of warmth about the poet's chest which figures in so many of the dream poems: "I am considerably better in health. . . . I felt as a man revisited by a familiar spirit the first morning, that I felt that sort of stirring warmth about the heart, which is with me the robe of incarnation of my genius, such as it is" (CL, III, 5).

Still, such associations are haphazard and unpredictable. It was inevitable, with his insistence upon method and unity, that Coleridge should seek more precise principles of association than the general cause and effect of physical sensation. His own rich mental life would have convinced him that such principles exist. But Coleridge did not need to rely upon this empirical psychology, except as verification of the associationist principles already fully articulated by the end of the eighteenth century. To some extent the scientific rationale of associationist psychology not only corroborated Coleridge's brilliant analyses of the life of his mind but also probably influenced what he looked for. Certainly his reports of the workings of his mind are phrased in terms of associationist theory. One principle which seems to have fascinated him was the relationship of bodily sensations to the vivification of memory: "Renew the state of affection or bodily feeling, same or similar—sometimes dimly similar —and instantly the trains of forgotten thought rise from their living catacombs" (*N,* I, 1575). A memorable experience recorded in his notebook on 19 July 1803 brilliantly substantiates his generalization.

> Intensely hot day—left off a waistcoat, & for yarn wore silk stockings— about 9 o'clock had unpleasant chillinesses—heard a noise which I thought Derwent's in sleep—listened anxiously, found it was a Calf bellowing— instantly came on my mind that night, I slept out at Ottery—& the Calf in the Field across the river whose lowing had so deeply impressed me—Chill + Child + Calf-lowing probably the rivers Greta and Otter. (*N,* I, 1416)

Contiguity, similarity, and contrast, Hartley had written, all control and shape the course of thought. And here Coleridge is using such laws to explain the association in his mind of the bellowing calf in the vicinity of the Greta with the lowing calf beside the Otter. With scholarly insouciance, Coleridge overlooks the fact that these laws of association are Hartleian in principle when he formulates them in the *Biographia Literaria* in a chapter criticizing Hartley's materialistic psychology. Either "proximity in time, or continuity in space" (*BL,* I, 87), or "the joint operation of likeness and contrast," he contends, may explain the seemingly random recall of ideas or images.

> Seeing a mackerel, it may happen, that I immediately think of gooseberries, because I at the same time ate mackerel with gooseberries as the sauce. The first syllable of the latter word, being that which had co-existed with the image of the bird so called, I may then think of a goose. In the next moment the image of a swan may arise before me, though I had never seen the two birds together. In the two former instances, I am conscious that their co-existence in *time* was the circumstance that enabled me to recollect them; and equally conscious am I that the latter was recalled to me by the joint operation of likeness and contrast. (*BL,* I, 86)

Another instance of the metamorphosis of his thought from object to object through the association of likeness occurs in a daydream recorded on 25 March 1801:

> Abed—nervous—had noticed the prismatic colours transmitted from the Tumbler—Wordsworth came—I talked with him—he left me alone—I shut

my eyes—beauteous spectra of two colours, orange and violet—then of green, which immediately changed to Peagreen, & then actually *grew* to my eye into a beautiful moss, the same as is on the mantle-piece at Grasmere— abstract Ideas—& unconscious Links!! (*N*, I, 925)

Finally, Coleridge found in Andrew Baxter's two volume work, *An Inquiry into the Nature of the Human Soul* (1745), read in 1795 and remembered as late as 1827, a discussion of dreams, which supported his respect for the conscious powers of the imagination. As Kathleen Coburn has pointed out (*N*, I, 188 n), Baxter's interest is in the role of the imagination and the union of opposites in dreams. His emphasis in 200 pages on dreams is on the "active principle," as opposed, for example, to Darwin's on "accumulation of sensorial power," an approach which Coleridge would undoubtedly have found attractive as a counterbalance to Alison's and the other associationists' stress on the passivity of the associative process in dreams.

This discussion of what Coleridge understood to be the phenomenon of the daydream is not meant as an argument for its appropriateness as poetic material—although there is good reason to believe that the scientific rationalists of the eighteenth century thought it to be so. Coleridge was a poet as well as a psychologist and knew that the poem is an artifact, and that "true poesy = making" (*N*, I, 1057 n). Fortuitously, however, the principles of association governing the images in a dream (as understood by Coleridge and his contemporaries) correspond in many respects to the principles of metaphor governing the language of a poem. Coleridge skillfully exploits this similarity in the dream poem. He selects and arranges the successive parts of his poem (1) according to the principle of connection obtaining between sensations felt and things remembered, and (2) according to that obtaining between objects co-existent in time or space and alike in shape or color. Just as the protean shapes of the reverie shift from object to object, each containing in itself a point of comparison suggestive of the next, so in the dream poem the images transmute from referent to referent, each similar to the last in at least one particular.

We can observe his artistry at work if we compare three renderings of the same experience: (1) a notebook entry of 1810 listing the facts and events associated in his mind with Sara Hutchinson, (2) a passage from the "Verse Epistle to Sara," written on 4 April 1802, and (3) "A Daydream," also composed probably in 1802. The presentation is strikingly different in each version. Here is the notebook entry:

I began strictly and as matter of fact to examine that subtle Vulcanian Spider-web Net of Steel—strong as Steel yet subtle as the Ether, in which my soul flutters inclosed with the Idea of your's—to pass rapidly as in a catalogue thro' the Images only, exclusive of the thousand Thoughts that possess the same force, which never fail instantly to awake into vivider flame the forever and ever Feeling of you—The fire/ Mary, you, & I at Gallow-Hill/—or if flamy, reflected in children's round faces—ah whose children?—a dog—that dog whose restless eyes oft catching the light of the fire used to watch your face, as you leaned your head on your hand and arm, & your feet on the *fender*/ the fender thence/—Fowls at Table—the last dinner at Gallow Hill, when you drest the two fowls in that delicious white Sauce which when very ill is the only idea of food that does not make me *sicker*/ all natural Scenery—ten thousand links, and if it please me, the very spasm & drawing-back of a pleasure which is half-pain you not being there—Cheese, at Middleham, too salt/ horses, my ride to Scarborough—asses, to that large living 2 or 3 miles from Middleham/ All Books—my Study at Keswick/—the Ceiling or Head of a Bed—the green watered Mazarine!—A Candle in its socket, with its alternate fits & dying flashes of lingering Light—*O God! O God!*—Books of abstruse Knowledge —the Thomas Aquinas & Saurez from the Durham Library/ (quoted by Whalley, p. 111)

The notebook entry consists of a series of objects and events jotted down as they came to mind. In effect, we are witnesses of the subterranean process of thought itself; we twist and turn with Coleridge's mind as it follows a trail of temporal, spatial, and emotive associations. This series of images, whose links are sometimes apparent, often missing, represents the raw material available to the memory.

In the "Verse Epistle to Sara," Coleridge has selected one incident from this random flux of many:

> It was as calm as this, that happy night
> When Mary, thou, & I together were,
> The low decaying Fire our only Light,
> And listen'd to the Stillness of the Air!
> O that affectionate & blameless Maid,
> Dear Mary! on her Lap my head she lay'd—
> Her Hand was on my Brow,
> Even as my own is now;
> And on my Cheek I felt thy eye-lash play.
>
> (*CL*, II, 792–93)

In keeping with the epistolary nature of the poem, the movement of the lines is conversational. There is no proliferation of related facts as occurs in the notebook entry; rather, the passage arranges the details of the incident into an orderly record of a past event.

When we turn to "A Day-dream," we find ourselves again in the eddy of spontaneous reminiscence, but with these differences: the flow of images is controlled and the links in thought are discernible. Dramatically separated into three scenes, the poem alternates between reverie and actuality. In the first scene, Coleridge visualizes a summer day when Sara and he lay with their heads on Mary Hutchinson's lap, while near them sparkled a fountain and over them bent a willow tree. In the second, he turns from this fantasy to note his present drowsy supineness out-of-doors on a June night. The momentary recurrence to the present acts as a bridge to the next retrospection which is a metamorphosis of these two scenes: now it is night in a shadowy room where Sara and he are again lying with their heads on Mary's lap. Soon, the shadows of the room fade into a "mild darkness" as the silent musings of Coleridge, who once more takes cognizance of his surroundings, merge with the quiet humming of the midnight air.

George Whalley (p. 125) contends that "it is not satisfactory to suppose" that "A Day-dream" represents a reworking of material rejected from the "Verse Epistle to Sara." Such a bald assertion is itself unsatisfactory. Why Coleridge conceivably could not have reworked an unused section of the "Verse Epistle to Sara" into another poem is difficult to understand, considering that "Dejection" originated in this fashion. Specifically, the difficulty with Whalley's assumption, I believe, is that it is based on a division of the poem into two, instead of three, scenes. Attempting to date "A Day-dream" by identifying its events with visits of Coleridge to the Hutchinson farm at Gallow Hill, he admits concerning the first scene (the daylight one under the willow tree) that he is "unable to identify an occasion in the spring or summer of 1800 or 1801 . . . which brings Coleridge, Sara, and Mary together in the absence of William and Dorothy." Possibly, he conjectures, "the 'June' of line 16 may simply be a rime-word"—a conjecture not very complimentary to the poet. Actually, the June designation clearly refers not to the first, but to the second scene (the nighttime one under a star-and-moonlit sky). What Whalley has to say about the rest of the poem, however, which he mistakenly conceives of as one scene, is more serious because of his misunderstanding of its structure. "The setting of the second part of the poem," he continues, "indicates the visit of March 1802, when Coleridge stopped at Gallow Hill on his way home from London." But, as I have already mentioned, the second scene, which Whalley believes comprises the entire second half of the poem, is dated by Coleridge as June, not March. Two conclusions immediately suggest themselves. First, the June date for the setting of "A Day-dream" indicates that it may have been written after the composition of the "Verse Epistle to Sara," which is dated 4 April. Second, the two dates of March and June serve to confirm that there are two scenes, not one, in the second half of the poem. As we have already seen, Coleridge is not sitting with Sara and Mary in a room at Gallow Hill in March and dreaming of a previous day when all three were similarly together. He is lying alone on a June night, alternately looking up at the stars and, with "eyes . . . shut," dreaming successive "pictures" of Sara, Mary, and himself: one of them in the daytime beside a fountain and a willow tree, and the other of them at night in a room lit only by the flames from a fireplace. The two women are present only in his mind's eye—although, admittedly, they are envisioned with such intensity that their presence seems to the poet almost palpable. He seems to be referring to the present moment (perhaps because the lines are carried over almost intact from the "Verse Epistle to Sara") in the statement:

> Thine eyelash on my cheek doth play—
> 'Tis Mary's hand upon my brow!

But the lines immediately preceding these make it clear that he is reminiscing. As the "deep shade" of the room blots its occupants from his mind's eye, the "mild darkness" of room and June night (of reverie and actuality) merge in his thought and prompt him to assert the unfading nature of his impressions:

> But not from me shall this mild darkness steal thee:
> I dream thee with mine eyes, and at my heart I feel thee!

More than a record of two visits with the Hutchinsons, "A Day-dream" is at its center a poetic rendition of the daydreaming mind alternating between reality and reminiscence. Like the conversation poem, it is made up of two cycles, each consisting of an expansion and contraction of thought. The difference between the two poetic modes is equally important. The conversation poem is concerned with the relationship of the mind to nature, each of which is presented as coexistent with, and yet independent of, the other. The dream poem concentrates on the ability of the mind to transform and combine things into new forms; it involves comparatively speaking an increased concentration on the thing as imaged in the mind. The objective world is not denied; it is still seen as an analog of the mind. The difference is that the objective world becomes more closely identified with the images of the mind than in the conversation poem, where it remains separate from, while continuing in active rapport with, the mind. To simplify this description of the two kinds of poems, one can say that they differ intrinsically in the way they organize their statements. The conversation poem is made up of several spatial complexes in juxtaposition to each other; it relates the private world of the speaker to the objective world external to him. On the other hand, the dream poem has a temporal arrangement; it relates a present experience to a past one. As a consequence, the conversation poem carefully distinguishes the external object from the mental impression and the present from the past, even when it draws analogies between the two. Contrariwise, the dream poem treats them as if they were not linear and chronological, but identical and simultaneous. The musing mind of the poet blurs past and present into one continuous moment, combines the fancied and the actual into a single action, and confuses the mental image with the real object. In "A Day-dream," for example, Coleridge sees the flickering lights of the glow-worm and stars, which are a part of the June night; but such perception includes his self-knowledge which combines them with other objects and experiences reminiscently identified with his drowsy feeling of warmth—with the sparkling fountain of the first scene ("fit stars for our sweet fountain") and the dancing flames of the third scene. The night sky vaulting over the poet similarly metamorphoses into a willow tree arching over three people. The shadow of a glow-worm flashing on the margin of the poet's sheet of paper alters to the shade of the willow tree and then to the shadows cast upon the wall of the darkened room by the "still dancing fire-flames" of an open hearth. Thus, the actual details of the June night initiate, modify, and coalesce with the visionary details of the scenes in the willow bower and the darkened room. And the poem ends with this fusion intact. Coleridge conceives of his silent musings, as well as Sara's and Mary's memories of the same events, as part of the still sounds of nature. He notes that the "tender lay" singing within him harmonizes with the "midnight hum" singing within the "still hive."

As is readily perceived the images do not change form capriciously. To explain their origin and to prescribe their forms, Coleridge links the metamorphosis of each scene to his sensations of warmth and tranquillity. The warmth of the June night reappears in the nostalgic memories of a *warm* sunlit day and of a hearth-*warmed* room. Similarly, the tranquil bliss overspreading the poet recurs in the serenity felt by the occupants of the willow bower and quiet room. In "A Day-dream," a "general principle of connection . . . pervades the whole" and gives to the train of images a "certain and definite character," to quote a passage from Alison so apposite that it could have supplied Coleridge with the form and content of his poem; "thus the prospect of a serene evening in summer, produces first an emotion of peacefulness and tranquillity, and then suggests a variety of images corresponding to this primary impression" (pp. 54–55).

"A Day-dream" is a beautiful poem delicately dreamlike in its fleeting and spontaneous recall of impressions from the well of memory. In it Coleridge creates a discursive structure of thought which suggests the seemingly spontaneous flux of a daydream, while paradoxically avoiding the byways which entice the streamy flow of association when reverie leaves it partly uncurbed and unruddered (cf. *N,* I, 1770). The notebook entry of 1810 shows us a brilliant analyst venturing along a trail of association which is a maze of new starts and trackless traverses of time and space; the dream poem shows us a skillful poet restricting himself to a few selected images which undergo a sea-change as they mediate between memory and actuality. Written in a minor key, the best of these poems express moods of tender reminiscence with considerable felicity. In "Recollections of Love," the hallucination that the "sweet bed of heath" "swells up, then sinks with [the] faint caress" of a loved one present there eight years before, conveys tastefully the poet's ardent nostalgia. Especially effective in "A Day-dream" and "Recollections of Love" is the image of the ceaseless sound of nature with which each ends. Coleridge's identification of nature's eternal undersong with "love's whisper" asserts with delicacy and reverence for life his faith in the constancy of "love's prompture deep" ("Recollections of Love").

Most important, Coleridge has not forgotten in the excitement of the reverie that he is constructing an artifact, which demands of him definite formal obligations. In its skillfully organized imagery, "A Day-dream" clearly conforms to the poetic requirements of order and unity. Coleridge also gives unity to the poem by depicting in each reverie essentially the same tableau of Sara and himself lying with their heads in Mary's lap. The carefully maintained, complex metrical pattern, besides supporting the poetic statement, also contributes much to the regularity of the poem. Each stanza has six lines, four of eight, one of eleven, and one of thirteen, syllables, which rhyme ababcc, with the first four rhymes masculine, and the final two feminine. The disparate lengths of the concluding couplet, plus the extra syllable in each line, reproduce metrically the wavering, involuntary movement of the dreaming mind and the fragmentary nature of the dream image; while the feminine rhymes add a "sweetness as of repose"[2] which accords well with the general dream fantasy. At the same time, just as the poet after each sortie into the past returns to the reality of the present, so the final lengthened couplet of each stanza brings the free-wheeling association of the dream image to a semi-conclusion, much as the Alexandrine halts a narrative in the Spenserian stanza.

*T*he tendency of the dream image to change continuously and involuntarily generally leaves it incomplete. Coleridge describes this phenomenon vividly in a marginal note in Tenneman's *Geschichte der Philosophie*. The state of dreaming, he writes, is like "the shifting current in the shoreless chaos of the fancy in which the *streaming* continuum of passive association is broken into *zig-zag* by sensations from within or from without" (*BL,* I, 225 n). And Hartley makes the same point in his chapter on imagination, reveries, and dreams: "We may observe, also, that the visible imagery in dreams is composed, in a considerable degree, of fragments of visible appearances lately impressed. For the disposition to these vibrations must be greater than to others, . . . at the same time that by the imperfection and interruption of the associations, only fragments, not whole images, will generally appear" (Hartley, I, 400). Just as it incorporates structurally the spontaneous flow of dream images, so the dream poem utilizes as a part of its form an inconclusive interaction of impressions and associations.

Unlike such an unfinished curiosity as "Limbo," however, which is a literary as well as psychological fragment representing some "still surviving recollections" of a "phantom world" fleetingly perceived by the poet (Preface to "Kubla Khan"), the dream poem is complete. In it, the poet's response to the reverie gives wholeness to the fragmented sequence of images. Thus, in "The Garden of Boccaccio," although Coleridge's vision of Tuscany stops abruptly the poem continues thematically to a conclusion: still musing on the make-believe garden of Boccaccio where a vestal maiden and a sly satyr peep forever through the leaves of a vine,

Coleridge expresses hope that the mazy pages of the Italian poet may long be his to con joyfully.

A sequence of physical impressions interrupted by less sharply realized associations, within a frame of commentary by the poet, characterizes each of the dream poems. Look, for example, at the drama enacted in "The Day-dream." At first, Coleridge has a sensation of a "soft and breeze-like feeling" caressing his lips, with which is associated a couch and quiet fire-warmed room. Without further elaboration, the incompletely realized room is succeeded by a second sensation of a warm weight on his chest, "as if some bird had taken shelter there," with which is associated a woman's form. Hopefully he wonders if she is Sara (Hutchinson?); but at the moment when he seems certain of recognizing her, the reverie is dispelled by the laugh of a child who has climbed up the poet's chair to peer into his face. The daydream continues, however, to linger in his mind and to touch his heart with the playful tenderness of an infant's finger. Although in this instance Coleridge's response to his reverie strikes us as forced and exaggerated, still this response completes the poem. His bittersweet commentary on the joy produced by the reverie and the pain of waking to find it an illusion incorporates the dream fragments into a statement which mirrors the inconclusive stream of reverie, while satisfying the esthetic demand of wholeness.

*T*o a great extent, the synthesizing act of "Kubla Khan," long heralded as Coleridge's great dream poem, conforms to the organization of statement that I have shown the other dream poems to have. As Humphry House (p. 114) reminds us, "If Coleridge had never published his Preface, who would have thought of 'Kubla Khan' as a fragment?" When read as a narrative, the poem undoubtedly strikes one as unfinished; but when read as a romantic daydream of one man's achievement of paradise on this earth, it is, in Coventry Patmore's words, "finished within."[3]

As a self-contained poem, "Kubla Khan" develops thematically and metrically two points of view and reaches two climaxes: first, a description as seen partly through Kubla's eyes, and partly through those of an omniscient observer, of how Kubla combined discordant details of the landscape to produce Xanadu; and second, a narration by the poet of how he came to see Xanadu and why he has not told us more about it.[4] Considered unfinished by readers from Coleridge's day to the present, especially if they thought that the description of the Khan's summer palace was meant as the introduction to a long narrative poem, "Kubla Khan" has considerable poetic unity and makes a satisfying statement capable of critical analysis, as the many readings of the poem testify.

Specifically, Kubla has been seen by Humphry House and others as the poet in action and most recently by J. B. Beer (pp. 226–29) as the man of commanding genius who strives to realize the ideal. He is also the dreamer who creates, or gives actuality to, his reveries—not an unfitting character for an inveterate daydreamer like Coleridge to imagine. That Coleridge thought of Kubla in this guise is evident by Collier's diary report of a conversation with him *c.* 1811–12. He recited, Collier comments, "some lines he had written many years ago upon the building of a dream-palace by Kubla-Khan" (*SC*, II, 47). "Dream-palace" may be Collier's words, reflecting his response—and many others, including Lowes'—to the poem. But it is reasonable to assume that Collier is trying to reproduce the words or intent of "his much-admired poet-acquaintance" (Schneider, p. 84) as accurately as possible. If so, "dream-palace" as a synonym for the pleasure-dome indicates that Coleridge was perhaps aware of the tradition that Kubla constructed his palace according to a dream (cf. Beer, p. 331 n); or, which is more likely, that Coleridge thought of Xanadu and the pleasure-dome as the epitome of all that man visualizes in his dreaming moments and longs to realize in life. In such a view, the figments of the mind are conceived of as more real and intense than the events of the day; and in the subsequent conversation about dreams which the recitation of "Kubla Khan" started, Collier tells us, Coleridge cited Scudamour's nightmare of Care nipping his side with burning cinders (*Faerie Queene*, IV, v, 44) as an instance of a dream which intensifies reality (*SC*, II, 48).

But dream projects such as Kubla's Xanadu represented more to Coleridge than simply idealized versions of reality. They were the raw material which the creative imagination must shape into finished forms if the visions were to have being. This view is implicit in a note which Coleridge jotted on the flyleaf of G. H. Schubert's *Allgemeine Naturgeschichte* (1826). In language which identifies dream visions with products of the imagination, he laments that his neglect of the study of mathematics in his youth has prevented him from productive work in the science of acoustics:

This day I read the account of Faraday's Microphone and instantly recognized a fond and earnest dream-project of my own of 30 years' standing—

with sundry other imaginations respecting what might be effected in the only embryo Science of Acoustics. (*Spirit,* p. 252)

Xanadu is a "dream-project" which has come into being through the creative imagination of Kubla, who has translated his dream of paradise into the daytime reality of gardens and pleasure-dome. Xanadu is not the Eden of God, however, (as House, p. 120, reminds us), but the creation of an oriental despot close to the rhythms of earthly existence and realistic enough to rest satisfied with a full realization of these. Another reason for the non-Edenic form that Xanadu takes may stem from the fact that the images of our dreaming mind ordinarily are a projection of our waking moments. Kubla's paradise comprises (as many critics have noted) a vision of reality in which are reconciled the measurable and immeasurable quantities of the birth-life-death cycle. His waking moments caught in the "sensual music" of life, Kubla has created a paradise which (to quote Yeats's vision of life in "Sailing to Byzantium") "commend[s] all summer long/ Whatever is begotten, born, and dies."

Fragmentary and contradictory as it may seem at each passing instant, life forms ultimately a completed gesture; and Xanadu within its confines contains in chasm, gardens, and caverns similar contraries of violence and repose, birth and death, and savagery and passivity. Girdled round with walls and towers, it reflects Kubla's realistic grasp of the human situation. On the one hand, it has a dark chasm, an intermittent fountain, and a sunless sea, all suggestive of the mysterious forces of life. A woman wails, the earth trembles as if breathing in fast, "thick pants," and a fountain flings up water and rocks intermittently. But paradise also contains the languid and the sensuous—even, perhaps, the voluptuous. Milton knew this when he pictured the "high groves of . . . earth" (as Coleridge puts it in "Religious Musings") and envisioned the conjugal joys of Adam and Eve. Coleridge also knew this as his daydreams in "The Eolian Harp" indicate:

> And that simplest Lute,
> Placed length-ways in the clasping casement, hark!
> How by the desultory breeze caress'd,
> Like some coy maid half yielding to her lover,
> It pours such sweet upbraiding, as must needs
> Tempt to repeat the wrong! And now, its strings
> Boldlier swept, the long sequacious notes
> Over delicious surges sink and rise,

Such a soft floating witchery of sound
As twilight Elfins make, when they at eve
Voyage on gentle gales from Fairy-Land,
Where Melodies round honey-dropping flowers,
Footless and wild, like birds of Paradise,
Nor pause, nor perch, hovering on untam'd wing!

And Kubla's creation of a perfectly balanced existence includes the exotic, inactive, and sensuous too. Xanadu contains the smothering green fecundity of gardens, ancient forests, and sunny spots of greenery. A sacred river connects this cycle of known and unknown experience. Its beginning and end shrouded in the incomprehensibility of the creative force, the river bursts from the unknown depths of the "deep romantic chasm," meanders through the enclosed certainty of the gardens, and sinks through "caverns measureless to man" "to a lifeless ocean." On this life line floats fittingly the shadow of a pleasure-dome, which Kubla's idea of the good life has prompted him to erect in the gardens. Rearing above river, gardens, and caves of ice, it both dominates Xanadu and combines within its dimensions the flux of the antithetical parts of Xanadu—the mundane and the transcendent, the temporal and the eternal. Its echoing walls resound with the "mingled measure" from the river's chasm origin, garden existence, and cave demise. Thus it objectifies and unites the diverse elements of Kubla's vision of life.

When we proceed to part 2, we find a new dimension added: specifically, another point of view and another level of statement. The literal accomplishments of Kubla are seen now through the wondering gaze of a second person, the "I" of the poem. Xanadu becomes in the context of the whole poem the creation of the poetic imagination, say House and others, and the "I" a portrait of the artist. But the speaker is more than that. He is first a dreamer, and then a poet. His knowledge of Xanadu came to him in a "vision" in which a maid sang on a dulcimer of the pleasure gardens of the Khan. If he wishes a second glimpse of Xanadu, he must revive the original vision in his mind's eye. He is thus forced to re-enact a vision which will not stay fixed but is forever dissolving. To his wondering eyes, Kubla, on the other hand, has decreed a daydream into substantial and permanent being. Within the context of the poem, then, Kubla stands as a surrogate of the dreamer, who similarly wishes to give being to his daydream, not like Kubla by erecting it solidly on earth, but like a poet by creating it in air "with music loud and long." So far, however, he has been unable to advance beyond some incomplete lines of verse because the airy edifice inevitably topples when the magical moment of the reverie ceases. The excited tone of voice which accompanies the opening description of the "deep romantic chasm" hints at the dreamer's identification with Kubla:

> But oh! that deep romantic chasm which slanted
> Down the green hill athwart a cedarn cover!
> A savage place! as holy and enchanted
> As e'er beneath a waning moon was haunted
> By woman wailing for her demon-lover!

The personal exclamation here is quite different from the objective description of the gardens in the preceding lines. It is as if both the sophisticated oriental despot and the enthusiastic romantic poet find the Gothic wildness of the setting simultaneously attractive and frightening. And again, at the end of the first section, the reference to the pleasure-dome seems to express the admiration of the poet as much as the self-satisfaction of Kubla:

> It was a miracle of rare device,
> A sunny pleasure-dome with caves of ice!

That Coleridge meant something like all this seems clear from the lines of verse he quotes in the Preface to "Kubla Khan." There, he likens his transient daydream of Xanadu to the fragile "images on the surface of a stream into which a stone has been cast":

> Then all the charm
> Is broken—all that phantom-world so fair
> Vanishes, and a thousand circlets spread,
> And each mis-shape the other.

These lines come from "The Picture." They appear in the context of a daydream. The speaker, "play[ing] the merry fool" because he thinks himself free of love's snares, stands beside a stream which, he exults, has never known the reflection of a woman:

> And thou too, desert stream! no pool of thine,
> Though clear as lake in latest summer-eve,
> Did e'er reflect the stately virgin's robe,
> The face, the form divine, the downcast look
> Contemplative!

But as he exults in his male privacy, he lapses into a daydream in which he sees such a reflection in the water:

> Behold! her open palm
> Presses her cheek and brow! her elbow rests
> On the bare branch of half-uprooted tree,
> That leans towards its mirror! Who erewhile
> Had from her countenance turned, or looked by stealth,
> (For Fear is true-love's cruel nurse), he now
> With steadfast gaze and unoffending eye,
> Worships the watery idol, dreaming hopes
> Delicious to the soul, but fleeting, vain,
> E'en as that phantom-world on which he gazed,
> But not unheeded gazed: for see, ah! see,
> The sportive tyrant with her left hand plucks
> The heads of tall flowers that behind her grow,
> Lychnis, and willow-herb, and fox-glove bells:
> And suddenly, as one that toys with time,
> Scatters them on the pool! Then all the charm
> Is broken. . . .

Without becoming ensnared by the mare's-nest about the truth of Coleridge's asseverations in the Preface (cf. Schneider, *passim*),[5] one can see that he associated his daydream of Xanadu, if not with "The Picture," certainly with the evanescent reveries which make up much of its content.

That the tone of part 2 is not pessimistic in spite of the conditional nature of the vision—

> Could I revive within me
> Her symphony and song
> . . . .
> I would build that dome in air

—can be attributed to several reasons. For one thing, in the lines,

> And 'mid this tumult Kubla heard from far
> Ancestral voices prophesying war!

there is an ironic commentary on the dreamer's desire to match Kubla's achievement, which defines the different approaches of the two men and the final success of each. The prophecy of the ancestral voices has ominous portents for Kubla. His pleasure in Xanadu is doomed by war. Furthermore, his "dream-palace" itself will vanish in time—a fact ominously underscored by the construction of the pleasure-dome: its caves of ice, like the "Russian palace of ice, glittering, cold and transitory" (*BL*, I, 12), hint at the precarious nature of Kubla's creation. Contrariwise, the poetic rendition of Coleridge will continue unaffected by war, time, or substance. Ironically, the pleasure from the insubstantial creation of the daydreamer who builds his reverie "in air" will survive that of Kubla who built his on the solid ground. And if Coleridge, by his own admission, has not realized his vision in full poetically, still he has formulated a portion of it, and that a considerable portion; for, as House points out, the reference to "that dome" reminds us that

> the dome . . . has been described in the first part. And if it had not there been fully described, the music of the singing and the dulcimer would not have any substantial and evident power. It is just because the first part presents the dome and the river with all its setting so completely, beautifully and finally, that we can accept the authenticity of the creative impulse in the second part, and find in the last word "Paradise" a fact, not a forlorn hope. (p. 116)

Once realized in a reverie, Xanadu is potentially summonable again and again, the images rising "as things" before the daydreamer's wondering eyes as they had originally. Coleridge may have lost faith finally in his capacity to create poetry, but he never lost faith in his capacity to daydream. He might half-heartedly—and unconvincingly—reject "these shapings of the unregenerate mind" under the reproving eye of poor conventional Sara in "The Eolian Harp" in 1795; but in the last thirty years of his life—no longer subject to her domesticating influence—he took joy in the permanence and recoverability of his reveries. "Stay awhile, poor youth!" he advises the daydreamer in "The Picture,"

> The stream will soon renew its smoothness, soon
> The visions will return! And lo! he stays:
> And soon the fragments dim of lovely forms
> Come trembling back, unite, and now once more
> The pool becomes a mirror; and behold
> Each wildflower on the marge inverted there,
> And there the half-uprooted tree. . . .

Not all his daydreams returned so easily. The girl fails to materialize, for example, in the reverie just quoted:

And there the half-uprooted tree—but where,
O where the virgin's snowy arm, that leaned
On its bare branch? He turns, and she is gone!

Despite the occasional obstinacy of a daydream—as with the music and song of the Abyssinian maid in "Kubla Khan" and the coy virgin in "The Picture"—Coleridge reiterates in poem after poem his faith in the constancy and immediacy of his reveries. And "A Day-dream," "Recollections of Love," and "The Garden of Boccaccio" are instances when he successfully recovered his daydream "with music loud and long." If " 'Kubla Khan' is a triumphant positive statement of the potentialities of poetry" (House, p. 116), it is even more positively a statement of the poetic potentialities of the daydream.

While "Kubla Khan" is a dream poem, it differs in degree from the later poems of the same type. In it Coleridge does not court his reverie with the single-mindedness that he does after 1800. In 1797–98 life was still sweet; a few more years had to elapse before daydreams became sweeter than living—and easier. For one thing, the "vision" is once removed from the dreamer, filtered through the song of an Abyssinian maid. Although the description of Xanadu, because of its initial position in the poem, makes it appear at first as if Xanadu were real, the second half of the poem indicates that the poet is able to stand aside and observe this creation for what it is: a figment of his mind. In the later poems he is a participant in the world of the daydream as well as in the world of actuality. This accounts for the confusion of fantasy and reality in a poem like "Recollections of Love."[6] In comparison to the later dream poems, the images in "Kubla Khan" do not slip and slide proteanlike from shape to shape as they alternate from fact to fancy. In it dream and reality remain essentially separate. The syntactical organization of the daydream, with its confusion of past and present, then, does not provide the basic form of "Kubla Khan" to the degree that it does in the later dream poems.

Nevertheless, despite this degree of departure from the dream structure, "Kubla Khan" manages to suggest the streamy world of the reverie. The abruptly changing landscape certainly works toward this effect. Part 1 of the poem shifts without transition from (1) a bird's-eye view of Xanadu and the river Alph emptying into "a sunless sea," (2) to a close-up of the "deep romantic chasm" where Alph has its fountain origin, (3) to a trip down the winding river Alph, (4) to a tour of the pleasure-dome, in which Alph is once more heard sinking "in tumult to a lifeless ocean." And the rhyme and meter correspondingly evolves through several forms. Coleridge describes the enclosed harmony of the garden (1–11) for the most part in masculine rhymes and short iambic octosyllabics. He depicts the savagery and sublimity of the chasm (12–24) in feminine rhymes and eleven-syllabled lines with some trisyllabic feet; and he suggests the forceful eruption of the fountain with masculine rhymes. He pictures the placid meandering of the river (25–28) in a quatrain (abba) of alliterated continuants (*m, r,* and *l*), long vowels, and eleven-syllabled lines (25 and 28).

Some merging of details also occurs between the maid's song about Xanadu, the dreamer's vision of the girl, and the dreamer's situation in the present—in short, between vision and reality. The "woman wailing for her demon-lover" evolves into the Abyssinian maid playing on her dulcimer. The note of the "holy and enchanted" reappears in the divine rapture of the dreamer as poet, the eyes closed with "holy dread," and the three circles to be woven around him to ward off the spell. In this context, the demon-lover echoes in the dreamer's vision of himself as poet-magician. The paradise of Xanadu recurs in the portrait of the dreamer who has "drunk the milk of Paradise." And of course the pleasure-dome, which stands

> Where Alph, the sacred river, ran
> Through caverns measureless to man
> Down to a sunless sea,

gathers beneath its dome the alpha and omega of existence, the sacred river of life and the icy caves of death, in its second and third appearances in the poem.

> The shadow of the dome of pleasure
> Floated midway on the waves;
> Where was heard the mingled measure
> From the fountain and the caves.
> It was a miracle of rare device,
> A sunny pleasure-dome with caves of ice!

Such fusion of time, place, and thing, besides reflecting somewhat that the past achievement of Kubla has become the present ambition of the poet, also suggests the syntax of the daydream.

Essentially, however, the temporal and spatial sequence of "Kubla Khan" is static rather than fluid and dynamic as in "A Day-dream." Structurally, part 1 (the past) stands in opposition to part 2 (the present). The details of the visionary, or dream, section do not merge, except in the few instances already mentioned, with those of the expository section. The paradigm of part 1, furthermore, with quite undreamlike order, consists of contraries which structurally compose a whole: the angular, dark, violent, and progenitive features of the garden juxtaposed to the round, sunny, languid, and fecund. Besides the unifying effect of these oppositions, the ubiquity of the river also helps to bind the components of the landscape into one pattern. The description of its birth in the chasm, journey through the garden, and disappearance into the caverns down to a "lifeless ocean" links the diverse elements of place and time, including the ominous note of destructive war prophesied by Kubla's ancestral voices, in a linear manner quite unlike the associative process of the other dream poems.

In the second half of the 1790's, as "The Eolian Harp" and "Kubla Khan" indicate, Coleridge was discovering and exploring the poetic possibilities of the world of the daydream. His concept of the daydream during these years was basically visionary and exotic. He seems to have accepted the aesthetics and psychology of his day, which identified the daydreaming faculty with the imaginative faculty, attributing to both the supreme power of creating things previously unseen and unknown to the senses and to the reason. The fantasy of love in "The Eolian Harp" and the vision of war in "Fears in Solitude" are essentially prophetic in form and intention, appearing to the wondering eyes of the poet as seer when, having stretched himself on a hillside and in a green and silent dell, he had surrendered his spirit "to the influxes/ Of shapes and sounds and shifting elements" ("The Nightingale"). In such reveries, Coleridge believed, "the veiling clouds retire," opening to view "the throne of the redeeming God/ Forth flashing unimaginable day" ("Religious Musings"). It is easy to see how the God-inspired poet of Platonic tradition—he with "flashing eyes" and "floating hair" ("Kubla Khan")—merged in Coleridge's mind with the visionary poet of eighteenth-century prosopopoetic tradition. The dreams of "Kubla Khan" and "The Eolian Harp," then, are closer to the intentions of the prophecy poems such as "Ode on the Departing Year," which he was writing during these same years, than to the conventions of the dream poems written after the turn of the century. A combination of visionary idealism and Pindarick extravagance prompted Coleridge to picture in these poems

The light that never was, on sea or land,
The consecration, and the Poet's dream.

Coleridge does not carry such visionary optimism, however, into the new century. He might daydream for a few happy years of dining on honey-dew gathered from honey-dropping flowers in a fairy-land paradise, but life with its tendency to restrict one's horizons inevitably forced him to question such "phantoms of sublimity" ("Apologia Pro Vita Sua"). J. B. Beer offers an impressive list of commentary on occult literature by Coleridge in letters, notebooks, and marginalia as proof that Coleridge was a visionary; but such a garner does not imply that Coleridge believed in these mysteries so much as that, with a truly modern mind, he saw these myths as attempts to explain the verities of human experience and had a healthy interest in, and respect for, all attempts to unite earth and heaven into "something one & indivisible" (CL, I, 349). Coleridge was very much a product of his age; and if he subscribed to the German idealism which attributed non-empirical insights to the reason, he still accepted the view, as Richard Haven[7] has shown, that his spiritual experience and insights, regardless of how much they coincided with the "facts of mind" (CL, I, 260) of the mystics and Neoplatonists, needed to be rationalized in relation to the facts of psychology and physics that his age accepted. Allsop records Coleridge as having once expressed the necessity he felt "of reconciling the restlessness of an ever-working fancy with an intense craving after a resting place for my thoughts in some *principle* that was derived from experience" (*Spirit,* pp. 33–34). As Haven puts it: "Coleridge's . . . studies and enthusiasms reveal . . . his attempt to find new answers to old questions, to explain in terms of contemporary science and psychology areas of experience which older writers had recognized but which they had discussed and interpreted in ways no longer acceptable."[8] The occult, then, could not hold Coleridge's interest for long if it could not be reconciled with the facts of nature as seen by an "enlightened" age. The exotic fantasies of "The Eolian Harp" and "Kubla Khan" are in their way unique. A sober Coleridge, chastened by unrequited love, domestic discord, and lack of worldly success, came to recognize ruefully after 1800 that these chimerical visions were a far cry from the reality of Georgian England. In subsequent dream poems, he chronicled those reveries which conformed to the principles of associationist psychology and squared with events in his past life. To this extent, the later dream poems are realistic and "Kubla Khan" fanciful.

The problem of realism brings up the large question of what Coleridge expected to find in observing and recording the life of his mind. In general, the dream poem depicts a "waking dream" (the phrase is August Wilhelm Schlegel's) which, to the wondering eyes of the poet, is as independently viable and mysteriously imperishable as all "thoughts seem to be" (*N*, I, 1575). As the studies of both R. C. Bald (pp. 37–41) and Elisabeth Schneider (pp. 91–105) have shown, Coleridge distinguishes between (1) the ordinary dream in which no judgment one way or the other is made about the reality of the vision, and (2) the waking dream, or reverie—which includes daydreams, nightmares, and even opium reveries—in which the voluntary power of comparison, although relaxed, is sufficiently active to cause the mind to pass judgment on the reality of the successive thoughts and images streaming by. One's reaction to the events of an ordinary dream, Coleridge believes, is similar to one's reaction to a play: in both there is "that willing suspension of disbelief for the moment" which the individual encourages in himself (*BL*, II, 6). Because the reveries incorporated into the dream poems can be momentarily illusory, they have little affinity with the "temporary half-faith" of the ordinary dream (*SC*, I, 200); rather, they impart the same hallucinatory sense of reality as Edward's nightmare at the end of "The Three Graves." In the instant of awaking, he reacts as if his dream were actual:

> He sat upright; and ere the dream
> Had had time to depart,
> 'O God, forgive me!' (he exclaimed)
> 'I have torn out her heart.'

Coleridge describes the psychological conditions and effects of this phenomenon in a passage of clinically brilliant self-observation, which can easily stand as a description of the reveries in the dream poems.

> When the waking state of the brain is re-commencing, and most often during a rapid alternation, a *twinkling,* as it were, of sleeping and waking, while either from pressure, [or] from some derangement in the stomach or other digesting organs acting on the external skin (which is still in sympathy with the stomach and bowels) and benumbing it, the sensations sent up to the brain by double touch (*ex. gr.,* when my own hand touches my side or breast) are so faint as to be merely equivalent to the sensation given by single touch (when another person's hand touches me). The mind, therefore, which at all times, with and without our distinct consciousness, seeks for and assumes some outward cause for every impression

from without, and which in sleep by aid of the imaginative faculty converts its judgements respecting the cause into a present image, as being the cause,—the mind, I say, in this case deceived by past experience, attributes the painful sensation received to a correspondent agent—an assassin, for instance, stabbing at the side, or a goblin sitting on the breast, etc. Add too that the impressions of the bed, curtains, room, etc., received by the eyes in the half-moments of their opening, blend with and add vividness and appropriate distance to the dream-image, which returns when they close again: and thus we unite the actual perceptions, or their immediate reliques, with the phantoms of the inward sense, and thus so confound the half-waking, half-sleeping, reasoning power, that we actually do pass a positive judgement for the reality of what we see and hear, tho' often accompanied by doubt and self-questioning, which, as I have myself experienced, will at times become strong enough even before we awake, to convince us that it is what it is—the nightmare. (*SC*, I, 202–03; cf. *N*, I, 1620 and 1726; II, 2468 and 2486)

Except for the emphasis upon nightmare—which fits the terrible experiences of "The Pains of Sleep" better than the nostalgic evocations of the dream poems—this brilliant analysis describes the situation and sequence of events occurring in "A Day-dream," "The Day-dream," "Recollections of Love," "The Garden of Boccaccio," and "Love's Apparition and Evanishment." Clearly these poems, originating in a common psychological experience, perform similar acts of integration. Dramatized in them are the same confounding of mental images and real objects by a half-awake, half-asleep reasoning power, and the same initiating (or accompanying) of the dream image by a physical sensation—invariably a brooding warmth pressing upon the poet's chest. Welling up from the depths of the mind and associated with the physical context of the immediate, waking moment, the daydream, combined with the imagination, becomes in these poems a "laboratory in which [the] thought elaborates essence into existence" (*N,* II, 3158).

At the same time, the poem which gives substance to the daydream is an artifact. Its integrating act involves a conscious manipulation of the poetic materials of narrative, description, and meter. In "Recollections of Love," for example, Coleridge's memory is activated by a return to once familiar scenes and by the pleasant sensation of the warm turf pressing against him. As a result the swell and sink of the grass and the "quiet sounds" which float "here and there" from "hidden rills" and a high-flying lark deceptively suggest to his impressionable senses the breathing and speaking, in short, the material, presence of a maiden who eight years

earlier had lain beside him in the same woodland recess. Coleridge deploys
the sequence of time and the details of nature with delicacy and taste to
give "factitious *Being*," or form (*N*, II, 3158), to this hallucination. A past
experience in which a loved one figured merges with the present experience in which she is absent until in the poet's self-deception she appears
beside him as she had the previous time. Two distinct moments are confused as one by the reminiscent poet. Literally the descriptive details realize the landscape; figuratively they evoke the absent girl. And the fifth (or
extra) line in each of the balladic stanzas underscores the impression of
an unaccountable addition to the scene. The daydream has the poetic illusion of substantiality without its confirmation of reality. At no time is
the reader tricked into believing that the apparition is present except in
the expectant thoughts of the speaker. Hence the blurring of the distinction between the woodland recess as it is now and as it was eight years before works to convey the intensity of the poet's nostalgia.

The confusion of the mental image with the real object in the dream
poem does more than parallel the situation occurring in a nightmare; it
also reflects the effort of Coleridge to find in his dreams a revelation of
subjective reality. "Those whispers just as you have fallen or are falling
asleep," he asks in 1805, "what are they and whence?" (*N*, II, 2470).
Again, in the same year, "On Friday Night, 8th Feb/ 1805," he records:
"my feeling, in sleep, of exceeding great Love for my Infant/ seen by me
in the Dream/ yet so as that it might be Sara, Derwent or Berkley/ and
still *it was an individual Babe and mine.*" In an effort to understand this
phenomenon he proceeds to generalize about the "sort of *universal-in-
particularness* of Form," which dreams prompted by love assume, quoting
some of his own verses in the process:

> "All Look or Likeness caught from Earth, All accident of Kin or Birth,
> Had pass'd Away: there seem'd no Trace of Aught upon her brighten'd
> Face Uprais'd beneath the rifted Stone, Save of one Spirit, all her own/
> She, she herself and only she Shone in her body visibly." This abstract
> Self is indeed in its nature a Universal personified—as Life, Soul, Spirit,
> &c. Will not this prove it to be a *deeper* Feeling, & of such intimate af-
> finity with ideas, so to modify them & become one with them, whereas
> the appetites and the feelings of Revenge and Anger co-exist with the
> Ideas, not combine with them; and alter the apparent effect of the Forms
> not the Forms themselves. (*N*, II, 2441)

Pursuing this idea in another notebook entry of about the same time, he
remarks that thought and reality are "two distinct corresponding sounds,

of which no man can say positively which is the voice and which the echo" (*N*, II, 2557). He expresses this uncertainty poetically when he wonders in "Phantom or Fact" about the reality of a vision he has had of his "spirit newly come from heaven":

> This riddling tale, to what does it belong?
> Is't history? vision? or an idle song?

In 1805 a need to see his "swarm of thoughts and feelings" as more than an "affrightful riddle . . . of limbs and trunk, tailless, headless, nothing begun and nothing ended," had lead him to seek universal significance in the "endlessly minute fragments" (*AP*, p. 246) of his experience. As he grew older, however, he tended more and more to explain such isolated instances in psychological, rather than metaphysical, terms—to see them as comprising the Gestalt of his being. "Phantom or Fact" was probably written late in his life. It reflects the wisdom of his old age, when he recognized the psychological significance of his visions. With sad resignation he expresses the view in this poem that life is the sum total of numberless fragmentary experiences:

> Call it a moment's work (and such it seems)
> This tale's a fragment from the life of dreams;
> But say, that years matur'd the silent strife,
> And 'tis a record from the dream of life.

To the extent that he seeks to find metaphysical significance in his dreams, Coleridge follows the tradition of the European Romantic poets who saw in the dream a means of transcending the limitations of the senses. In the dream poem, he sometimes tries to see his personal experiences as expressive of universal ideals, as in "Love's Apparition and Evanishment." At other times, he contrasts the emptiness or meaninglessness of the actual moment with the ideal world of Kubla and Boccaccio's paradisal gardens. Usually, however, he fuses past and present into an idealized reminiscence which murmurs in his mind a dear, ceaseless undersong ("Recollections of Love") like "the still hive at quiet midnight humming" ("A Day-dream") when all other voices sleep. Regardless of the explicit point of view they adopt, all these poems reflect Coleridge's unflagging interest in the life of his mind as a mode of apprehending the eternal verities.

On the other hand, to emphasize the psychological and metaphysical under-carriage of the dream poem in this fashion is perhaps to weight these artifacts with too much philosophical machinery, for each pretends to do no more than give actuality to a few memories. As nostalgic evocations of the past, "A Day-dream," "Recollections of Love," and "The Garden of Boccaccio," particularly, are artful dramatizations of psychological reality. To the extent that he was satisfied to pursue this limited poetic objective, Coleridge follows the mainstream of English empiricism. The form of the dream poem thus represents a structure of emotion and thought erected by Coleridge out of his response to the observed reality of his experience. So defined, these poems are controlled expressions of the dream phenomenon. As instances of poetic creativity acting under laws of its own origination, they are comparable to the conversation poems; both illustrate the fidelity with which Coleridge's artistry recreates the substance and manner of his experience. In their sensitive representation of his interior life, the dream poems also show an affinity with the confession poems which we shall examine next.

I sit down to write you, not that I have any thing particular to say— but it is a relief, and forms a very respectable part in my Theory of Escapes from the Folly of Melancholy. I am so habituated to philosophizing, that I cannot divest myself of it even when my own Wretchedness is the subject. I appear to myself like a sick Physician, feeling the pang acutely, yet deriving a wonted pleasure from examining its progress and developing its causes.

—Letter to Robert Southey, 11 December 1794

VII

THE CONFESSION VOICE

*T*he conversation poems celebrate a joyous period in Coleridge's life, roughly the three years extending from his marriage in the fall of 1795 to his departure for Germany in the fall of 1798. Although egocentric in origin, they irradiate outward, embracing the loved ones of the Coleridge-Wordsworth-Lamb circle and the unassuming landscape of Somerset. And the spatial arrangement of the contents, the subjective impressions of the poet balanced by, and reconciled to, the objective facts of the world, supports this intuition of oneness. A sense of fraternity with man and nature permeates these poems.

Less joyous than the conversation poems but still serene, for the most part, are the dream poems written almost entirely after 1800. Although retrospective and personal, they do not entirely reject the present for the past nor the anticipation of human relationships for the remembrance of lost friendships and completed events. In keeping with this harmonious vision, places and objects associated with different times are seen by the poet as parts of a continuum which seems to merge into one place and one time; while the temporal arrangement of reminiscence and actuality insures that the references remain essentially distinct and meaningful.

Forming a melancholy antiphonal to the happiness of the conversation poems and the serenity of the dream poems are many *pensées* best described as confessions. They recount the death agonies of Coleridge's spirit and thus constitute one of his most persistent poetic voices in the second half of his life. They include the "Verse Epistle to Sara Hutchinson" (and "Dejection"), "The Picture," "The Day-dream" ("If thou wert here, these tears were tears of light"), "The Pains of Sleep," "The Blossoming of the Solitary Date-tree," "To Two Sisters," "Youth and Age," "Work Without Hope," "Constancy to an Ideal Object," "The Pang More Sharp Than All," and "Love's Apparition and Evanishment." Dating from the early years of the new century, when his life is assuming the pattern familiar to most students of Coleridge—domestic estrangement, hopeless love for Sara Hutchinson, opium addiction, waning poetic powers, expanding interest in psychological and philosophical problems, and homeless wandering—these poems trail across the last thirty years of his life, a record of his unhappy isolation from the rest of loving mankind.

Like the conversation group, the confession poems are personal and introspective. Unlike the early group, however, in which Coleridge's thought inscribes a huge parabola, swinging outward and away from himself to embrace the living world before curving back again unto himself, the confession poems depict him circling endlessly around the mysterious but painful drama being enacted in his mind. From a detailed observation of the outside world in the conversation poems, Coleridge shifts more and more in the dream and confession poems to the detailed consideration of the inner world of his mind and heart. Crabb Robinson comments testily in reference to the lectures of 1808 that Coleridge "too often interwove himself into the texture of his lecture" (*SC*, II, 20). This remark characterizes the orientation of the confession poem. Thus, in "To Two Sisters," Coleridge turns his note of thanks for hospitality into a complaint about his loveless, wandering existence. Loneliness rather than fraternalism predominates. Although the conversational note is still heard, the poet now speaks to himself; he has become a clinician, a prober of the abscesses irritating his mind and heart. Like the conversation poems, the confession poems are reminiscent; but in the conversation pieces Coleridge also looks forward to the intimacy of married love, the blessing of nature, the harmony of friendship, and the joy of fatherhood. In the confession poems, on the other hand, he gazes unswervingly at the past; the future does not figure in them. If a failure to look at the future, or to admit the possibility of its existence, is an indication of despair, then these poems express a deep pessimism.

One hears this dirge of confession interrupting the celebration in "To William Wordsworth" of an early idyllic existence and once warm friendship, rekindled for an instant through the magical presence of the Wordsworths and the "deep voice" of William reciting the "long sustainéd song" of his soul's growth. Except for this momentary rebirth of springlike feeling and the conversational tone I hesitated to include "To William Wordsworth" in the conversation group; yet, like R. H. Fogle, one "reluctantly defers to [George McLean Harper's] judgment in admitting" it (*C*, 103). Eight years separate it from the Nether Stowey idyl. The date and place of its composition—January 1807 and Coleorton—lie well within the despairing decades of the confession poems. It reflects equally, then, as might be expected, the comradeship of the Somerset days and the self-absorption of the Westmorland period. Thus, if not transitional in time, at least in mood and form, "To William Wordsworth" links the antiphonal voices of conversation and confession.

Many characteristics of the confession poem appear in "To William Wordsworth": (1) the swift alternation of emotions, of "life's joy rekindling" only to arouse a "throng of pains"; (2) the cry of unrequited love and the lament for "past youth and manhood come in vain,/ And genius given and knowledge won in vain"; (3) the hopeless feeling that the future lies dead in the unfulfilled promise of the past; and (4) the sense of isolation that results from being pitied rather than loved. Coleridge attempts to understand the cause of these misgivings; but he is momentarily under the heaven-soaring influence of William's song, so he impatiently shrugs off his own unhappiness to celebrate his fellow-poet's joy. When he arises after Wordsworth has finished reading *The Prelude,* he finds himself, however, involuntarily praying.

So far in this comparison of the conversation and confession voices, I have considered only tone and subject. Unquestionably tone contributes to the total structure of any poetic statement. Without its cynicism, Donne's song "Go and catch a falling star," for example, would convey little sense. And without its gentle irony, "Mr. Flood's Party" by Edwin Arlington Robinson would be simply a distasteful portrait of a drunkard instead of a richly ambiguous vision of the poignant isolation and ludicrous perseverance of old age. Structurally, the first half of "To William Wordsworth" eulogizes Wordsworth's depiction in *The Prelude* of "moments awful,/ Now in [his] inner life and now abroad" in nature and society, and hence the first part of the poem conforms to the man-nature, subject-object, vision of life that controls the organization of the conversation poem. In the second half of the poem, however, Coleridge turns from his consideration of Wordsworth's tale of the "vernal growth" of "a human spirit" to evaluate his own life. And the parallels are deliberate and significant. "Power streamed from" Wordsworth, and his "soul received"

> The light reflected, as a light bestowed—
> Of fancies fair, and milder hours of youth,
> Hyblean murmurs of poetic thought
> Industrious in its joy, in vales and glens

> Native or outland, lakes and famous hills!
> Or on the lonely high-road, when the stars
> Were rising; or by secret mountain-streams,
> The guides and the companions of thy way!

Coleridge has known the same "vital breathings secret as the soul/ Of vernal growth"; but his knowledge, he laments, addressing Wordsworth, has been won in vain,

> And all which I had culled in wood-walks wild,
> And all which patient toil had reared, and all,
> Commune with thee had opened out—but flowers
> Strewed on my corse, and borne upon my bier
> In the same coffin, for the self-same grave!

Whereas Wordsworth's communion with nature has produced the magnificent foliage of *The Prelude,* Coleridge's has brought forth only enough posies to make him aware of how far short of his goal he has fallen. "To William Wordsworth" is one of these funereal flowers which commemorates the death of his spirit. The form of the poem has evolved into a comparison of the past with the present—the past as portrayed in *The Prelude,* when Coleridge

> . . . on Quantock's grassy Hills
> Far ranging, and among her sylvan Combs,
> . . . in delicious words, with happy heart,
> Didst speak the Vision of that Ancient Man,
> The bright-eyed Mariner, and rueful woes
> Didst utter of the Lady Christabel,
> (1805–06, XIII, 393–98)

with the present as pictured in "To William Wordsworth," in which his life no longer "hears the voice of vernal hours" but listens "with a heart forlorn" to the "howl of more than wintry storms."

In the confession poem, Coleridge recalls over and over the two gifts granted him—his creative imagination and his capacity for love—with the subsequent shriveling of the one and the dying of the other. In "Work Without Hope," "Dejection," "Constancy to an Ideal Object," and "Love's Apparition and Evanishment," he depicts the present as a death-in-life and the future an abyss—all nature is at work while he cowers over the sickly vacuum that reigns in his heart. In "The Pains of Sleep," "The Daydream," "To Two Sisters," "Youth and Age," and "Dejection," he juxtaposes past and present in an effort to fathom the "one guiltless fault" wasting his soul and body "daily with the poison of sad thought." Like the dream poem, the organization of the confession poem derives from this preoccupation with time.

Many of the poems begin with a remembrance of things past, then turn to the present in the light of the things remembered. This view of the present through a window in the past comprises the structure of the confession poem. Coleridge cannot understand why a "sense of intolerable wrong" afflicts him, filling him with "shame and terror" over

> Deeds to be hid which were not hid,
> Which all confused I could not know
> Whether I suffered, or I did. ("The Pains of Sleep")

Consequently, he is forever reviewing his past actions, feelings, and thoughts, hoping to find in them a clue to his present "throng of pains . . . and fears self-willed, that shunned the eye of hope" ("To William Wordsworth"). "The Pains of Sleep," for example, opens with a stanza recounting how the poet used to resign himself gently to sleep. This commendation of his spirit to love and God is then contrasted in the second stanza to his present supplication "aloud/ In anguish and in agony" for peaceful slumber. But quiet sleep is a thing of the past: now he feels bereft of love, besieged by

> . . . guilt, remorse or woe,
> My own or others still the same
> Life-stifling fear, soul-stifling shame.

He starts up in terror from nightmares, awakened by his own wild screams. Contrasting his previous sense of security with his current state of uncertainty, he looks deeply into his soul, searching among his personal faults for an explanation of his present desolation of spirit:

> But I—O wherefore this on me?
> Frail is my Soul, yea, strengthless wholly,
> Unequal, restless, melancholy;
> But free from Hate, & sensual Folly!
> To live belov'd is all I need,
> And whom I love, I love indeed.[1]

As this last quotation indicates, another distinctive feature of the confession poem—besides its juxtaposition of a promising past to a hopeless present—is its inconclusiveness. Many of the poems end in a question: "But wherefore, wherefore fall on me?" he asks in "The Pains of Sleep"; "Why was I made for love and love denied to me?" he queries in "The Blossoming of the Solitary Date-tree." He questions, but no answer is forthcoming. Coleridge ends "To William Wordsworth" with the statement "And when I rose, I found myself in prayer." In a real sense the poem itself is the prayer—as is true also of the other confession poems. In each Coleridge seeks self-knowledge, but always with discouraging results. And the key to this inconclusiveness lies in the difference between poetic and religious prayer. Ordinarily, prayer consists of a lonely vigil in which the suppliant confesses extemporaneously his thoughts and actions. Like such prayer, the confession poem is introspective, psychologically searching, fiercely sincere, and retrospective. It dwells upon human failure and the succumbing of the spirit to temptation. There is, however, an essential difference between religious confession and the confession poem. The religious confessor concludes with a feeling of hope for the future; Coleridge ends with his despair unassuaged and his questions unanswered. The one employs spiritual self-abasement and supplication; the other lay-psychology and analysis. The one begins despondent and ends joyous; the other starts and finishes in bewildered pain. Neither Coleridge's science nor his artistry, so far as the poems disclose, can advance to the initial cause of his depression. The confession poem remains for the most part a repository for avowals of unspecified guilt.

Coleridge early acquired the habit of writing confessional poems. In a letter to Southey of 11 December 1794, which is quoted in the epigraph to this chapter, he confesses the relief derived from examining the progress and developing the causes of his wretchedness. "Lines on a Friend Who Died of a Frenzy Fever Induced by Calumnious Reports," which first appears in a letter of 6 November 1794 to his brother George, reflects this habit of introspection as well as his tendency to measure his actions against those of another and his compulsion to disclose what he has found. The thought, here, proceeds from the "popular creed"[2] to the personal consideration. This order is characteristic of the confession poem and is the extreme form taken by Coleridge's romantic tendency to reduce all things to the common denominator of the self—or, to put it in Wordsworthian terms, to see "the life/ Of all things and the mighty unity/ In all which we behold, and feel, and are" as converging in the "dark/ Invisible workmanship" of the self (*The Prelude,* 1805–06, XIII, 253–55 and I, 352–53). Coleridge turns from contemplation of the fate of his friend to examine "with introverted eye" his similar soul—perhaps fate:

> To me hath Heaven with liberal hand assign'd
> Energetic Reason & a shaping Mind,
> The daring ken of Truth, the patriot's part,
> And Pity's Sigh, that breathes the gentle heart
> Sloth-jaundic'd all! and from my graspless hand
> Drop Friendship's precious Pearls, like hour glass sand.

"Of course," he adds, these rhymes "are meant for a brother's eye" (*CL,* I, 127–28). But his zeal for publication soon overcame his desire for privacy and they appeared in the 1796 edition of his poems. Thus began for Coleridge a life-time of introspective poetizing, which gained impetus after 1800 when, for sixteen years, he wandered through an intellectual and emotional Walpurgisnacht and felt the need of unburdening himself through confessional poems.

A comparison of "The Picture" and Salomon Gessner's prose poem, "Der feste Vorsatz," from which Coleridge borrowed the conception of the lover's broken resolution, illustrates the contorted pattern of ingenuous self-disclosure and subtle-souled psychology traced by Coleridge's confessional voice.

"Der feste Vorsatz" reflects the typical responses of the romantic solitary. A fugitive from love, the poet wanders with melancholy pleasure through grottos formed by the forest trees. Here, he dallies with thoughts of fair-haired Chloe and brown-tressed Melande, transforming flesh-and-bone girls into idealized nymphs whom he wafts on the summer breeze into a pastoral setting where the kisses of the sprightly maidens and the gentle breezes naively and unrealistically intermingle.

Coleridge's adaptation of "Der feste Vorsatz," published in the *Morning Post* for 6 September 1802, is less sentimental in its treatment of love. During the previous summer months his hopeless love for Sara Hutchinson had tormented him with days and nights of restlessness. He knew that one does not dally coyly with such despairing love, as Gessner's Theocritean swains and damsels with "girlish fancy" do (*CL,* II, 810, 813); rather, one strives to stifle it, strives

> not to think of what I needs must feel,
> But to be still and patient, all I can;

> And haply by abstruse research to steal
> From my own nature all the natural man. ("Dejection")

In his poem, Coleridge introduces a psychological realism lacking in "Der feste Vorsatz." Whereas Gessner's lover glories in the sad pensiveness of the lovelorn and seeks to intensify his despair by frequenting the melancholy forest, Coleridge's lover in "The Picture" exults in the illusion of "the master-passion quelled" and searches out a "tangle wild of bush and brake" as a barrier against which his new-born feeling of freedom can assert itself.

But Coleridge knew from experience the self-delusions of unrequited passion. Even as the lover, delighting in the fitness of associating his person (unmastered by love's tyranny) with nature (untamed by the gardener's rake), praises the virginal wind that "liftest the feathers of the robin's breast," his heart betrays him into revealing the agitated thoughts, lurking in the hidden recesses of his mind:

> The breeze, that visits me,
> Was never Love's accomplice, never raised
> The tendril ringlets from the maiden's brow,
> And the blue, delicate veins above her cheek;
> Ne'er played the wanton—never half disclosed
> The maiden's snowy bosom, scattering thence
> Eye-poisons for some love-distempered youth,
> Who ne'er henceforth may see an aspen-grove
> Shiver in sunshine, but his feeble heart
> Shall flow away like a dissolving thing.

With keen insight, Coleridge dramatizes the self-deception of the mind. Under the pretense of condemning the "sickly thoughts" of the "love-lorn man," the speaker scornfully itemizes the wanton tricks that his excited eyes might have seen played on his inamorata by the breeze. By means of this device and the additional one of attributing to nature the designs of his fevered thoughts, he savors the "eye-poisons" which he is self-righteously condemning.

The dissemblance of the mind is also disclosed in the conclusion to the poem. Gessner's lover, after many protestations of absenting himself a while from the joys of love, suddenly espies the dainty footprint of an unknown girl. He starts in pursuit, anticipating the kisses that he will claim if he overtakes her. Coleridge's lover, after congratulating himself on his escape from the toils of love, stumbles upon a picture freshly drawn on bark by his beloved. Gusts of attraction and repulsion alternately sway him as he realizes that she too is in the forest. Finally, his heart supplies his mind with reasons for pursuing her:

> She is alone!
> The night draws on—such ways are hard to hit—
> And fit it is I should restore this sketch,
> Dropt unawares, no doubt. Why should I yearn
> To keep the relique? 'twill but idly feed
> The passion that consumes me. Let me haste!
> The picture in my hand which she has left;
> She cannot blame me that I followed her:
> And I may be her guide the long wood through.

Ingenuously, the lover progresses from disinterested desire to return a lost article to its owner, to rationalization that the girl, like the article, means nothing to him, to realization that the picture offers a reason for his seeking her, to anticipation of a long walk through the woods with her.

Coleridge's mature years witnessed a succession of such intellectual compromises. The ever lengthening list of books projected but never completed, for example, was a sop to a conscience nagging him to correct his inertia. Epistolary confession also gave him a semblance of productivity. By 1802 the habit of self-incrimination had crystallized into a ready anticipation of, and hence defense against, the accusation of others that he had wasted his talents. "During my illness," he writes to Godwin, 4 June 1803, "I was exceedingly affected by the thought that month had glided away after month, and year after year, and still had found and left me only *preparing* for the experiments, which are to ascertain whether the hopes of those, who have hoped proudly of me, have been auspicious omens, or mere delusions—and the anxiety to realize something and finish something has, no doubt, in some measure retarded my recovery" (*CL,* II, 946–47; cf. II, 814, 876, and 950). The confession poems are similar avowals of his guilt-stricken conscience—which, he confides on the back flyleaf of G. H. Schubert's *Allgemeine Naturgeschichte* (1826), is "the avenging daemon of my life" (*Spirit,* p. 251). They also represent a few shards dug up from the ruins of his mind and heart as evidence that life and industry had once flourished in him, if only beneath the surface, and that he had tried to keep faith with those who had believed in him.

Considering the human need to look good in at least one's own eyes, it is surprising to find that in the confession poems Coleridge attempts, as much as his very great skill in psychological analysis and his all too-human proclivities toward self-justification permit, to diagnose his infirmities of resolution and love with candor. He may camouflage the self-revelation by railing at the conventions of the pastoral idyll, as in "The Picture," or by recasting his intimately confessional verse letter to Sara Hutchinson into a formal ode, as in "Dejection"; yet, in poem after poem, he faces up courageously to the emptiness of his life, foregoing the cant that so frequently turns us away from his letters. His poetic references to his love for Sara Hutchinson illustrate this honesty. For over twenty years, while abjectly confessing to personal inadequacies, he clung to a faith in his affection for her. Yet, rich in bitterly earned wisdom, he knew that,

> If Hope prostrate lie,
> Love too will sink and die.
> ("Love, Hope, and Patience in Education")

And he finally acknowledges without equivocation that even his love for Sara, the pain that he has nursed in his heart as the one real ache in a life of stingless vacancy, has faded away as has so much of his life:

> In vain we supplicate the Powers above;
> There is no resurrection for the Love
> That, nursed in tenderest care, yet fades away
> In the chill'd heart by gradual self-decay.
> ("Love's Apparition and Evanishment")

Written on 24 April 1824, these lines may not commemorate a specific occasion, such as his several meetings with Sara in the previous year—as "The Pang More Sharp Than All" probably records his reaction to a meeting in October 1823.[3] Still, as George Whalley has so sensitively written, the "longings, recollections, laments upon a past unfulfilled and a broken but visionary hope" stirred in Coleridge during the last decade of his life. As a result the sentiments of the late confession poems "have moved into an ambience of their own, image-haunted, rooted in the past, indifferent to the accidental and the particular substance of unaccountable human events" (p. 140), honestly describing the death of his spirit and the agony of his wry self-reproach.

We can see by hindsight, of course, that at least some of Coleridge's stagnancy of will and spirit is attributable to opium, whose debilitating effects morally, mentally, and physically he records in "The Pains of Sleep." Marshall Suther would add that this stagnancy comes from his agonizing realization that neither the power of poetry (expressed in "Dejection" in 1802) nor the power of love (expressed in "Constancy to an Ideal Object" c. 1826) could lead him to God.[4] But when all the evidence is in, the mystery of Coleridge's creative life still contains large areas of unfathomed and uncharted depths. As I have already mentioned, even the traditional view about Coleridge's loss of creativity after the *annus mirabilis* can overstate the case if one does not observe due caution. The fact is that many passages can be culled from his letters, prose writings, and notebooks—not to mention his poems—to illustrate that the flow of his imagination, while rising to the surface only fitfully in the form of a poem, ran like a subterranean river deep and strong to his death. That he shifted steadily between 1800 and 1810 from poetry to prose as his principal medium of expression is undeniable. That he wrote poems in every year but five or six after 1800 is equally undeniable. Many of these poems are of the first order. And it is with the measurable fact of these poems that we are concerned here. Although the confession poems express the perplexities of a man reviewing the supposed failures of his life, their method of expression derives from a mind reproducing with artistry the process of self-analysis. Coleridge and his age might have believed that feeling expresses itself spontaneously— and the confession poem certainly originates in strong emotion—but he took the making of poetry seriously and knew that the emotional experience (and the psychological analysis of it) were not the same as the artistic elaboration of a poem.

One of the best of the confession poems, "Youth and Age," demonstrates that Coleridge could still occasionally summon in the last ten years of his life the creative imagination and artistic discipline which we find in operation in "The Ancient Mariner," "Dejection," and in many of the conversation and dream poems. Praised by Leigh Hunt in *Imagination and Fancy* (1844) as one of the most perfect poems for style and feeling ever written, it systematically contrasts the present with the past in three strophes which progress dialectically from thesis and antithesis to synthesis. Prefacing each of the three strophes is a five-line ballad stanza ending in a refrain which indicates the changing attitude and age of the poet. Thus, the thesis ("When I was young") recalls a time when

> Life went a-maying
> With Nature, Hope, and Poesy.

Then, the antithesis ("Ere I was old") acknowledges that in middle age "Friendship is a sheltering tree." Finally, the synthesis ("When we are old") admits the unavoidable truth that

> Dew-drops are the gems of morning,
> But the tears of mournful eve!

Harmonizing with this thesis-antithesis-synthesis development of idea are two conceits which elaborate the theme into a series of counterpointing statements. The prefatory ballad stanzas objectify their thought through flower, rain, and wind imagery celebrating the immutable and joyous freedom of nature. The strophes develop their thought through a body image mirroring the inevitable, disheartening imprisonment of man by time. In the thesis—which celebrates a time when youth and nature lived together in one body—the two conceits combine, with the imagery of flower, wind, and rain dominant. In the antithesis—which heralds middle age— the two conceits alternately converge and diverge. Echoes are still heard of the time when spring tide blossomed on the poet's lips and his body ("this breathing house") raced with nature out of doors "o'er aery cliffs and glittering sands." But a new note of physical confinement and emotional isolation is also heard. "Locks in silvery slips" and "drooping gait" deny that spring tide and he are "house-mates still." Finally, in the synthesis—which accepts the advent of old age—the body image emerges dominant. The dewdrops are transformed into tears and the flower motif does not appear, all of which is expressive of the poet's hopeless conclusion that

> . . . life's a warning
> . . . .
> That only serves to make us grieve
> With oft and tedious taking-leave,
> Like some poor nigh-related guest,
> That may not rudely be dismist,
> Yet hath outstay'd his welcome while,
> And tells the jest without the smile.

During most of his life Coleridge lived as a guest in another's house. He frequently felt "the stranger's shame" ("To Two Sisters"). In "Youth and Age" the poignancy of that situation acquires poetic objectivity through the image of a man living out his life in a world that he, guest-like, can never call his own.

Coleridge did not arrive at this superb blend of themes without effort. Lines 1–43 (the sections on youth and middle age and the prefatory stanza on old age) were drafted in a notebook dated 10 September 1823; but only the first and second sections, lines 1–38 (youth and middle age), were subsequently printed as "Youth and Age" in 1828 in the *Literary Souvenir* and the *Bijou*. The third section, lines 39–49 (old age), referred to by Coleridge as an "out-slough or hypertrophic stanza of a certain poem called 'Youth and Age,'" was published separately as "The Old Man's Sigh: A Sonnet" in *Blackwood's Magazine* for June 1832. He had attempted to combine the two poems but had failed because, as he comments in a manuscript entry appended to a notebook version of the third section, he decided that the first two sections (the 1828 version of "Youth and Age") "formed a whole without it: and I must have either made a cheerless conclusion or a religious one too elevated for the character of the Ode."[5] Sometime between the 1832 publication of "The Old Man's Sigh" and the 1834 edition of his *Poetical Works,* however, he reworked the two poems, and this time, after making several changes, succeeded in combining them into a three-fold structure. First, he deleted from "The Old Man's Sigh" the line

> Whose bruised wings quarrel with the bars of the
> still narrowing cage.

The idea expressed here that life is increasingly one of constraint and isolation fits the thought of the preceding sections, but the image of the caged bird conflicts superfluously with the human image developed throughout. Second, he dropped the last two lines,

> O! might Life cease! and Selfless Mind,
> Whose total *Being* is *Act,* alone remain behind!

because they involved the finished poem in a gratuitous debate over the corpuscular theory of life (cf. *PW,* p. 641). Then, by changing line 21, which had been printed in the 1828 version of "Youth and Age" as "Of beauty, truth, and liberty," to "Of friendship, love, and liberty," he made the second ballad stanza thematically consistent with the description in the third section of old age as a friendless guest who has overstayed his welcome. Thus revised, the final structure of "Youth and Age," while dialectically opposing the present to the past, interweaves a dense complex of motifs: youth-age, freedom-confinement, joy-sorrow, immutability-mutability, nature-man, union-isolation, beloved-friendless.

*T*he note of isolation on which "Youth and Age" ends is a motif found in all the confession poems. A paralyzing fear of not belonging pervades them in the same way that a quickening joy pervades the conversation group. Yet, despite their general unity of tone, the confession poems are a less homogeneous collection than the conversation group. In many of them can be heard the other poetic voices of Coleridge. "The Picture" is ironic in the manner of the farrago voice, "Dejection" and "Youth and Age" sublime in the manner of the prophecy voice, "The Day-dream" and "Love's Apparition and Evanishment" reminiscent in the manner of the dream voice, and "The Blossoming of the Solitary Date-tree" spontaneous in the manner of the improvisation voice.

The confession poems succeed less uniformly than those celebrating the Clevedon and Nether Stowey days for the very human reasons that Coleridge had difficulty getting at the crux of his problem and that he responded in time with less intensity to his supposed failures as man and artist.

To focus the light of the past onto the present is sometimes a disturbing experience. No one relishes facing the unpleasant fact of failure. With the uncertainty of a man who confesses what is ultimately beyond his comprehension, Coleridge sometimes misinterprets the facts, contradicts himself, digresses from the subject, or misunderstands a momentary uplift of spirit. Marshall Suther shows in a close analysis of the "Verse Epistle to Sara Hutchinson" that Coleridge offers both incorrect and contradictory definitions of the afflictions which bow him down to earth and suspend his "shaping spirit of imagination" ("Dejection"). Coleridge contends that his "coarse domestic life" has known

> No Habits of heart-nursing Sympathy,
> No Griefs but such as dull and deaden me,
> No mutual mild Enjoyments of its own,
> No Hopes of its own Vintage.

But as Suther illustrates from the "Verse Epistle" itself, Coleridge's married life was not an emotional blank; it had joys and griefs which Coleridge keenly felt:

My little children are a Joy, a Love,
  A good Gift from above!
But what is Bliss, that still calls up a Woe,
  And makes it doubly keen
Compelling me to *feel,* as well as KNOW
What a most blessed Lot mine might have been.

Furthermore, Coleridge's brief against his marriage conflicts with his contention that he can no longer feel how beautiful is nature because he strove to be still and patient

And haply by abstruse Research to steal
From my own Nature all the Natural Man.

In the one he claims that he cannot feel sorrow or pain because his domestic life has not offered the occasion for such fears and sorrows; and in the other he claims that he has felt such soul-shattering sorrows that he has deliberately pursued abstract studies to deaden his capacity for feeling.[6] In another of the confession poems, "The Picture," the ambiguity assumes a literary form. Besides psychological subterfuges, described in my previous analysis of the poem, Coleridge pursues multiple poetic goals. His failure to focus them into a unified vision leaves the central statement of the poem fuzzy and obscure. The depiction of the briars and thorns and low stumps of nature as a threat to lovers' gay plumes and dainty feet is too exaggerated not to be meant as an indictment of the "gaudy verse" of the day which idealized and falsified nature (*CL,* I, 612). Also, the roll call of oreads, nymphs, and dryades is too ostentatious not to be meant as a jibe at Gessner's gauche union of the pastoral idyls of classical poetry and the back-to-nature sentiment of the eighteenth century. At the same time, Coleridge appears to employ these same pastoral conventions seriously, as in the tableau of the virgin and her lover at the edge of the pool. Furthermore, the poem partakes of the ambulatory, pictorial world of Gray and the Wartons. And most important for this chapter, it contains Coleridge's satirical analysis of the self-deception employed by a man in love. Adding to the disunity is the tendency of the verse to shift disconcertingly from eighteenth-century Miltonics:

But hence, fond wretch! breathe not contagion here!

to Wordsworthian prosiness:

Sweet breeze! thou only, if I guess aright,

[or]   Two crescent hills
Fold in behind each other, and so make
A circular vale, and land-locked, as might seem,
With brook and bridge, and grey stone cottages,
Half hid by rocks and fruit-trees.

In short, the tone of the poem is uncertain, and consequently the self-indictment softened. The multiplicity of voices which the confession poem assumes reflects the compulsion of Coleridge's soul-searching and under-scores sadly the price such soul-searching cost him in artistry. When Coleridge wrote a confessional poem he often found it difficult to follow the counsel he once gave to Southey in earlier more optimistic days: "Before you write a poem, you should say to yourself . . . which feature is to be predominant in it?" (*CL,* I, 139).

This uncertainty of direction undoubtedly contributed to the incon-clusiveness of the confession poem. In a letter to Thelwall in 1796, Cole-ridge remarked: "Whatever a man's excellence is, that will be likewise his fault" (*CL,* I, 279). Faithfully reflective of Coleridge's introspective habits, the confession poem also reflected his inability to resolve his sense of guilt. Consequently, an unanswered question in his mind led inevitably to an unanswered question in the poem, for he could find no explanation except the unacceptable one of being a nature "deepliest stained with sin" ("The Pains of Sleep"). If he had been content to dramatize his sense of in-adequacy and incompleteness, as a modern poet like John Crowe Ransom dramatizes a similar ambivalence of attitude in "The Equilibrists," Cole-ridge might have transformed his experience into great poetry. But he was "incapable of remaining content with half knowledge" (to use Keats' ver-sion of Coleridge's problem); he persisted in his "irritable reaching after fact and reason," ever hopeful of reaching the "penetralium of mystery."[7] When he did refrain from probing for first causes, willing simply to re-alize his experience of growing old and unwanted in the form of a poem, he produced "Youth and Age," a moving poem in which his shortcomings and disappointments merge into the universal experience of man. "Youth and Age" is one of the most esthetically satisfying of the confession poems because it is complete.

Coleridge tried, of course, to universalize his experience in poems other than "Youth and Age." In "The Pang More Sharp Than All," he abstracts from the bitter-sweet knowledge of his love for Sara Hutchinson a disquisition on the pain of finding kindness substituted for love. And in "Constancy to an Ideal Object," he treats his unchanging emotions as part of the larger problem of what is the real object of one's affections: the person or the ideal concept of that person. Yet these poems have a disturbing vagueness which leaves them curiously unfinished. In "The Pang More Sharp Than All" the emotions involved appear in place of the persons, the allegorical figures of Kindness, Esteem, and Love playing out a pretty charade about metamorphosed feelings. In "Constancy to an Ideal Object" "she" and "that shining swarm" seem arbitrarily shadowy figures. As a love poem, it gives only hints and inferences about the details and situation of the lovers. Why cannot the poet, for example, have "a home, an English home, and thee"? The answer is not forthcoming from the poem. Only biography—facts external to the poem—will elucidate this and similar lacunas in the poetic statement. Coleridge is guilty here of what Yvor Winters calls the structural method of pseudo-reference. Even the ideal nature of the "thou" is not clear until at least a third of the poem is read. In his effort to transcend the particulars of his life, Coleridge has become elliptical and general in these two poems. Complicating his problem is the fact that the events of the past, the eyes through which the confession poem views the misfortunes of the present, had no doubt lost for him their sharpness of detail.

An eventual diminishment of emotional intensity in Coleridge accounts probably for the sterile formalism of the late confession poems. After he found anchorage at Highgate, Coleridge felt with less poignancy the guilt of lost love and thwarted ambition. As the sage of Highgate, he employed the tone and form of self-examination and abnegation rather perfunctorily. In the late confession poems, especially "Constancy to an Ideal Object," "The Pang More Sharp Than All," and "Love's Apparition and Evanishment," he removed himself poetically from the immediacy of a pain once eagerly scrutinized; he retired to the fairy court of Spenser and the artificial, wondering world of archaic words, where the emotions of hope, love, and kindness became allegorical figures drained of bodily heat, like "elfin knight[s]" trapped by Merlin's art in an orb of glass ("The Pang More Sharp Than All"). As a consequence the late confession poems lack surface tension and underlying intensity of emotion. For the felt experience, Coleridge substituted poetic formula.

The revision of "Love's Apparition and Evanishment" illustrates this failure of imagination. In the opening lines of an early draft (c. 1824), Coleridge confesses to the "inward self-decay" of his feelings. Then follows an "Arab" image which restates this confession in much the same way that the "grave Tyrian trader" and "merry Grecian coaster" image in

Arnold's "The Scholar Gipsy" metaphorically summarizes for us the contrast between the faith and simplicity of the scholar gipsy and the doubts and divided aims of Arnold and his age. When it was finally published ten years later in *Friendship's Offering,* however, the poem, now much elaborated and subtitled "An Allegoric Romance," begins with the "Arab" simile rather than with the confession. Thus read before we know of its referent, the "Arab" image fails to synthesize the poet's insight with the aptness of the original version but conveys instead an impression of self-conscious poetizing. Unquestionably, the 1834 version of the poem has gained in verbal clarity—no mixed metaphors nor ambiguous references mar its surface as they do the earlier draft—but it has lost in emotional intensity. Coleridge has mitigated the terrible intuition that his empty, loveless heart is like an unused, waterless well in which no echo is heard, sound it as often as he wishes; in place of that harrowing insight, he has substituted a less shocking experience: a momentary stagnancy of mind for which he makes God responsible.

In the second half of the poem the same resort to poetic formula occurs. The allegory of Hope and Love, which is inobtrusive in the 1824 version, is enlarged into a labored wedding ceremony in which Hope ("drest as a bridesmaid") and Love ("a sylph in bridal trim") perform like painted figures on an eighteenth-century music box. Safely harbored at Highgate from gusts of emotion, Coleridge slowly lost the capacity to feel his disappointments intensely. Since he continued to employ the confession form, these late poems enact a relatively empty ritual.

If there are few satisfactory poems in the confession group, there are nevertheless, single lines and whole passages taut with the immediacy of Coleridge's introspection. His nightmares are depicted in "The Pains of Sleep" with an accuracy of observation which is vividly apparent when we compare them with his effort in "Ode on the Departing Year" to realize the same kind of experience with the convention of the dream-vision. His tribute in "To William Wordsworth" to the healing power of Wordsworth's blank verse is a revelation of self-pity and selfless generosity. Such passages have often been noted. Less frequently cited is this admission of sterility, which prefigures Gerard Manley Hopkins's greater sonnet "Thou Art Indeed Just, Lord":

> All Nature seems at work. Slugs leave their lair—
> The bees are stirring—birds are on the wing—
> And Winter slumbering in the open air,

> Wears on his smiling face a dream of Spring!
> And I the while, the sole unbusy thing,
> Nor honey make, nor pair, nor build, nor sing.
>
> ("Work Without Hope")

or this confession of loneliness, which voices a love of country traditional to English poetry from Chaucer to Rupert Brooke:

> "Ah! Loveliest friend!
> That this the meed of all my toils might be,
> To have a home, an English home, and thee!"
> Vain repetition! Home and Thou are one.
> The peacefull'st cot, the moon shall shine upon,
> Lulled by the thrush and wakened by the lark,
> Without thee were but a becalméd bark,
> Whose helmsman on an ocean waste and wide
> Sits mute and pale his mouldering helm beside.
>
> ("Constancy to an Ideal Object")

or this recognition that he is the object of pity:

> One pang more blighting-keen than hope betray'd!
> And this it is my woeful hap to feel,
>
> . . . .
>
> O worse than all! O pang all pangs above
> Is Kindness counterfeiting absent Love!
>
> ("The Pang More Sharp Than All")

or this picture of himself suspended over the vacancy of his own heart:

> Like a lone Arab, old and blind,
> Some caravan had left behind,
> Who sits beside a ruin'd well,
>
> . . . .
>
> And listens for a human sound—in vain!
>
> ("Love's Apparition and Evanishment")

But Coleridge would be the first to deny "the praises of a just poem" to the above "series of striking lines or distiches, each of which, absorbing the whole attention of the reader to itself, disjoins it from its context, and makes it a separate whole, instead of an harmonizing part" (*BL,* II, 10).

Perhaps only in "Dejection" and "Youth and Age" has Coleridge written confessional poems in which the parts have their intrinsic interest and the whole its proper importance. In them he translated into poetic form his passionate interest in the intricacies of his mind. In them he confessed with all mankind his yearning for love and his fear of having abused the gift of life. In them he found, in the words of A. O. Lovejoy, "a certain triumph in defeat; for he [was] able to derive, and to impart, aesthetic pleasure from the very emotion aroused by his inability to experience aesthetic pleasure—or at all events, from the poetic utterance of that emotion." He did not merely make melancholy enjoyable but achieved beauty by the description of his loss of the feeling for beauty and of the will for life. "Dejection" and "Youth and Age" are then "welcome example[s] of the 'reconciliation of opposites.' "[8] In the other confession poems, unfortunately, Coleridge transformed the unalloyed particulars of lovelessness and loneliness into the universals of art only fitfully. To the extent that they succeeded, however, the confession poems supplied a literary vehicle responsive to his emotional stagnancy and enervation in the second half of his life and to his yearning for the regenerative "spice-islands of youth and hope" (TT, II, 341), symbolized by the recurrent images of a baby,[9] a blossoming plant, and an oasis.[10]

[I learned] not to consider too nicely the expressions I should employ, but to trust mainly to the extemporaneous ebullition of my thoughts. . . . It is true that my matter may not be so accurately arranged: it may not dovetail and fit at all times as nicely as could be wished; but you shall have my thoughts warm from my hearth, and fresh from my understanding.

—Sixth Lecture of 1811–12, Collier Report

. . . Meantime the grey-haired philosopher, left to his own musings, continued playing with the thoughts that Alia and Alia's question had excited, till he murmured them to himself in half-audible words, which at first casually, and then for the amusement of his ear, he *punctuated* with rhymes, without however conceiting that he had by these means changed them into poetry.

—Introductory Note to MS. Version of "Duty Surviving Self-love"

VIII

THE IMPROVISATION VOICE

"*P*oor Coleridge" was a phrase frequently whispered among acquaintances of the poet during the last thirty years of his life, and it reflects the disappointment felt by all over his seeming failure to realize the promise of his youth. That Coleridge knew of this condescension is evident by his continuing references to it in his poetry, beginning as early as January 1807 in "To William Wordsworth" and appearing as late as the mid-1820's in "The Pang More Sharp Than All."

But few men can long endure such disesteem, not even the S. T. C. for whom Pecksniffian humility was second nature. Catering to Coleridge's very human need to find favor with himself is a group of poems written principally during the years of snug harborage at Highgate, when the shuffling, snuff-taking, prematurely aged poet and philosopher had collected around him a coterie of young disciples. Basking in the congenial warmth of their admiration, the impetuous, animated poet who twenty-five years before at Racedown had leaped a gate and bounded across a pathless field to meet Dorothy and William Wordsworth had evolved into a venerable but slightly foolish parlor rhapsodizer who shone in the reflected light of guests come to sit respectfully for a moment at his feet and be astounded with his "charades and extempore verses at Christmas times" ("The Improvisatore"). Coleridge justifies—even celebrates— this bardic role in the poems "A Tombless Epitaph," "The Reproof and Reply," "*Sancti Dominici Pallium*," "A Character," "Duty Surviving Self-love," "Lines Suggested by the Last Words of Berengarius ob. Anno. Dom. 1088," and "The Improvisatore."[1]

Carlyle describes Coleridge in those years as perched "on the brow of Highgate Hill . . . looking down on London and its smoke-tumult, like a sage escaped from the inanity of life's battle; attracting towards him the thoughts of innumerable brave souls still engaged there."[2] In contrast to this famous portrait, Coleridge depicts himself in these poems as the good grey warrior, still carrying on the battle for truth, still faithful to his youthful ideals amid a world of sycophancy and dishonesty. Sickness and slander have besieged him with "whole years of weary days" but have not dimmed his passion for the ancient truths nor dislodged him from the "citadel unconquered" ("A Tombless Epitaph"). Although "old friends burn dim" ("Duty Surviving Self-love"), he does not love them the less. Steadfast in love, he has remained firm also in principles, "his own whim his only bribe"; he has "never left in lurch/ His king, his country, or his church" ("A Character"). Sometimes, if the cause were just, he has fought with good will even his enemy's battles. Ever the unwearied warrior-poet, he sees himself in many guises but always with armor dented yet sword held high. He calls himself Constantius in a prose introduction to the first draft of "Duty Surviving Self-love"; and Idoloclastes Satyrane, "breaker of idols," and child of "wild-wood fancy and impetuous zeal" in "A Tombless Epitaph."

The man pictured in the confession poems is lonely, bewildered, and pain-wracked, but he does not flinch at the failure of his life. We feel a vague distaste for his insistent self-advertising; yet we are forced to admire the honesty with which he acknowledges the ruin of his hopes.

The same man sits for his portrait in the improvisation poems; but he is garbed now in the robes of a semi-retired oracle. He wears a nimbus of otherworldliness as an explanation of his threadbare station in life. He is the "studious poet"

> . . . framed for calmer times and nobler hearts!
> . . . eloquent for truth!
> Philosopher! contemning wealth and death,
> Yet docile, childlike, full of Life and Love!
>
> ("A Tombless Epitaph")

Despite Herculean labors, he is perennially indigent, a "silly bard, unfed, untended," who has

> . . . plough'd and sow'd, while others reapt;
> The work was his, but theirs the glory.
>
> ("A Character")

He sees in his heroic struggle against suffocating odds a repetition of Berengarius' fate. Born into a dark age in which congenial minds were rare, he has been forced to move in the "scanty circlet" of his own light. Is it any wonder then, he asks, that he "withdrew the ray/ That did but guide the night-birds to their prey"? Do not criticize him for unfulfilled promises, he pleads; it is the time in which he was born which is to blame. Meant for the warmth of noon, he came too early in the harsh, struggling light of dawn ("Berengarius"). A "meek Parnassian" beguiled by the beauty of flowers, music, and feminine charm, he has retreated to the safety of the drawing room. There, a modest oracle divorced from the ambitions of the world, he dispenses gracious "extempores" in answer to questions put to him by his morning callers.

In the poem as improvisation, then, Coleridge portrays himself as a buffeted warrior for truth, with a reputation as an inspired maker of verses, who occasionally emerges from semi-retirement to instruct friends at feasts and entertainments.

So much for the content and tone of these poems. Something must also be said about their form and origin. The speaking voice, with its suggestion of the casual talk of friends, is a characteristic of the conversation pieces. With the improvisation poem, Coleridge extends his experiments along this line, except that an *improvisatore,* who is both originator and subject of the poem, replaces the dramatis personae of the Coleridge and Wordsworth families. Before our fascinated eyes he brings a poem into being where before there was nothing. This incorporation of the creative process into the poetic structure represents the furthest point reached by Coleridge in his search for a form conveying an air of spontaneity.

He did not conceive this kind of poem miraculously out of whole cloth. For one thing, it mirrors well his own extemporizing powers; the bard of the poems remains an idealized transcription of himself. For another, it reflects his flair for the dramatic. We should not forget that he alone of the major English Romantic poets wrote a play which had a successful London run.

Equally important is the social context out of which the improvisation poems grew. The improviser was a favorite literary figure in the early nineteenth century. Like his troubadour ancestor, he is able to sing a song or tell a story at a moment's notice. He provides narrative poems of the day with heroes, as in Praed's *The Troubadour* (1823–24), and heroines, as in Letitia Landon's *The Improvisatore* (1824). He also gives narrative unity to such collections of stories as Beddoes' *The Improvisatore* (1821) and Miss Landon's *The Golden Violet* (1827). In European literature he furnishes the title of an early (1835) Hans Christian Andersen novel. He figures in Pushkin's prose tale, *The Egyptian Nights* (1835), and in Mickiewicz's verse drama, *Forefathers' Eve,* Part III (1832).

The Romantic poets claimed the same impromptu powers for themselves as they did for their fictional troubadours. Moore incarnated the national bard, enchanting lords and ladies of the concert-room with songs that celebrated the glories and misfortunes of his race, in much the same way as had his bardic predecessors. Burns, Wordsworth, Coleridge, Southey, and Byron all published poems which were supposedly inspired by the divine afflatus of Orpheus. Thus the improvisation poem reflects the literary fashion of the 1820's.

It also reflects Coleridge's belief that poetry originates in a spontaneous overflow of feeling. During his Bristol and Nether Stowey days, he had frequently claimed impromptu origins for his poems. But his efforts to suggest spontaneity through the structure of the poem had been jejune and inorganic. The simplest expedient had been to narrate in the subtitle the circumstances giving rise to the poem. Thus, "To Fortune [was] Composed During a Walk to and from the Queen's Head, Gray's Inn Lane, Holborn, and Hornsky's and Co., Cornhill."[3] Occasionally a preface was drafted, instructing the reader that the poem "was struck off in a great hurry." The "Ode on the Departing Year," written with "unusual rapidity" "in the course of the last three days," had this sort of introduction at its first printing. The professional bard's pride in a spur-of-the-moment facility with words is again evident in the prefatorial account of how the first canto of "The Wanderings of Cain" was "despatched . . . at full finger-speed" "in one night!" Infrequently such exposition was incorporated into the poem:

> The indignant Bard composed this furious ode,
> As tired he dragg'd his way thro' Plimtree road!
>
> ("Devonshire Roads")

Impromptu renderings in guest-books at inns ("Lines Written in the Album at Albingerode, in the Hartz Forest") also measured the extemporaneous gifts of the poet. Even Coleridge's "Religious Musings . . . on the Christmas Eve of 1794" were not sacred if they called attention to the impromptu ebullience of his thoughts.

About half these assertions of impromptu composition were made for poems written before 1798. The decline in such claims after 1800[4] was an inevitable result of Coleridge's ceaseless struggle to write poetry that was "form as proceeding" rather than "shape as superinduced" (*BL,* II, 262). His call in the introduction to *A Sheet of Sonnets* for a union of meter and thought was bearing fruit during these same years. By 1798 he was using a supple, conversational idiom which implied the natural tones of speech more effectively than "impromptu" or "extempore" tags. His dropping of "conversation" from the subtitle of "The Nightingale" in the 1800 *Lyrical Ballads*[5] is indicative of his growing dissatisfaction with external devices. If the poem suggests conversation in its syntax, rhythm, and diction, no tag is necessary; if not, no tag is an adequate substitute.

The ideal of the poet as *improvisatore,* however, was not entirely forgotten amid the excitement of exploring new ways of submerging the artificial in the natural. Like Pushkin and Mickiewicz, Coleridge was famous for his extemporizing power; and he retained a pardonable pride in it throughout his life. During the years of homelessness and laudanum addiction and the years of semi-invalidism at Highgate, his reputation as a versifier who could contribute a few appropriate lines for any occasion was a remnant of poetic renown worth clinging to. There flowed from his pen between 1807 and 1834, years when he relied upon friends and strangers rather than his family for succor, a stream of gratuitous and pontifical compliments. They include a "bread and butter" note ("To Two Sisters"), welcome of a sick friend to the ranks of the healthy ("The Two Founts: Stanzas Addressed to a Lady on Her Recovery with Unblemished Looks, from a Severe Attack of Pain"), praise of another's poetry ("The Snowdrop" and "To Matilda Betham from a Stranger"), an inscription in a book sent as a present ("Written in a Blank Leaf of Faulkner's *Shipwreck,* Presented by a Friend to Miss K")[6] and compliments in ladies' albums or commonplace books ("To Mary Pridham"; "Love, Hope, and Patience in Education"; and "Lines Written in Commonplace Book of Miss Barbour, Daughter of the Minister of the U.S.A. to England").

That Coleridge delighted in displaying his extemporaneous gifts is further testified to by Dr. Carlyon's report that stanzas 1, 3, and 4 of "Homesick" were written in the Brockenstammbuch at the little inn on the Brocken from Coleridge's dictation.[7] He was also forever including in his letters examples of his unpremeditated effusions. Even on manuscript versions of his poems and in his notebooks—work sheets presumably for his eyes only—Coleridge is careful to note those fathered by impromptu urgings of the muse. He characterizes a first draft of "Youth and Age" as an "Aria Spontanea" (*CPW*, II, 1085) and brags that the envoy to "Love's Apparition and Evanishment" was written "without taking my pen off the paper" (*PW*, p. 644).

There are psychological implications in all this, of course. Coleridge's emphasis on his extemporaneous gifts can be interpreted as another variety of self-effacement—like his apologies for hasty or faulty workmanship and his disavowals of serious intentions—calculated to protect him from the judgment of the public. Yet one should not overlook as an influence the esteem that the bard enjoyed in his day. The vogue of the *improvisatore,* plus his effort to write poetry that sounds natural, undoubtedly explains, in part, his continuing interest in poetic improvisation.

If the 1790's is the decade when Coleridge is most active in claiming through tags that his poems are spontaneous effusions, the second half of the 1820's is the period when he is most intent on trying to write poems which convince us of their extemporaneity by letting us watch them come into being.

An extreme instance of a poem in the process of shaping an inchoate thought into a meaningful expression is "The Blossoming of the Solitary Date-tree." In a preface, Coleridge furnishes us with the source of the title and the theme of the poem. He then confesses that the "first leaf of the manuscript from which the poem has been transcribed, and which contained the two or three introductory stanzas, is wanting. . . . But a rude draught of the poem contains the substance of the stanzas, and the reader is requested to receive it as the substitute." After this ingenious request for our tolerance, Coleridge adroitly suggests that "it is not impossible, that some congenial spirit, whose years do not exceed those of the author at the time the poem was written [another veiled excuse for the unfinished form of the poem?], may find a pleasure in restoring the lament to its original integrity by a reduction of the thoughts to the requisite metre." Coleridge is inviting us to help create the poem. He can hardly bring us closer to experiencing the spontaneity of the creative act than this.

There follows a remarkable poem of six stanzas, of which the first three are in varying stages of completion. Stanzas 1 and 2, like the introductory remarks, are prose statements. Stanza 3, although printed in poetic lines, is obviously still an early draft; its appositives look as if they had been jotted down as the ideas sprang into the poet's mind. However, a chance rhyme in the first seven lines and the rhyming of the last three lines indicate the poet's growing control of his material. In stanzas 4 to 6 the theme emerges fully developed and arranged in seven-line staves of iambic pentameter and an intricate rhyme scheme of ababccc.

Thus "The Blossoming of the Solitary Date-tree" allows us to watch the imagination create a new whole, object by object, out of the "multeity" of experience. As a result, a startlingly effective air of improvisation marks Coleridge's success in this poem.

Nor is there much question that such was his intention with this poem. The sentiment and content suggest the Malta period (about 1805), when Coleridge was thirty-three years old. Yet the preface implies that the poem was composed at a more youthful time in the author's life (unless thirty-three may be considered youthful when viewed with the eyes of fifty-six, the age of Coleridge in 1828, the year the poem was published). Coleridge was adept at concocting prefaces which placed his endeavors in the best light possible, while absolving him of criticism if the reader found the work diffident, incomplete, or unpolished (cf. the prefaces to "The Wanderings of Cain," "Kubla Khan," "The Three Graves," and "Ode on the Departing Year"). If, then, one statement in his prefatory comments about "The Blossoming of the Solitary Date-tree" is suspect, or ambiguous at best, why not others? particularly the claim that several opening stanzas of the poem were lost. Could not the story of the lost stanzas represent an "Estecian" apology for a never completed work? How a poem drafted in 1805 came to be published in 1828 as an improvisation can be explained, I think, in the following fashion. While in Malta, he jotted down the lines constituting stanzas 3–6, which are expressive of his unhappy exile and unrequited love for Sara Hutchinson. Since they were personally revelatory as well as unfinished, he did not publish them in 1817 in *Sibylline Leaves*. And when he printed stanzas 4–6 in the *New Times* of 31 January 1818, by way of advertisement for his lectures at the London Philosophical Society, he fobbed them off, with fitting modifications, as an "Imitation of One of the Minnesinger of the Thirteenth Century." As for stanza 3, either he had not yet written it or, more likely, had recognized the inappropriateness of its Lake Country *mystique* and deleted it. In any case, the deception practiced so deftly on the reader was worthy of a man who had developed to a high degree the skill of adjusting poems to different occasions and new themes. But these stanzas were fated ten years later to be the instrument of a more embellished subterfuge. In 1828 a collected edition of his poems was projected. Desirous of including as large an offering as possible, he searched through his juvenilia and unfinished poems for anything which might be usable. "The Wanderings of Cain" was published with its "Prefatory Note" for the first time, and so were these lines about his inability to "delight in little things" unless he shared his delight with a loved one. In the two preceding years he had been experimenting with such poems as "Berengarius," "Duty Surviving Self-love," and "The Improvisatore." With this emphasis on improvisation, what was more natural than for Coleridge, apparently forgetful of the version buried in the *New Times*, to take these unfinished lines which the years had rendered less personal, write a preface—(1) relating two anecdotes elucidative of the poem, the first about God's refusal to separate Adam and Eve and the second about a solitary date tree's inability to bear fruit; (2) explaining the misfortune of the lost stanzas; and (3) inviting the reader to complete the poem—add two prose stanzas to the lines already written, and print the results as an interesting example of improvisation? Precedent for using such elaborate machinery to introduce a poem had been established as early as 1809 and repeated in 1816 when he had excused the printing of "The Three Graves" and "Kubla Khan" with the plea that each was a "psychological curiosity."

Coleridge never again used the form of "The Blossoming of the Solitary Date-tree." Rather, in most of the improvisation poems, he exploits the figure and situation of the drawing-room monologist. In them he pretends to have recorded an unrehearsed exchange of talk; but the rejoinder is mainly illusory. Thus he may bill "*Sancti Dominici Pallium*" as "A Dialogue between Poet and Friend";[8] yet one hears, for the most part, only the improviser whose words open and close the poem and monopolize forty-three of the fifty-eight lines. And not without justification is the preface to the manuscript version of "Duty Surviving Self-love" headed, "Question, Answer, *and Soliloquy*" (my italics).

It is not surprising, therefore, to learn that Coleridge experimented with several methods of conveying the effect of colloquy while retaining the solo performance of the *improvisatore*: (1) He has the *improvisatore* imagine the speech of a second person. (2) He prefaces the *improvisatore's* words with a narrative of the events preceding the moment of actual versifying. (3) He sets the stage and dramatizes the action leading up to the *improvisatore's* impromptu poem.

"The Reproof and Reply" is an example of the first method. The poet envisions the reprimand which he may receive for stealing flowers on a Sunday morning from a lady's garden. This fancied chastisement allows him to plead at some length that music, a lovely woman, and the month of

May conspired to enchant his senses. The effect is that of a conversation, although the form remains technically that of a monolog.

An example of the second method occurs in a manuscript draft of "Duty Surviving Self-love." Here, Coleridge introduces the poet's impromptu triumph with a narrative explaining the occasion:

> And are *you* (said Alia to Constantius, on whose head sickness and sorrow had antedated Winter, ere yet the time of Vintage had passed), Are you the happier for your Philosophy? And the smile of Constantius was as the light from a purple cluster of the vine, gleaming through snowflakes, as he replied, The Boons of Philosophy are of higher worth, than what you, O Alia, mean by Happiness. But I will not seem to evade the question—Am *I* the happier for my Philosophy? The calmer at least and the less unhappy, answered Constantius, for it has enabled me to find that selfless Reason is the best Comforter and only sure friend of declining Life. At this moment the sounds of a carriage followed by the usual bravura executed on the brazen knocker announced a morning visit: and Alia hastened to receive the party. Meantime the grey-haired philosopher, left to his own musings, continued playing with the thoughts that Alia and Alia's question had excited, till he murmured them to himself in half audible words, which at first casually, and then for the amusement of his ear, he *punctuated* with rhymes, without however conceiting that he had by these means changed them into poetry.

Here are the ingredients *sui generis* for the poem as an improvisation: the serious, inquiring female who unwittingly simplifies life, literature, and philosophy (Mrs. Barbauld on "The Ancient Mariner" comes to mind immediately); the benign philosopher who perceives the complexity of the questions put to him;[9] the soliloquy with its shift from silent musing to utterance in prose to improvisation in verse; and the humble insistence that such rhymed thoughts are not poetry. Out of such familiar Coleridgean ingredients is born a neatly turned sonnet on the constancy of the poet's heart in contrast to the fickleness of the world, an extemporaneous feat which any troubadour could be proud of.

Although "Duty Surviving Self-love" was subsequently published minus its prose introduction, "The Improvisatore" (an example of the third method) did reach print with an integrated stage-setting. In fact, this strange composition, which presents a nineteenth-century *improvisatore* during one of his inspired performances, exploits all the conventions introduced individually in the other improvisation poems: scene description, prose preamble, dialog structure, and poetic monolog.

The opening scene discloses "a spacious drawing-room, with music-room adjoining." Present are the *improvisatore* and two young disciples. Since the poem purports to be an overheard portion of salon chatter, it has no formal beginning. The speakers are in the middle of a discussion:

> *Katherine.* What are the words?
> *Eliza.* Ask our friend, the Improvisatore; here he comes. Kate has a favour to ask of you, Sir; it is that you will repeat the ballad that Mr. —— sang so sweetly.

The *improvisatore* identifies the song as one of Moore's *Irish Melodies.* Unable to recollect the words distinctly, he extemporizes, in true bardic fashion, a quatrain which summarizes the moral of the song, and then supplements this verse with lines from Beaumont and Fletcher's *The Elder Brother* which illustrate the same sentiment. Responsive to the sensibilities of his auditors, this Victorian bard expurgates as he recites, ad-libbing "neighbor" for the less delicate "wanton" in Beaumont and Fletcher's line, "We'll live together, like two wanton vines." Similarly, a nineteenth-century gentility prompts a young man, who has just joined the group, to whisper when he asks the *improvisatore* about the union of friendship and passion in love—lest the vulgarity of his question offend the ladies. Thus interrogated about the nature of love, the *improvisatore* begins a prose discourse on the subject. He posits a series of definitions, or first principles: first, a general idea of what love is not; second, a notion of what love is. After adumbrating the characteristics of true love, he examines the reasons why ideal love is rarely found united in both husband and wife and then analyzes the distinction between misery and happiness. Deftly he leads his auditors from topic to topic toward a final triumphant poetic improvisation. In answer to the suggestion of one of his feminine interlocutors that surely he who has described so well the human qualities necessary for experiencing true love must have possessed them himself, the *improvisatore,* "after a pause of a few minutes," begins a verse autobiography, "ex improviso."

Throughout this discourse, we hear the intonations of Coleridge's voice and detect the idiosyncrasies of his mind as he approaches an idea, picks it up, examines it, sets it down, and moves on to another idea in a steady progress toward the fruition of his thought in the form of a poem. In "The Improvisatore," he fashions out of the streamy nature of experience an organic form which combines both becoming and being. Thus, with its argument originating and developing before our eyes, the improvisation poem acts as its own "self-witnessing and self-effected sphere of agency" ("On Poesy or Art," *BL*, II, 262).

Obviously the expedient of including with the poem a background against which it figures as part of a flow of talk lends to the poem an air of spontaneity. At the same time, since it functions in this setting as a culmination of the talk, the poem imparts a sense of design to the entire drama. With such a poem our attention remains divided, now seeing the unrehearsed performer, now hearing the polished performance.

Coleridge puts the verse to a similar dual purpose. Much of it duplicates the now halting, now headlong, rush of talk. At the same time the rhyme and meter remind us that the poet is exercising firm control of his material. Irregular patterns prevail for the most part, however, giving the impression that the poetic line is not forced into a preconceived scheme but is allowed to follow the twists and turns of impromptu speech, as, for example, in these lines from "The Improvisatore":

> Crown of his cup, and garnish of his dish!
> The boon, prefigured in his earliest wish,
> The fair fulfillment of his poesy,
> When his young heart first yearn'd for sympathy!
> But e'en the meteor offspring of the brain
>   Unnourished wane;
> Faith asks her daily bread,
> And Fancy must be fed!
> Now so it chanced—from wet or dry,
> It boots not how—I know not why—
> She missed her wonted food; and quickly
> Poor Fancy stagger'd and grew sickly.
> Then came a restless state, 'twixt yea and nay,
> His faith was fix'd, his heart all ebb and flow;
> Or like a bark, in some half-shelter'd bay,
> Above its anchor driving to and fro.

In the improvisation poem, Coleridge writes heroic couplets reminiscent of Dryden's supple lines. Although he retains a firm feel for the couplet as the controlling unit of expression, he does not always allow the rhymed couplet to segment his thought into isolated pairs of lines, but frequently combines three and four lines when the thought demands it, as in these lines from "Berengarius":

> Lynx amid moles! had I stood by thy bed,
> Be of good cheer, meek soul! I would have said:
> I see a hope spring from that humble fear.
> All are not strong alike through storms to steer
> Right onward. What? though dread of threatened death
> And dungeon torture made thy hand and breath
> Inconstant to the truth within thy heart!

Here, the abrupt stop of the enjambed rhythm at "what?" and then the renewed impetus of the meter as the poet answers the question give the hallucinatory impression that the departed ghost of Berengarius has just spoken—a use of implied query and explicit rejoinder to advance the thought which reaches perfection in Browning's monologs. Coleridge's range with the couplet extends from the conversational, relaxed rhythm of "The Reproof and Reply" to the colloquial diction yet balanced antithesis of thought and meter of "*Sancti Dominici Pallium*," this last a shrill reminder of the bite and scorn of Pope's Horatian satires. In the verse of all three poets—in Dryden's reasoned discourse, Pope's urbane tone, and Coleridge's pulpit manner—is heard the accent of the speaking voice transcending the meter.

One has to admire Coleridge's mastery of his medium. There is in this voice of his old age the same deliberate, even insouciant, disregard for rules that one finds in the late Shakespeare. Unfortunately, the improvisation poems do not move us to awe as do *Antony and Cleopatra* and *The Tempest*. Although he displays great technical proficiency, Coleridge the *improvisatore* lacks dignity, humility, universal interest, and vitality. These are serious defects.

First, he lacks dignity. The society poet as impersonated by Coleridge retains little of the social importance which the role had for his heroic predecessors. He no longer fulfills a necessary function in society; he is the monologist who is tolerantly heard on dull mornings but left to his own thoughts when, as in "Duty Surviving Self-love," a carriage full of visitors is announced. One has only to recall diminutive Tom Moore trilling his way through a saccharine song before an audience of solicitous ladies to realize the low level to which the bardic office had sunk.

Second, like Wordsworth, he is egocentric, without the grace of

Wordsworth's humility before nature and honesty of vision. We may, as R. P. Blackmur maintains, have to overlook systems of thought or belief which we no longer accept if we are to continue to read certain poems, *The Divine Comedy* for instance, but no persuasion says that we must countenance the humbug of the *improvisatore*. Coleridge may have evolved during the Highgate years into a benign seer; certainly he liked to see himself as such a person and there is sufficient testimony from contemporaries to corroborate his having acted such a part; but we are reluctant to accept the truth or wholeness of view of this portrayal, especially if it originated in fragmented experience and circumscribed emotions. Like the side-show medicine man anxious to dispense his oracular cure-alls "free" to all, he is suspect and hence distasteful.

Third, although the poems interest us as experiments in improvising form, the *improvisatore* bores us. This is the unforgivable sin of art. Coleridge fails to enlist our sympathy or our interest, as he does in many of his poems of confession, principally because he has stopped searching out the human riddle of himself and is intent, instead, upon erecting a soul-satisfying effigy of himself. No such pathos may be found in the improvisation poem as invigorates the concluding lines of "The Pains of Sleep"; instead, one must tolerate the noisome smugness of "Duty Surviving Self-love," the enervating righteousness of "Berengarius," or the Pollyanna cant of "The Improvisatore" who stuffs himself with nostrums:

> Though heart be lonesome, Hope laid low,
> Yet, Lady! deem him not unblest:
> The certainty that struck Hope dead,
> Hath left Contentment in her stead:
> And that is next to Best!

In short, the conversation of the *improvisatore* is dully complacent and proverbial. And even though he has the dubious honor of siring a long line of self-nominated victims of a divorce between poet and society, this nostalgically sentimental "outsider" remains a literary curiosity. Despite his interesting progeny, who have become ruthlessly self-excoriating by the time one reaches Laforgue and Corbière, one feels little desire or finds little reason for seeing in his portrait the "soul of universal significance" which Coleridge felt was a necessary ingredient "in a true poet's composition, in addition to the specific meaning" (*AP*, p. 293).

Finally, the *improvisatore* is the product of a relaxed imagination, illustrated by the crystallization of the meaning of the words, *hope, joy, love,* and *fancy.* In the poems written during the Nether Stowey idyll and the Keswick interlude before the Malta sojourn, especially the conversation group, these concepts acquired a personal reference that enriches and deepens the meaning of the poems in which they appear. A feeling of hope, for example, contributes to "Frost at Midnight" a motif which is integral to the evolving statement of the poem: the hope Coleridge had as a Christ's Hospital boy of entertaining a visitor metamorphoses into the hope he has as a father of raising his son in full communion with nature. Four years later, in "Dejection," he explains his loss of creative imagination in terms of the absence of joy and fancy in his life. And the hope that his senses, once active but now listless, will quicken to the stimulus of nature as they used to do accompanies like a sweet undersong his anticipation of a coming storm. With the improvisation poems, the concepts have lost their vitality. Hope and fancy have become fixed ingredients of a recipe for love:

> Poor Fancy stagger'd and grew sickly.
>
> . . . .
> Doubts toss'd him to and fro:
> Hope keeping Love, Love Hope alive.
>
> . . . .
> Those sparkling colours, once his boast
>   Fading, one by one away,
> Thin and hueless as a ghost,
>   Poor Fancy on her sick bed lay.
>
> ("The Improvisatore")

Paul Valery has said that an artist can construct in an orderly fashion only with the aid of a set of conventions. Here a rich convention has hardened into a sterile formula.[10] It is unintentional irony that the poems featuring an improvising bard should illustrate an imaginatively tired Coleridge.

Thus, the improvisation poem fails to achieve the status of living poetry. It lacks the passion, simplicity, and sensuousness which Milton, seconded by Coleridge *(CL,* II, 830), considered requisite for great poetry. Central to it is a straw figure who, like the scarecrow, is a caricature of reality.

Yet we should not entirely dismiss these poems because they are abortive experiments, for they remind us that Coleridge never stood still poetically. Structurally they represent his last important effort to write poetry combining spontaneity and order. Metrically they reveal a steady evolution in his handling of verse. The conversational ease of the blank verse in the conversation poem and the colloquial verve of the rhymed couplets in the improvisation poem differ in kind as much as in degree. If the improvisation poem recalls the metrics of Augustan verse, it also miraculously reproduces the cadences of Regency speech.

On the other hand, the nearness of the improvisation poem to the society verse of Gay and Prior reveals the distance Browning still had to travel before perfecting the dramatic monolog. Although it anticipates the fascination felt by the Victorians for man as a phenomenon of civilization, the improvisation poem remains a soliloquy rather than a dramatic monolog. Concerned with constructing an apologia for his actions (or lack of action), the speaker in Coleridge's poems strives to convince himself that his point of view and version of truth are disinterested. Unconcerned about the truth and beginning with an established point of view, the speakers in Browning's poems direct their attention outward in an attempt to impress their views on the outside world. Coleridge's soliloquist turns the accepted moral perspective upon himself as he acts the role of self-apologist; Browning's monologist is oblivious of moral perspective as he pursues his strategy.[11] Consequently, in the improvisation poems, we have subjective didacticism, ultimately, rather than objective drama. Like such monologs as "My Last Duchess" or "The Bishop Orders His Tomb at Saint Praxed's Church," the improvisation poems arise out of specific situations: a stolen flower, a controversy between Southey and two Catholic theologians, the deathbed utterance of an eleventh-century scholastic, and a polite drawing-room conversation about love; but, in contrast to Browning's many-sided figures who unwittingly disclose themselves as they speak about people, things, and events, Coleridge's one-dimensional character, renowned for his unrehearsed lectures on any subject supplied by the ladies and gentlemen of the soirée, forever discourses about himself. Such egocentricity gives the improvisation poems their shape and being, but also accounts for their limited psychological and dramatic development.

Moreover, the impromptu nature of the *improvisatore*'s oral performance comprises the *end* of the improvisation poem. The Browning poem has gone beyond this; it uses process, for example, in *The Ring and the Book,* as a *means* of exploring and communicating the psychological and historical truths implicit in human actions. Browning's speakers do not self-consciously display a naive delight in their extemporaneous skill as does Coleridge's *improvisatore* who, like the bard of old composing against the clock, shows off by adding needless difficulties to his feat, proudly rendering his "extempores" in rhymed couplets and even in sonnet form. These efforts too frequently produce the effect of a set speech and hence sacrifice the dramatic impact of the unseen and the unheard, but nevertheless forceful, presence of a second person; they substitute the social art of deceit for the living drama of revelation. Thus, instead of an artistic achievement, the poem as an improvisation became in Coleridge's hands simply a drawing-room diversion and survives for students of Coleridge as a literary curiosity.

The delight in richness and sweetness of sound, even to a faulty excess, if it be evidently original, and not the result of an easily imitable mechanism, I regard as a highly favourable promise in the compositions of a young man. "The man that hath not music in his soul" can indeed never be a genuine poet. Imagery (even taken from nature, much more when transplanted from books, as travels, voyages, and works of natural history); affecting incidents; just thoughts; interesting personal or domestic feelings; and with these the art of their combination or intertexture in the form of a poem; may all by incessant effort be acquired as a trade, by a man of talents and much reading, who, as I once before observed, has mistaken an intense desire of poetic reputation for a natural poetic genius; the love of the arbitrary end for a possession of the peculiar means. But the sense of musical delight, with the power of producing it, is a gift of imagination; and this together with the power of reducing multitude into unity of effect, and modifying a series of thoughts by some one predominant thought or feeling, may be cultivated and improved, but can never be learned. It is in these that "poeta nascitur non fit."

—*Biographia Literaria,* Chapter XV

IX

THE SONG VOICE

*I*t is appropriate to end this study with a consideration of Coleridge as a singer of songs, for he was concerned throughout his life with the problems of rhythm and sound. And for 150 years, from Sir Walter Scott, who felt the bewitching influence of "Christabel," to the most recent college student, who responds for the first time to the hypnotic tale of "The Ancient Mariner," readers have succumbed to the spell of his music. The nineteenth century virtually canonized him as a lyricist second only to Shakespeare. Designating poets as either painters or musicians, Henry Nelson Coleridge officially inaugurated this worship in 1834 when he characterized Coleridge as a poet of "verbal harmony" from whose pen flows "a magnificant mirage of words" remarkable for their "perfection of . . . rhythm and metrical arrangement."[1] The idea of Coleridge as a lark circling with lyrical grandeur at Heaven's gate appealed to the Victorians. Rossetti worshiped him "on the right side of idolatry," claiming that the "three greatest English imaginations are Shakespeare, Coleridge, and Shelley";[2] the coupling of Coleridge and Shelley tells us where Rossetti's emphasis lies, if his continual appreciation of "Christabel" and "The Ancient Mariner" in letters and conversations and his sonnet on Coleridge "the father songster" has not already made it plain. Swinburne saw Coleridge as "a winged and footless" "bird of paradise" whose flight and song are "outside all law and jurisdiction of ours" and "beyond all praise and all words of men"; inevitably Swinburne, like the other nineteenth-century critics, compares Coleridge with Shelley, conceding the laurel to Coleridge as "the greatest of lyric poets," and the garland to "Kubla Khan" as "the supreme model of music in our language."[3] And at the close of the Victorian age, Arthur Symons finds the distinctive Coleridgean note still to be "his lucid and liquid melody, his imagery of moving light and the faintly veiled transparency of air, his vague, wildly romantic subject-matter, coming from no one knows where, meaning one hardly knows what; but already a magic, an incantation" (p. 140).

The sensibilities of the Victorians responded accurately enough to the music of Coleridge's verse. Unfortunately, their exaggeration of this side of his genius, to the exclusion of his other poetic achievements, fostered the belief that the "main phenomenon of Coleridge's poetic life," to quote Pater, "is not, as with most true poets, the gradual development of a poetic gift, determined, enriched, retarded, by the actual circumstances of the poet's life, but the sudden blossoming, through one short season, of such a gift already perfect in its kind, which therefore deteriorates as suddenly, with something like premature old age."[4] I have attempted in this study to counteract such easy generalizing—which conveniently overlooks not only the eighteen years, from 1797 to 1815, stretching from the composition of An Invocation in *Remorse* to Glycine's song in *Zapolya* but also the multiplicity of Coleridge's poetic voices—by illustrating the evolution in form and the drive toward order which characterize much of his poetry. Still, in spite of our antithetical conclusions, neither the Victorian sensibility nor mine is necessarily faulty, for our responses to these poems are not mutually exclusive; and in his songs (which, alas, considering their exquisite perfection, number all too few) may be seen Coleridge's two-fold ability to hear "the music of the spheres" and to give poetic form to this experience. All the songs were written for plays: "Tell me, on what holy ground" for *The Fall of Robespierre;* the Invocation ("Hear, sweet Spirit, hear the spell") for *Remorse;* Thekla's song ("The cloud doth gather, the greenwood roar") for *The Piccolomini;* and Glycine's song ("A sunny shaft did I behold") and the hunting song ("Up, Up! ye dames, and lasses gay!") for *Zapolya*. With these five lyrics, which charm one's Caliban ear with "sounds and sweet airs, that give delight, and hurt not," one might include "The Knight's Tomb." To limit oneself to the songs in what becomes, in part at least, a discussion of Coleridge's music is, of course, arbitrary; for most of his poetry sings—as the nineteenth century was quick to recognize. This fact is a commonplace of Coleridgean studies. But such criticism, in the past, has concentrated on the metrical wizardry of "The Ancient Mariner," "Christabel," and "Kubla Khan," while almost completely ignoring Coleridge's achievement in the song itself. For this reason, I believe that his little appreciated artistry in this difficult form deserves to be explored.

In most of Coleridge's drinking songs, *jeux d'esprit,* and adaptations of German lyrics, we miss the creative energy which pulsates through Burns's "The Jolly Beggars," for instance. Only when we turn to the songs from the plays do we find the deft touch of the song-master in his fusion of sound and sense. That Coleridge sought for this fusion is corroborated by the history, so far as it can be reconstructed, of the composition of Glycine's song. Since he adapted it from Tieck's "Herbstlied," by way of two prose redactions,[5] we can watch him reworking the basic ingredients—a bird singing farewell in the fleeting sunshine at the end of summer—into a new poem reflective of his sensibility.

One redaction, which I take to be first in point of time, occurs in the notebooks (*N*, II, 2791), dated conjecturally by Kathleen Coburn 5 January–6 March 1806. The other is printed by Ernest Hartley Coleridge (*CPW*, II, 1109–10) without indication of his source and seemingly without knowledge of the Tieck original (he cites the redaction vaguely as "probably a translation from the German," *CPW*, I, 426 n). Kathleen Coburn identifies this redaction as the one that she prints in *Notebooks*. Yet the variants between the two versions are so extensive that I find difficulty in believing they are the same. To believe so is to attribute all the changes in the *CPW* version to Ernest Hartley Coleridge. Can the poetic creativity which ran lamentably thin in the lifetime of the illustrious grandfather have flowed again in the grandson? The most likely explanation of the two redactions is that Coleridge under the immediate influence of making the acquaintance of Tieck in Rome in 1806 attempted a free translation of "Herbstlied." At some later date between this *terminus a quo* and the *terminus ad quem* of the song as it appears in *Zapolya* (1817), he reworked this initial redaction into the version printed by Ernest Hartley Coleridge. The first redaction (*N*) is clearly closer to the German original than is the second redaction (*CPW*). For example, Tieck's lines,

> Doch als ich Blätter fallen sah,
> Da sagt' ich: Ach! der Herbst ist da,
> Der Sommergast, die Schwalbe, zieht,
> Vielleicht so Lieb' und Sehnsucht flieht,

are literally, if somewhat loosely, rendered by Coleridge in the *Notebook* version as

> Yet, when I saw the Leaves fall, and all was cloudy,
> Then said I, Ah! Autumn is here/
> The Swallow, the Summer Bird, is gone/
> And so will my Beauty fall, like the Leaves,
> From my pining in Absence/
> And so will his love fly away. . . .

The additions, such as "and all was cloudy," do not distort Tieck's intentions, but represent elaborations of ideas expressed elsewhere in "Herbstlied." In the *CPW* version, however, Coleridge has substituted "Heavens falling" for "Leaves fall" and "Summer" for "Autumn." Neither idea appears in the German poem. Similarly, Tieck's implication that the day is cloudy, which Coleridge had at first prosaically rendered,

> on a day when the Sky had but few lines & openings of Blue,

is compressed in the second redaction to "liquid openings of Blue." Besides suggesting that Redaction 2 is a revised version of Redaction 1, these variants indicate the shaping process which ultimately produced Glycine's song.

With striking innovation, Coleridge is working to depict a singing bird in the summer sunshine, which simultaneously holds out to us the hope of permanence, and reminds us sadly of the mutability of all things. He gives a connotation of substantiality to the sunshine by transmuting "muntern Sonnenschein" into a slanted "shaft of sunny mist" ("column of Sunshine" in *N* and "slanting pillar of sun mist" and "slanting sun-shaft" in *CPW*)—an observation of nature which haunted him for many years (cf. *N*, I, 781, 798, 808, 862, 1577, 1603, and 1788). He also alters some of the other statements of the German poem. Tieck's emphasis on the arrival of autumn is changed to a nostalgic recall of warmer months. His allusion to falling leaves, a sure sign of approaching winter, metamorphoses into a hallucinatory vision of the heavens appearing to fall, a brilliant metaphoric fusion of two images: sunshine descending in shafts of light and clouds wheeling across the sky. Whereas Tieck responds to the life-cycle of nature and laments that love may not survive the winter, Coleridge embraces a metaphysical abstraction and insists that true love kindles its own summer in the heart. Most important for the eventual form of the new poem is Coleridge's effort to reduce the multiple allusions of "Herbstlied" to oneness. Tieck bases the structure of his poem on a series of explicit antitheses (what probably first attracted Coleridge to it): he contrasts summer with autumn, sunshine with cloudiness, fullness of love with death of love, and the carefree happiness of the bird and the joyousness of the sunshine with the melancholy of the speaker. He resolves these antitheses by having the bird at the end of the poem reassure the speaker that

"Die Liebe wintert nicht,
Nein! nein!
Ist und bleibt Frühlingeschein,"

and thus closes on a facile note of optimism. Coleridge is striving in Redaction 2 to restrict the poem to the single image of a bird perched on a column of sunlight singing about the mutability of love and nature, to an image at once suggestive of the joyous continuity and sad impermanence of life.

In the final version—Glycine's song—Coleridge has succeeded in transforming the German silver and potter's clay of "Herbstlied" into a bird of "hammered gold and gold enamelling," to quote Yeats's not altogether irrelevant poem "Sailing to Byzantium." He has eliminated the meaningless second appearance of the bird in the sunlight, the redundant references to approaching autumn, and the intrusive allusion to the speaker's short-lived love affair—all of which occur in "Herbstlied." In their place, he has substituted a jeweled bird of gold and amethyst whose appearance of immutability and whose song of mutability fuse into that singleness of form for which he was constantly struggling:

A sunny shaft did I behold,
From sky to earth it slanted:
And poised therein a bird so bold—
Sweet bird, thou wert enchanted!

He sank, he rose, he twinkled, he trolled
Within that shaft of sunny mist;
His eyes of fire, his beak of gold,
All else of amethyst!

And thus he sang: 'Adieu! adieu!
Love's dreams prove seldom true.
The blossoms they make no delay:
The sparkling dew-drops will not stay.
Sweet month of May,
We must away;
Far, far away;
To-day! to-day!'

Rather than Tieck's real-bone-and-feathers swallow, a bird of paradise that might have come from Cellini's furnaces now perches on an insubstantial shaft of golden sunlight slanting "from sky [heaven] to earth" and trolls an enchanted song. For a moment, Coleridge's vision encompasses the eternal and the temporal. The airy actions of the bird suggest that it is not subject to change. A transitory note of reality in its song, however, reminds us that everything must eventually pass, that blossoms wither, dew evaporates, and May quickly ends. Much as hammer blows might shatter a golden bird, so the lingering notes of the bird's song dispel its appearance of permanency. In this picture of a bird poised on a beam of sunshine singing a sad song of summer's brevity, we have an instance of the wizardry with which Coleridge gives structural equilibrium to contraries. Paralleling this fusion of the mutable and immutable is his daring repetition, in stanza 3, of the long vowels in the rhymed words, "adieu-true" and "delay-stay-May-away-today." Repeated like a plaintive refrain by other words in the stanza and elaborated upon by a third strain in "he-dreams-sweet-we," these rhymes form a structure of sound which simultaneously supports the fusion of mutable and immutable and brings the theme of the transiency of this life, an undertone in stanzas 1 and 2, to the surface in a peal of music that diminishes to an echo—a pattern all life must inevitably trace.

A reconciliation of sense and meter also occurs. Thus, the extra syllable in the third foot of line 5 reinforces metrically the meaning of "twinkle"; and the unvarying accents of "they make no delay," in reference to the inexorable passing of the flowers, corroborate the inevitable end of summer.

Such a structural use of sound and meter as support of meaning is not an isolated phenomenon restricted to Glycine's song only, but is a characteristic of Coleridge's best poetry, as well as a cardinal point of his criticism. The elements of a poem, he insisted, "are formed into metre artificially, by a voluntary act, with the design and for the purpose of blending delight with emotion, so the traces of present volition should throughout the metrical language be proportionately discernible." The effects of meter, he continues, although "too slight indeed to be at any one moment objects of distinct consciousness, yet become considerable in their aggregate influence. As a medicated atmosphere, or as wine during animated conversation, they act powerfully, though themselves unnoticed" (*BL,* II, 50–51). Although verses "are not logic," he argues in a marginal note in a copy of Selden's *Table Talk,* "they are, or ought to be, the envoys and representatives of that vital passion, which is the practical cement of logic" (*MC,* p. 277).

Meter and sound also support the meaning of the Invocation in *Remorse:*

> Hear, sweet Spirit, hear the spell,
> Lest a blacker charm compel!
> So shall the midnight breezes swell
> With thy deep long-lingering knell.
>
> And at evening evermore,
> In a chapel on the shore,
> Shall the chaunter, sad and saintly,
> Yellow tapers burning faintly,
> Doleful masses chaunt for thee,
> Miserere Domine!
>
> Hush! the cadence dies away
> On the quiet moonlight sea:
> The boatmen rest their oars and say,
> Miserere Domine!

Coleridge reinforces his vision of the dying cadences of a midnight mass in lines 11 and 12 by means of trochees, accentuation of the long vowel sounds, and caesuras after the unaccented syllables in "cadence" and "quiet." By using a seven-syllabled line, he achieves metrically a note of incompleteness, suggestive of the troubled suspense felt when one cannot hear distinctly words lingering faintly in the air. With the introduction of the boatmen in line 13, he shifts to iambics and a full eight-syllabled line, only to return with the reference to the indistinctly heard words of the mass in line 14 to a prosodically incomplete line again. Similarly, the depiction of a swelling breeze in line 3 is emphasized by a full eight syllables and an iambic measure; while the lingering knell of a distantly tolling bell, communicated in the next line, is accentuated by the prolonged notes of an anapest, spondee, and then another anapest. Furthermore, Coleridge knew about the device of linking long syllables to suggest concentration of sight and sound. In a letter to Thelwall of 17 December 1796, he praises the scribbling parson of Wiltshire for just such a skillful use of prosody. "As to Bowles, I affirm, that the manner of his accentuation in the words 'broad day-light['] (three long syllables) is a beauty, as it admirably expresses the captive's dwelling on the sight of noon—with rapture and a kind of wonder" (*CL,* I, 278). It is not surprising, then, after this expression of admiration for Bowles' accentuation to find Coleridge employing the same technique in the Invocation written not too many months after the letter. Thus, the long accents on "deep"-"long"-"linger" convey admirably a sense of the reverberations of the chapel bell drifting on the breeze across the water, while onomatopoetically the overtones of the bell ring out brazenly at first in the rhymes of the first stanza ("spell"-"compel"-"swell"-"knell") but soften to a whisper, as the sounds become faint, in the rhymes of the third stanza ("away"-"sea"-"say"-"Domine"). In addition, the long vowels in the rhyme words emphasize the idea of the lingering tones of the bell.

The metrics of Glycine's song and the Invocation reflect the trend of the times. As Burns, Blake, Moore, Scott, and Beddoes were doing in their lyrics, Coleridge is exploring the resources of accentualism and trisyllabic substitution. When we compare his songs, however, with those of Beddoes, another master lyricist, we are struck not only by the occasional unnatural diction and syntax, but also by the lack of metrical subtlety. Compared with the song in *Torrismond* or "Wolfram's Dirge," in which almost all the syllables are equally accented, Coleridge's songs keep time like a metronome. It is well to remember that the relative regularity of their meter is, in part at least, conscious policy: that Coleridge once described verse as a "covey of poetic partridges with whirring wings of music," but immediately changed the image in the interests of accuracy to "wild ducks shaping their rapid flight in forms always regular" (*CL,* II, 814). It is also worth recalling that he argues in *Biographia Literaria* (II, 50) that the design and purpose of a poem should be discernible in the meter.

In such regularity lies the lyrical—and structural—strength of Coleridge's songs. Ironically, Coleridge, who never mastered the sonnet, uses the form with skill as a structural aid in these lyrics. He organizes Glycine's song into two quatrains and a sestet, which exploit the contrapuntal possibilities of the Petrarchan sonnet: (1) the two quatrains portray the apparent immutability of the bird, while (2) the sestet, contrariwise, conveys its song of earthly mutability. Although the Invocation does not have a regular octave-sestet form, it too relies somewhat for organization on the structural principles of the sonnet. Coleridge divides the song into an introductory quatrain, a sestet, and a concluding quatrain. In short, he has split the octave into two halves, which he has then separated with the six-line stanza. This allows him to counterpoint the *sound* of the bell (stanza 1) and chant (stanza 3) with the *sight* of the chapel and yellow tapers (stanza 2). In both lyrics, then, Coleridge is extending the resources of the sonnet twenty years before Keats experimented along the same lines to produce his great odes.

One need not go to Wordsworth to learn that when Coleridge "was intent on a new experiment in metre, the time and labour he bestowed were inconceivable";[6] his songs clearly show that he sought a structure of sound as well as of meaning. Part of the enjoyment of reading his poetry undoubtedly comes from its "sweetness of . . . versification" producing a "continued excitement of surprize" and "quick reciprocations of curiosity still gratified and still re-excited" (*BL*, II, 14, 51). And his range is wide, from the full orchestration of "Kubla Khan" to the clear, thin resonance, like the notes of a distantly heard oboe, of Glycine's song.

Coleridge may have unduly stressed rhythm and sound, but with our emphasis on the cognitive in poetry, we have difficulty preserving a judicious objectivity concerning the relative proportions of sound and sense which should compose a poem. We can see, however, that his critical dictum about meter unquestionably affected his attitude toward his own poetry. Any man of talent, he believed, may by incessant effort combine interesting personal or domestic feelings into the form of a poem; but only the man of natural poetic genius has the sense of musical delight, with the power of producing it (*BL*, II, 14). Might not such critical strictures partly explain Coleridge's low opinion of his conversation poems with their personal and domestic matter and their prosaic presentation which "affects not to be poetry"? And here, in respect to his own poems, Coleridge's critical acumen may have faltered. For if the songs illustrate in a fine tone the rhythmical and auditory resources of his poetic voices, they appear, nevertheless, in comparison to the conversation, dream, and improvisation poems, like a nosegay of hothouse orchids beside an English meadow of wind-tossed posies. The "deliberate and formal poetry" (*CL*, III, 434) of the songs is antithetical to the organic form of the conversation, dream, and improvisation poems—and we in this century, following Coleridge's own theory of poetry, have elevated "organic" to a major critical touchstone.

The songs also lie outside the mainstream of Coleridge's poetry because of the philosophy of life that they express. Instead of transcendental optimism, they communicate a sense of the transience of life that is almost Keatsian in its yearning for the immutable. In the Invocation, for example, the evocation of an evening chant heard faintly across silent waters renders with exquisite music a strong presentiment of temporality. It expresses a mood that my memory tricked me into believing is also evoked by Shelley in "Julian and Maddalo" when he describes the Bay of Venice under the spell of a fiery sunset and tolling madhouse bell. A comparison of these two descriptions, however, points up the mysterious suggestiveness of Coleridge's achievement. His presentation of an evening scene lit by pale moonlight and "yellow tapers burning faintly" produces a subtle impressionism that compares favorably with Shelley's glaring collage of black bell, red tower, purple sea, orange heaven, and grey gloom of churches, ships, and palaces huddling between horizon and foreground. The Invocation suggests the same brooding reverie, with a hint of violence lurking in the Gothic gloom, that is depicted graphically in Washington Allston's "The Moonlit Landscape." Even the grave in "The Knight's Tomb" becomes a prey to change and decay:

> Where is the grave of Sir Arthur O'Kellyn?
> Where may the grave of that good man be?—
> By the side of a spring, on the breast of Helvellyn,
> Under the twigs of a young birch tree!
> The oak that in summer was sweet to hear,
> And rustled its leaves in the fall of the year,
> Is gone,—and the birch in its stead is grown.—
> The Knight's bones are dust,
> And his good sword rust;—
> His soul is with the saints, I trust.

The quiet dactyls and anapests of the first seven lines poignantly enforce the contrast between the impermanent tomb and eternal nature, while the spondees of the last three lines sound repetitively the heavy note of human mutability. Nor is it wholly fortuitous that Coleridge in translating Thekla's song expands "Ich habe genossen das irdische Glück" into a full-throated comment on the inevitability of death: "Make ready my grave-clothes to-morrow."

Melancholy, then, is the prevailing mood; but these songs differ from the eighteenth-century meditative lyric by not dressing up such moods as abstract personifications. The enchanted, yet recognizably concrete, world of singing birds, wolf hunts, vanished graves, fleeting sunlight, and evening chants—much of it made up of the evanescent world of sound and time—forms the matrix of these lyrics. In them Coleridge reconciles for an instant the fleeting and the permanent: the vision and the artifact, spontaneity and form. A bird of gold and precious stones eternally trills a song about the passage of time. The chant of a mass forever fades to unheard murmurs. Springtime perennially obliterates man's monuments to death. We are reminded of the silent, frozen form of Keats's Grecian urn, which similarly tells a tale of a melodist who is "for ever piping songs for ever new," of leaves that will never "bid the spring adieu," and of lovers who will forever love and be fair.

With the deceptive ease and simplicity of Blake, Coleridge transforms in his songs the "metaphysical bustard" of his thoughts into "a covey of poetic partridges," and then fashions the irregular music of their whirring wings into a formation like "wild ducks shaping their rapid flight in forms always regular" (*CL,* II, 814). Using the insubstantial materials of sound and light, he works the miracle of art: a singing bird poises on the airy nothing of a sunbeam; an evening chant hovers suspended on a breeze over a quiet moonlit sea. We can see this sensibility at work in much of his most successful verse. His vision of an Abyssinian maid singing of a pleasure-dome comes immediately to mind. If he could revive "her symphony and song" in his mind, he promises, he would "build that dome in air" "with music loud and long." Not without reason did Wordsworth, with the Invocation in mind, call Coleridge the "harp of Quantock." And with Wordsworth, while grateful for the songs Coleridge wrote, we regret that he did not mine the ore of this lode with more diligence.

Be wise! be bold! fulfil my auspices!
Tho' sweet thy measures, stern must be thy thought,
Patient thy study, watchful thy mild eye!
Poetic feelings, like the stretching boughs
Of mighty oaks, pay homage to the gales,
Toss in the strong winds, drive before the gust,
Themselves one giddy storm of fluttering leaves;
Yet, all the while self-limited, remain
Equally near the fixed and solid trunk
Of Truth and Nature in the howling storm,
As in the calm that stills the aspen grove.
Be bold, meek Woman! but be wisely bold!
Fly, ostrich-like, firm land beneath thy feet,
Yet hurried onward by thy wings of fancy
Swift as the whirlwind, singing in their quills.
Look round thee! look within thee! think and feel!

—"To Matilda Betham from a Stranger"

X

CONCLUSION

W e have been considering Coleridge's poems as they reflect in form and content the voices which he essayed: the farrago, prophecy, ventriloquism, conversation, dream, confession, improvisation and song. The poems in these voices differ radically from each other. Some of them, however, while conforming broadly to the traits of one voice, also incorporate those of another. A few words need to be said about this overlapping of voices, especially since time has judged many of the poems blending two or more voices to be Coleridge's most successful. In general, this hybridization combines the conversational mode of development, reminiscent point of view, and "one world" frame of reference.

It is probably no accident that the conversation poems bulk large among Coleridge's characteristic utterances. As a great conversationalist, he was most at ease with an informal mode of expression. He found prepared lectures distasteful, preferring "to trust mainly to the extemporaneous ebullition" of his thoughts (*SC,* II, 114). He stresses this point on 18 November 1811 about a series of lectures on Shakespeare and Milton which he was to begin that day. In a directive to Crabb Robinson outlining a puff of the lectures, he writes:

> After the Lecture write about 20 lines [for the newspaper]—notice that it was not in etymologic severity a Lecture—for tho' the reasoning, the arrangement, the &c bore the clearest marks of long premeditation, yet the language, illustrations &c were as evidently the children of the Moment. (*CL,* III, 348)

Coleridge seems to have found the social situation of a conversation most congenial as a means of confronting the world. Significantly, the passage he culled from *Osorio* to swell his contribution to the *Lyrical Ballads*— "The Foster-Mother's Tale"—presents not just the life history of a "poor mad youth" who was found as a baby beneath a tree, grew up learned, was imprisoned for heretical and lawless talk, escaped to the new world where he "set sail by silent moonlight/ Up a great river, great as any sea,/ And ne'er was heard of more," but includes also the dramatic situation of the foster-mother telling this tale to another. An inspired monologist, the characteristic communicative arrangement for Coleridge throughout his life consisted of himself and an audience vis-a-vis.

Although we identify the colloquial mode with the conversation and improvisation voices, we find not unsurprisingly that poems of the other voices are also cast in this form. "Dejection" specifically addresses Sara Hutchinson ("dear lady, friend devoutest of my choice"). The natural syntax and diction, testimony of its origin as a versified letter, matches the clausal sentence structure of "Frost at Midnight"—of the conversation poems—rather than the cumulative phrasal and adjectival sentence structure of such an eighteenth-century poem as "Ode on the Departing Year." Probably no serious ode in English literature begins with quite the degree of facetiousness and condescension that "Dejection" develops in its opening remarks about the folk meteorology of "the grand old ballad of Sir Patrick Spence." From the initial "Well" to the "For lo" of the second sentence, the tone is that of the fun-loving Coleridge who had puckishly prefixed a motto from Isaiah (XV, 2), "Wherefore my bowels shall sound like an harp," to an essay "On National Fasts" in *The Watchman*. The irreverence is more subdued in "Dejection," but the same sensibility obviously concocted both sallies. There is expressed in each a desire to enlighten the reader at the expense of a classic, but slightly pontifical, statement. Many of the ballad narratives also use some kind of address machinery, usually a speaker relating a tale—which makes up most of the poem—to one or more auditors. In "The Three Graves" a garrulous "old sexton, in a country church-yard" (to quote the Preface) tells the pitiful history of Edward, his wife Mary, and her mother "to a traveller whose curiosity had been awakened by the appearance of three graves, close by each other, to two only of which there were gravestones." In "The Ancient Mariner" the adventures and misfortunes of a voyage to the Pacific Ocean and the lessons learned from that experience are narrated by the sole survivor to one of three wedding guests. In "Love" the speaker recalls how he won Genevieve, his "bright and beauteous bride," by singing to her a doleful tale—which he now retells—of a knight whose love for a lady was scornfully rejected. The best of the dream poems similarly involve speaker and auditor: in "A Day-dream," the poet fancies that Sara and Mary Hutchinson hear his musings and in "Recollections of Love" that the spirit of an old love harkens to him; and in "Kubla Khan," in an odd reversal of events, the poet becomes the auditor, hearing in a reverie the beauties of Xanadu sung by a phantom Abyssinian maid. Coleridge even develops several confession poems in the form of a discussion: in "The Picture" the misogynist takes the lovelorn in himself to task; in "Constancy to an Ideal Object" the poet asks the ideal of love, which has haunted him for years, if it is real or a spectre; and in "Youth and Age" the aged poet complains to his youthful spirit about its departure from his body. Clearly Coleridge, though embued like Wordsworth with the egotistical sublime, shows a marked inclination for a dramatic confrontation of speakers in his poems. Significantly, he laments in "The Blossoming of the Solitary Date-tree" having no one to share his joys. It is no wonder, then, that the conversation poems, which are unabashed colloquies, strike us as reflecting Coleridge at his most natural and spontaneous.

As we have seen, the colloquial mode is organic to the conversation and improvisation poems, but appears in hybrid form in poems of the other voices. The same may be said about the reminiscent point of view, which is organic to the dream and confession poems, but also appears in poems of the prophecy, ventriloquism, improvisation, and conversation voices, where one is not prepared to find such nostalgia because of the commitment of these voices to the present, and even to the future. The prophecy poems, for example, may start in the present, but most of them soon revert to reviewing the past. As its title indicates, "Ode on the Departing Year" surveys events that have happened; only at the conclusion does it struggle to a consideration of present and future actions:

> Away, my soul, away!
> In vain, in vain the Birds of warning sing—
> And hark! I hear the famish'd brood of prey
> Flap their lank pennons on the groaning wind!
> Away, my soul, away!
> I unpartaking of the evil thing,
> With daily prayer and daily toil
> Soliciting for food my scanty soil,
> Have wail'd my country with a loud Lament.
> Now I recentre my immortal mind
> In the deep Sabbath of meek self-content;
> Cleans'd from the vaporous passions that bedim
> God's Image, sister of the Seraphim.

"France: An Ode" is frankly autobiographical in its recollection of how the author became disillusioned with France as the champion of liberty. And the central portions of "Dejection" nostalgically recall the time when

> though my path was rough,
> This joy within me dallied with distress,
> And all misfortunes were but as the stuff
> Whence Fancy made me dreams of happiness:
> For hope grew round me, like the twining vine,
> And fruits, and foliage, not my own, seemed mine.

The remembrance of things past also controls the viewpoint of the ventriloquism poems "The Three Graves," "The Ancient Mariner," and "Love." Although the setting, the external frame, of each poem is the present, the central action, which is told by a narrator, has occurred in the distant past. The backward glance also prevails in such improvisation poems as "Berengarius," "Duty Surviving Self-love," and "The Improvisatore"—a point of view which strikes one as incongruous in the light of the contemporary scene and impromptu form of the improvisation poem. This mood of reminiscence reaches major proportions in the conversation poems, superimposing on the spatial relationship of mind and world a temporal perspective which gives to these seemingly simple poems a complex structure of statement. In each the poet not only oscillates between apprehension and the thing apprehended, but also between the event remembered and the event in process. Each poem includes one or more incidents from the past: the noon-day reverie on a sunny slope in "The Eolian Harp," the sight of the roaring dell and the sunset in "This Lime-tree Bower," the memory of school days in "Frost at Midnight," the tales of Hartley's and a gentle maid's responses to nature in "The Nightingale," the review of Wordsworth's spiritual growth in "To William Wordsworth," and—as the title implies—all of "Reflections on Having Left a Place of Retirement," the honeymoon cottage, the Bristol visitor, and the hilltop view of the countryside. The point has been often made that Coleridge's analysis of Hamlet is essentially a portrait of himself once removed. Nowhere is this analogy more pertinent than in his characterization of Hamlet as one

> in whose view the external world, and all its incidents and objects, were comparatively dim, and of no interest in themselves, and which began to interest only when they were reflected in the mirror of his mind. (*SC,* II, 192)

Coleridge similarly found the world of his thoughts as fascinating as the world of reality, constantly moving in his poetry from consideration of the external object to consideration of its impression on his mind. Like Wordsworth, who formally defined poetry as passion recollected in tranquillity, Coleridge illustrates in poem after poem that retrospection is an intrinsic part of his *rapprochement* to experience. The two poets may have differed in personality, Wordsworth emotionally reserved and morally stern, Coleridge ebullient and impulsive; and they may have differed ultimately in poetic aims and critical theory, each eventually going his separate way; but they clearly and unequivocally shared in spite of these apparent differences a profoundly similar vision of life.

An aspect of this vision of life, which has become a commonplace of Wordsworthian and Coleridgean criticism, was their belief in the oneness of man and nature. This sacramental vision of nature, as Robert Penn Warren calls it in his essay on "The Ancient Mariner," while developed with most consistency and quiet certainty in the poems written before 1802, particularly the conversation poems, lies also at the center of the best poems of the late voices. In the dream poems "A Day-dream" and "Recollections of Love" Coleridge uses the rapport of mind and things, with its assumption of the oneness of all being, as a *raison d'etre* for organizing the isolated facts of reverie and actuality into a meaningful apprehension of past and present. The memories Coleridge has been recounting in "A Day-dream" dilate, becoming a part of the thoughts of Sara and Mary Hutchinson and the sounds of the midnight setting:

> But let me check this tender lay
> Which none may hear but she and thou!
> Like the still hive at quiet midnight humming,
> Murmur it to yourselves, ye two beloved women!

Similarly, the whisper of love within Coleridge's heart merges with the ceaseless roar of the Greta as an affirmation of the oneness of life in "Recollections of Love." Contrariwise, in "Dejection," written about the same time as "A Day-dream," Coleridge laments his inability to be a partner to this joyous wedding of man with thing. Several months later in "Hymn Before Sun-rise" he is still striving to patch up the divorce between himself and nature by coercing his "dilating soul, enrapt, transfused," to become a part of the soaring form of Mont Blanc. The effort is forced, however, and the strained texture of the poem reflects this. Coleridge continued to write poems after 1802; but missing from most of them is his early joyous sense of the light, the glory, the fair luminous mist of nature ("This beautiful and beauty-making power," as he puts it in "Dejection"), which was simultaneously the agent and the recipient of his genial engagement with the world. This does not mean that the old compatibility between nature and himself, which he had celebrated in the conversation poems, was permanently lost. It recurred intermittently to the end of his life; and the experience usually resulted in a moving poem of reminiscence. His return home from Malta, communion with the Wordsworth household, and reading of *The Prelude* combined to allow him briefly in 1807 to re-call his once happy marriage with nature in "To William Wordworth." His revisit to Nether Stowey in the same year continued this "second honeymoon" for a few more months; and "Recollections of Love" com-memorates the experience. Vestiges of the old glorious union reappear in "Youth and Age," written nineteen years after "Dejection" and "Hymn Before Sun-rise," when he alluded to "the one life within us and abroad" with the interlocking imagery of flower and body.

Besides the dramatic interaction of mind and nature, Coleridge also uses an interlocking leit-motif of silence, sound, and light to convey on the level of the imagery his vision of the oneness of life. The motif appears in its most fused form in the beautiful lines which he added to "The Eolian Harp" when he issued *Sibylline Leaves* in 1817:

> O! the one Life within us and abroad,
> Which meets all motion and becomes its soul,
> A light in sound, a sound-like power in light,
> Rhythm in all thought, and joyance every where—
> Methinks, it should have been impossible
> Not to love all things in a world so fill'd;
> Where the breeze warbles, and the mute still air
> Is Music slumbering on her instrument;

and in the lines ending "Frost at Midnight":

> Therefore all seasons shall be sweet to thee,
> . . . .
> . . . . . . whether the eave-drops fall
> Heard only in the trances of the blast,
> Or if the secret ministry of frost
> Shall hang them up in silent icicles,
> Quietly shining to the quiet Moon.

The implication of this survey seems clear. For the past several pages I have been defining the voice which can be heard as an undersong, like "love's prompture deep" ("Recollections of Love"), in the best of the generic voices. Its presence in such diverse poems as "The Ancient Mariner," "Dejection," "The Eolian Harp," "This Lime-tree Bower," "Frost at Midnight," "Kubla Khan," "A Day-dream," "Recollections of Love," and "Youth and Age" explains, in part, why they are among Coleridge's most successful poems. Simultaneously, each pursues the defined objective of a specific form, while transcending that form to reflect the dominant vision of a constantly synthesizing and unifying sensibility. Throughout his life, Coleridge felt

> the necessity of reconciling the restlessness of an ever-working Fancy with an intense craving after a resting-place for my Thoughts in some *principle* that was derived from experience, but of which all other knowledge should be but so many repetitions under various limitations, even as circles, squares, triangles, etc., etc., are but so many positions of space. And, lastly, that my eloquence was most commonly excited by the desire of running away and hiding myself from my personal and inward feelings, *and not for the expression of them,* while doubtless this very effort of feeling gave a passion and glow to my thoughts . . . and language on subjects of a general nature, that they otherwise would not have had. I fled in a Circle, still overtaken by the Feelings, from which I was ever more fleeing, with my back turned towards them; but above all, my growing deepening conviction of the *transcendency of the moral to the intellectual,* and the inexpressible comfort and inward strength which I experience myself to derive as often as I contemplate truth realized into Being by a human Will; so that, *as I cannot love without esteem, neither can I esteem without loving.* Hence I *love* but few, but those I love as my own Soul; for I feel that without them I should—not indeed cease to be kind and effluent, but by little and little become a soul-less fixed Star, receiving no rays nor influences into my Being, *a Solitude which I so tremble at, that I cannot attribute it even to the Divine Nature.* (*Spirit,* pp. 33–34)

The central principle of one life, the dramatic concept of a community of conversants, and the concentering force of personal feeling and memory which, Coleridge asserts in this note to Allsop, have been the intellectual and emotional needs of his life are the means by which Coleridge confronted and gave pattern to the stream of events. They supply the world created by his poems with its syntax and angle of sight. In their configurations we recognize the naked voice—the poetic experience and shaping spirit—that is Coleridge's. To the degree that a poem is not shaped by one or more of these conventions—as is the case with the farrago, improvisation, and most of the confession poems—that poem strikes us as inflated, unfinished, and derivative.

Coleridge struggled to combine in his verse the values of spontaneity and form. Most of his poetic life reflects his varying responses to this Scylla and Charybdis of the poetic world. Beginning with the sublime tradition of verse current in his youth, he tried successively and concurrently with the various voices to unite this dualism of heart and head (*BL,* I, 16). In this study I have examined only those poems which figure directly in this effort. Inevitably some poems have been neglected. There are the satires which do not qualify as farrago poems, some in mock-heroic vein, others in Hudibrastic measures, and still others in light-hearted burlesque of a poetic genre (for example, "The Silver Thimble," "Recantation Illustrated in the Story of the Mad Ox," "The Raven," "The Two Round Spaces on the Tombstone," "The Devil's Thoughts," "The Madman and the Lethargist," and "An Ode to the Rain"). I do not think that these and other *jeux d'esprit* are important to a study of Coleridge's evolving poetic style. True, they reflect both fun-loving and political-minded sides of him too frequently overlooked. They do not represent him, however, learning to speak different poetic languages but display him either divested of his poet's cape, carelessly lounging in his living-room in stocking feet and undershirt, prating about wife and children and friends; or engaged in the hurly-burly of Fleet Street and Parliament Row for pay and party (as Carl R. Woodring epitomizes his political activities),[1] sleeves rolled up, fighting for freedom, enlightenment, and social mercy. Instead of flowing in the mainstream of his changing voices, these verses eddy in a poetic backwater. Many represent "merely the emptying out of [his] desk" (*CL,* II, 876). Thus Coleridge confided to Tom Wedgewood on 20 October 1802 his opinion of "An Ode to the Rain" and several epigrams published in the *Morning Post* that autumn, a statement which unwittingly characterizes others as well.

Quite different are the effusions of Coleridge's youth, which constitute one of his earliest and most persistent poetic voices (for example, "To a Young Lady with a Poem on the French Revolution," "Lines on a Friend Who Died of a Frenzy Fever Induced by Calumnious Reports," and "To the Nightingale"). Since the farrago poem derives from this poetry of sensibility, I decided to spare the reader a lengthy discussion of his juvenilia by discussing this style only as it relates to the farrago poem, which has been generally misunderstood in most studies of Coleridge's poetry. Similarly, I confined my reference to the Gothic accent—less widespread than the facetious and the Della Cruscan—to my consideration of the ventriloquism voice, in whose articulation its labored cadence is most often heard.

Coleridge's love poems also present a problem. Although many are written in the mode of the dream and confession voices, just as many are not. I have been unable to classify such individual expressions of feeling as "The Keepsake," "On Revisiting the Seashore," "To Asra," "Inscription for a Fountain on a Heath," and "Separation."

Then there are those poems which do not fit satisfactorily into any category used in this study because they comprise a patchwork of voices. "Religious Musings" and "The Destiny of Nations," for instance, have the structural amorphousness of the farrago, the linguistic sublimity of the prophecy, and the nature metaphysic of the conversation poems.

Coleridge's effort to maintain an equilibrium between abandonment to spontaneity and subservience to form produced many varied and notable successes: "The Ancient Mariner," "Dejection," "Frost at Midnight," "This Lime-tree Bower," "Kubla Khan," "A Day-dream," "Recollections of Love," and "Youth and Age." Two contrary and deflecting forces, however, were forever frustrating his attainment of simplicity and order and an even more impressive list of successes. First, he was a child of the eighteenth century, with a fatal taste for sublime flights of rhetoric. The "empyreal air" ("Religious Musings") of "th' impassion'd theme" ("To the Author of Poems") remained an easily summoned panacea when calmer and more honest emotions did not materialize. Second, his initial success with the ventriloquism voice spurred him on to repeat that which could not be repeated and paled by comparison his solid achievements in a minor mode. The ballad seemed for a while to offer a shortcut to his poetic ideal; unfortunately he found increasing difficulty in satisfying its narrative demands. Every line of "Christabel," he complains to James Tobin in a letter of 17 September 1800, "has been produced by me with labor-pangs" (CL, I, 623). His inability to finish the poem served to convince him that he was less of a poet than his friend Wordsworth, from whose pen flowed copious lines of narrative verse. "The poet is dead in me," he proclaims to Godwin in 1801. "If I die, and the booksellers will give you any thing for my life, be sure to say—'Wordsworth descended on him, like the Γνῶθι σεαυτόν from Heaven; by shewing to him what true poetry was, he made him know that he himself was no poet'" (CL, II, 714). And the emphasis that Wordsworth placed on narrative realism only substantiated Coleridge's doubts about his own poetic talents. "True poetry"—"real-life poems" he calls them in a letter to Southey, 10 November 1799 (CL, I, 545)—consisted of such narratives as "Michael" and "The Brothers," whose psychological truth and narrative simplicity, Coleridge boasts to Humphry Davy on 25 July 1800, will "rive the Enchanter Gaudyverse from his crown to his fork" (CL, I, 612). To the end of his life, as if he were embarked on a literary crusade, he attempted ballad tales suggestive of primitive simplicity but merely succeeded in writing poems which are pastiches of Spenserian knights and castles and eighteenth-century descriptive-meditative sentiments.

Still, if the faults of Coleridge's poetic talent grew out of the ethos of the late eighteenth century, so too did the virtues. It was a time of tender sensibility and humanitarian impulse, Sterne's *Sentimental Journey* and Mmes. Barbauld and Robinson's tender emotions, a time when a man could weep unashamedly, as Coleridge frequently did. The hopes and views of his generation were Coleridge's, for his ordinary daydreams were not cast in the tragic or the heroic mold but were sweetly sentimental, domestic, and commonplace.[2] The quiet conversational voice and contemplative reminiscent tone were pervasive and persistent sides of his genius. He automatically adopted these accents when he had something personal to say.

Coleridge the critic wished to act as "arbitrator between the old school and the new school" (CL, II, 830). As a poet he achieved this goal in a qualified way. His age was seeking new poetic means of expressing its emotions and thoughts simply, sincerely, and spontaneously. He grafted these new sensitivities onto the old literary forms: the ode, the ballad, and the descriptive and society verse of the eighteenth century. His effort to combine the old and new produced a low-keyed style expressive alike of his unique vision and of the yearning of Englishmen during the Napoleonic era for peace and security. In the best poems of each of the voices, Coleridge retains the love of nature rediscovered by the Georgians, adds a nostalgic view of the one world haunting his generation, and anticipates the preoccupation of man with his own thoughts soon to fascinate the Victorians. In them, he introduces a new colloquial ease without abandoning the regularity of the traditional rules. If we take the accomplished fact of his poetry as an indication of his aims, then we cannot disregard the evidence that Coleridge was an innovator, tirelessly seeking new poetic ways of speaking naturally in an artful manner.

Clive Bell has written that "the supreme masterpieces derive their splendour, their supernatural power, not from flashes of insight, nor yet from characterization, nor from an understanding of the human heart even, but from form—I use the word in its richest sense, I mean the thing that artists create, their expression. Whether you call it 'significant form' or something else, the supreme quality in art is formal; it has to do with order, sequence, movement and shape."[3] Without exaggeration, we can say that a passion for form characterizes Coleridge's artistic life.

It is a cardinal tenet of his criticism. He condemns Landor for a lack of "that modifying faculty, which compresses several units into one whole" (*TT*, II, 279) and praises Defoe for sacrificing in *Robinson Crusoe* many opportunities for delightful but irrelevant details to the greater interest of universal representation and organic unity (*MC*, pp. 299–300). He may define poetry from the viewpoint of the poet, as he does in the *Biographia Literaria,* but inevitably he turns in his practical criticism to the poem and an insistence on a "total completeness," a "shapeliness—*forma formosa*"—of the whole and its parts (Allsop, pp. 118–19). For in theory he believed that "the great thing in poetry is, *quocunque modo,* to effect a unity of impression upon the whole; and a too great fulness and profusion of point in the parts will prevent this" (*TT*, II, 215). Grand lines or fine stanzas must never distract our attention from the central thought of the poem (*MC*, p. 137).

To submit to esthetic discipline is not an easy task; yet in his own poetry he conscientiously strove for unity of effect, with the histories of "Frost at Midnight," "Youth and Age," and "The Ancient Mariner" furnishing classic examples. There were times when Coleridge wished that he might, like Southey, have the facility to please himself with what he wrote (*CL,* I, 320), for he knew moments when his execution did not measure up to his conception. "My taste in judging is far, far more perfect than my power to execute," he laments to Daniel Stuart on 7 October 1800; "I do nothing, but almost instantly its defects and sillinesses come to my mind and haunt me, till I am completely disgusted with my performance and wish myself a tanner, or a printer, or any thing but an author" (*CL,* I, 629). But the artistic spirit was strong in Coleridge, and even in minor efforts he trudged the disciplined route that leads to major works. As late as 1829, when no longer goaded by poetic ambition, he deleted several lines from "Love, Hope, and Patience in Education," prompted, he assures Sotheby in a letter, by the desire to maintain the artistic integrity of the poem:

> They [lines 24–29, initial draft] were struck out by the author, not because he thought them bad lines in themselves (quamvis Della Cruscam fortasse nimis redolere videantur), but because they diverted and retarded the stream of the thought, and injured the organic unity of the composition. *Più nel uno* is Francesco de Sallez' brief and happy definition of the beautiful, and the shorter the poem the more indispensable is it that the *Più* should not overlay the *Uno*, that the unity should be evident. But to sacrifice the *gratification*, the sting of *pleasure*, from a fine *passage* to the *satisfaction*, the sense of complacency arising from the contemplation of a symmetrical *Whole* is among the last conquests achieved by men of genial powers. (*CPW*, I, 481 n)

As F. L. Lucas[4] has asserted, derisively to be sure, unity of form represented to Coleridge the mystical perfection which the legendary quincunx represented to Sir Thomas Browne. That his pursuit of the ideal was no wooly-minded yearning for cloud-cuckoo land, Albert Gérard has recently argued forcefully. He points out that the English Romantic poets, perceiving reality as a matter-spirit continuum, elevated the poetic experience to a position of supreme importance in apprehending and interpenetrating the two contrary forces: "the unity and organising power . . . of the spirit and the diversity and chaos of matter."[5] Hence, Coleridge's search for poetic unity is no artistic dilettantism but is representative of his greater search for order in his life. Viewed thus, his poetic voices are not simply esthetic achievements of the creative imagination, but are also, on a psychological and philosophical plane, efforts to give meaning and wholeness to the fragmentary impingement of experience.

That he never succeeded for a lasting time in any voice is an indication of the difficulty of the task as much as a reflection of his poetic genius. If Blake is an example of the artist who breaks radically with the literary conventions of his time, Coleridge is an example of the one who never entirely frees himself from its inhibiting shackles. He pushed beyond the frontiers of his own day in his poetry but had trouble realizing the potentialities of his exploration. He wrote the greatest non-folk ballad in English literature but could not profit from the experience enough to write another. He fashioned the conversation poem, but the supreme example of its stately informality is Wordsworth's "Tintern Abbey." His experiments in the improvisation voice are crude first steps beside Browning's dramatic monologs. He explored the dream as a mode of reality and as a new technique of poetry; but the greatest of the dream poems, "Kubla Khan," carries the stigma of the unfinished work of art, and the other dream poems have been almost entirely neglected by the modern reader.[6] Although the dream poem inaugurated the dramatization of the subliminal associations of the mind, English poetry had to wait for Eliot's "The Love Song of J. Alfred Prufrock" before the possibilities of the form were fully realized. Unlike Eliot and Pound, who faced the same problem in 1910 that he and Wordsworth faced in 1797, Coleridge (and to a lesser extent Wordsworth) was unable to formulate an idiom which was responsive on all occasions to his thoughts and feelings. Again and again, when he appears to have solved the problem in one voice, his muse falters, inhibited by the poetic diction and forms which he had learned in his youth. The literary tastes and conventions of his age hampered as much as they aided his effort to give form to his visions. They supplied him initially with tools of expression but also left him ultimately dependent on them. His is the tragedy of the artist who sees, if only fitfully, beyond his ability to do.

The "showy" chestnut tree rotten at the heart was applied by Coleridge to himself as an emblem of his poetic failure (*N*, II, 2914). He was thinking of wasted potentialities. To assess his accomplishments, however, instead of decrying his unfulfilled promises is to judge at once less romantically and less incriminatively. Coleridge asked nothing more of his critics. "By what I *have* effected am I to be judged by my fellow men," he wrote in his literary biography; "what I *could* have done is a question for my own conscience" (*BL*, I, 151). His was a true but thin vein of poetic talent. It explored rather than exploited, was seminal rather than developmental. Restlessly, he stopped with each voice only long enough to realize one or two finished examples of the form: "Dejection" in the prophecy voice; "The Ancient Mariner" in the ventriloquism; almost everything in the conversation (where we find a charm in the infelicities of the verse even as we find a sympathy for the faults in the man) but especially "The Eolian Harp," "This Lime-tree Bower," and "Frost at Midnight"; "Kubla Khan," "A Day-dream," and "Recollections of Love," in the dream; "Youth and Age" in the confession; and Glycine's song and the Invocation in the song. Only in the farrago and improvisation voices— his earliest and his latest—did he fail to produce distinguished poems, although "To a Friend [Lamb] Who Had Declared His Intention of Writing No More Poetry," "On a Ruined House in a Romantic Country," "The Blossoming of the Solitary Date-tree," and "The Improvisatore" are fully realized and interesting experiments.

Leigh Hunt wrote in *Imagination and Fancy* that Coleridge's poetry "is so beautiful, and was so quietly content with its beauty, making no call on the critics, and receiving hardly any notice, that people are but now beginning to awake to a full sense of its merits." One hundred years have passed; yet Hunt's prophecy is still not fully realized. To be sure, we now number Coleridge among the great English poets, but primarily on the basis of one poem and two fragments. These three poems give a false picture of his poetic range and idiom. He traveled gregariously from one set of friends to another. He was equally facile in moving about among the poetic conventions familiar to his day. In the past thirty years, we have acclaimed the breadth and pertinency of his criticism and philosophy; it is time that we recognize and acclaim similarly the range and creativity of his poetic sensibility.

APPENDIX I

A Subspecies of the Farrago Poem

*A*n inconstant tone and multiple themes are traits of the farrago poem. Coleridge also wrote satirical poetry which employs half this formula. While remaining unmistakably clear about the object under attack, it scrambles linguistic and literary levels of usage as the manner of attack.

Thus, "Parliamentary Oscillators" attacks the unprincipled wavering of "Sir John Sinclair, S. Thornton, Alderman Lushington, and the whole Troop of Parliamentary Oscillators" (*CPW*, I, 211 n) who deferred to Pitt and his war budget of 1798 in spite of their professed moral and patriotic reservations, but veers in tone from mock-courteous inquiry about the parliamentary members' restful sleep to outright name-calling. The mock-heroic machinery of "pullies" lifts the politicians' tired eyes. Hudibrastic rhymes ("chicken"-"licking," "quack"-"back," and "crew"-"tu-whoo") terminate the insulting sallies of the poet. Elevated rhetoric jostles with irreverent slang: the "ivy-haunting . . . bird of wisdom" with the "slapdash" of an impish scampering devil. Coleridge further objectifies his scorn for the oscillating parliamentarians by likening their duplicity to a scavenging barnyard chicken, glozening serpent, quacking water-fowl, and dozing blindness. The poem is truly shapeless, a rambling spontaneous vituperation. It begins without exposition, proceeds in a disorderly off-the-cuff manner, and stops inconclusively when Coleridge has run out of breath and insults. To insure that we do not miss this point, Coleridge calls our attention to its extemporaneity:

If you can stay so long from slumber free,
  My muse shall make an effort to salute 'e:
For lo! a very dainty simile
  Flash'd sudden through my brain, and 'twill just suit 'e!

Then follows for one-third of the poem an elaborate metaphor of quacking statesmen who duck-like follow the leader and of tu-whooing ministers who owl-like profess wise leadership.

Similarly, the metrical epistle "Talleyrand to Lord Grenville" sneers in mixed diction and random sequence at Lord Grenville's warmongering through the discreet indirection of lampooning the French bid for recognition as a peace-loving, civilized nation. (On 4 January 1800 Grenville in the name of George III had rejected a peace overture sent by letter from Napoleon to the English king; Coleridge's poem appeared 10 January 1800 in the *Morning Post.*) A hoax in the manner of Ben Franklin's "Edict by the King of Prussia," the poem has Talleyrand striving with such ardor to portray France as conservative rather than Jacobinical that he succeeds in picturing it as arch-reactionary. Thus, Coleridge sees little distinction between Grenville's Tory jingoism and Talleyrand's republican imperialism and quickly indicates his scorn for both by rapid shifts in tone. The letter begins with a formal salutation, and then shifts to jaunty colloquialisms. There follows helter-skelter Talleyrand's views on a variety of subjects, mostly political, which readers of the *Morning Post* would have recognized as allusions to the expedient and oppressive measures sponsored by Grenville. Talleyrand comments on the folly of mob rule; the civilized statecraft of bribery, perjury, and theft; the shocking precedent of the American congress; his apostasy from the church; Grenville's reputation for leading the War Party and ruthlessly smothering parliamentary opposition and bothersome truth; the beauty of a crooked line; the legitimate, aristocratic membership of the English House of Lords; the muzzling of the press; and the digressive nature of his style. With insulting familiarity, he likens his rambling commentary to Grenville's long and disorganized speeches:

> Your goodness, my Lord, I conceive as excessive,
> Or I dar'd not present you a scroll so digressive;
> And in truth with my pen thro' and thro' I should strike it;
> But I hear that your Lordship's own style is just like it.

After 107 lines, Talleyrand checks himself:

> . . . but perhaps it were better
> To proceed to the absolute point of my letter:
> For the deep wounds of France, Bonaparte, my master,
> Has found out a new sort of *basilicon* plaister.

The letter, however, has run too long. So Talleyrand apologizes for intruding upon Grenville's time and promises to outline Napoleon's plan in a second letter. Thus, this poem calls attention more slyly than "Parliamentary Oscillators" to its unpremeditated development and amorphous structure; it pretends to have rambled for so long, unintentionally discussing irrelevant items, that it no longer has space or time to take up the main pretence for writing the letter in the first place. To the vices and crimes of the war-minded parties of France and England Coleridge has artfully added the charge of ineptitude.

In "The Delinquent Travellers," a late poem (1824), much of the asperity of the early satire has softened into a spoof of the ubiquitous world-traveling Englishman. Still recognizable, however, is the method of development. Coleridge meanders from fancy to fancy, much as the delinquent Englishman pursuing his aimless itinerary. Gayly Coleridge lists the many-faced travelers milling about: tourist, professional travel-litterateur, bankrupt, and debtor. The poem grows more serious in its satire towards the end. Taking *"French leave"* of such commercial purveyors of English culture, the "ugly Englishmen" of his century, he opts for the felons transported to Australia, as delinquent travelers whose private vices will produce good. Fated to farm for their livelihood, they will transform New Holland into "Old England with some elbow-room," that is, into the rural England of the pre-industrial eighteenth century.

In these poems, Coleridge speaks with an insouciance usually dismissed by the critics as impromptu doggerel. To do so is to overlook the satirical effect that shapelessness and linguistic or tonal meanness contribute to the statement of the poem. Viewed thus, these poems may represent a serious effort of Coleridge to give poetic form to social and political commentary. That the effort proves ultimately misguided and the poems, artistic failures, does not preclude the original seriousness of his intentions.

APPENDIX II

The Conclusion to "Dejection"

*T*he conclusion to "Dejection" has puzzled countless readers. What finally happens to the poet's despair? Does it continue? Is it partly ameliorated? Or does it give way unreservedly to joy? And what does Coleridge mean when he wishes the storm to "be but a mountain-birth"? Interpretations range from the suggestion that the poem describes a rebirth of Coleridge's imagination (Fogle, *D,* 71–77), to the belief that the poem is "not primarily about modes of perception . . . [but] about unhappiness and about love and about joy" (House, p. 138), to the generally held view that the poem pictures Coleridge lamenting the momentary loss of his ability to write poetry. I have no illusions about settling these questions once and for all. I merely wish to define the problem and to add another interpretation to the record.

*A*lthough R. H. Fogle presents a persuasive and almost unassailable case for the re-awakening of Coleridge's genial spirit, I think that such an interpretation, while properly emphasizing the structural components of the poem, tends to minimize the poetic function of the imagery and the mood of dejection conveyed by it. The crucial sections are the last two strophes. Fogle reads the tragic actor and epic poet impersonations of the lute as an indication of Coleridge's re-activated imagination, his feelings awake and at work, although still painful and disorganized. This reading would be reasonable if the interpretation of the second lay were not perhaps too narrow. Quoting part of it:

> And all that noise, as of a rushing crowd,
> With groans, and tremulous shudderings—all is over—
> It tells another tale, with sounds less deep and loud!
> A tale of less affright,

> And tempered with delight,
> As Otway's self had framed the tender lay,

he concludes: "These lines express a further development of the imagination, a more complex organization in which the shaping power moulds into unity the diverse elements of grief, fear, and their opposite delight (see l. 124). Strife, in effect, has given way to reconciliation, and for Coleridge only the imagination can reconcile. The mind, recalled to activity, has regained its wholeness" (Fōgle, *D*, 76).

There is certainly from the first to the second tale an advance in the organization of the sounds wrung from the lute. But does the story recounted in the second lay really indicate that Coleridge's imagination has regained its equilibrium? Can we claim that joy or delight really appears as one of the elements of the imaginative reconciliation effected in the second tale? Fogle says yes, basing his answer on lines 117–120, where Coleridge, commenting on the sound of the wind through the lute, says that the second tale is "tempered with delight"; and also on the Coleridgean assumption that any unified poem must embrace a reconciliation of opposites, so that if there is grief, there must also be joy. But significantly the actual contents of the lay contain little comfort:

> 'Tis of a little child
> Upon a lonesome wild,
> Not far from home, but she hath lost her way:
> And now moans low in bitter grief and fear,
> And now screams loud, and hopes to make her mother hear.

Of grief there is "God's plenty" here, but of delight there is no trace whatever. Could not "Otway's . . . tender lay" be "a tale of less affright" only in comparison to the "groans and tremulous shudderings" of the previous lay? The tale of the little child wandering lost on the lonely heath is tenderer than the epic song of martial struggles but no less plaintive. For the outcome of the action, which paraphrases Wordsworth's "Lucy Gray," is paralyzing fear and blighted hope. And if the raving of the wind harp ("a crystallizing symbol of mind and nature," Fogle, *D*, 73) accurately portrays the state of Coleridge's mind, as Fogle agrees it does, then one can hardly contend that the second lay indicates a return of the poet's mind to wholeness. Coleridge's imagination, furthermore, is not recreating and reshaping his own experience through the agency of the lute into a new, meaningful reality as the creative imagination, according to Coleridge (and Fogle concurs), customarily does. It is merely imitating another man's rendering of life—and, it should be noted, imitating just a part of it. The second tale of the wind harp remains incomplete, hardly a convincing indication of a healthy, synthesizing mind. Coleridge is in much the same predicament as the poets who, echoing Milton, call the nightingale a "most melancholy" bird. His imagination, even after the arrival of the energizing rain, continues closed "to the influxes/ Of shapes and sounds and shifting elements" of nature, where "there is nothing melancholy." Instead, like "some night-wandering man," his heart pierced "with the remembrance of a grievous wrong,/ Or slow distemper, or neglected love," he has

> filled all things with himself,
> And made all gentle sounds tell back the tale
> Of his own sorrow. ("The Nightingale")

Thus, Coleridge's emotion has certainly been activated into something other than a drowsy, unimpassioned grief; but it is a far cry from that joyous wholeness from which flow all the melodies that charm the ear or sight (see vv. 73–74). Rather, his stifled grief has simply found a voice which vents his distress like a mad lutanist with screams of agony and unhappy songs of the death of the flesh and the spirit. Sharpness of feeling has returned to the poet, but it is not the imaginatively creative, life-giving wholeness of joy; it is still the death-dealing fragmentation of dejection.

Nor does the outward soaring of Coleridge's thoughts in the final strophe, that is, simply the act itself, indicate necessarily and solely that Coleridge has won through to imaginative joy and equilibrium. Those outward soaring thoughts use words expressing definite meanings. I question if one can ignore the words in favor of the gesture, particularly when the words indicate a sentiment contrary to the supposed meaning of the gesture. Coleridge's dejection, at first passive and finally throbbingly active, prompts him to pray that the screaming wind and pelting rain which have symbolically kept pace with the increasing violence of his emotions have had "a mountain-birth" and "the stars hang bright above [Sara Hutchinson's] dwelling." That is, he hopes that the April storm has a local origin and that this atmospheric disturbance does not extend beyond the mountains encircling Keswick to the Hutchinson farm at Gallow Hill, Yorkshire, where Sara, he prays, is resting peacefully, not keeping a grief-stricken, sleepless vigil as he is. He hopes this because the storm has not brought him joy and wholeness of spirit as he had anticipated. It has failed to materialize into a natural, fecund power restoring his genial spirit. It remains a blustering April shower noisily parroting his own for-lorn feelings, the random wailings of the wind symbolizing the disor-ganized, unwholesome products of his imagination.

*I*t is apparent that the storm has a dual reference. Literally it posits a potential threat to Sara's peaceful slumber. Symbolically it de-scribes the fragmented fancies of Coleridge's creative imagination. Much of the difficulty critics have found in reading the "mountain-birth" pas-sage can be blamed, I think, upon this ambiguous reference.

For example, both Humphry House (pp. 165–66) and Florence Marsh[1] conjecture that the passage means a wish that what seems to be terrible may be a mere trifle. House bases his interpretation on the possi-bility that the "mountain-birth" line is a reminiscence of Horace's famous one in *Ars Poetica* ("Parturient montes, nascetur ridiculus mus"). If the "evils, torments, and sorrows" which "the creativeness of the wind (as actor and poet) . . . appears to create" are the consequence of a passing mountain storm, then perhaps, Coleridge pleads, the twisted fancies of his imagination may similarly pass, leaving as its aftermath, like the wet evidence of a rain storm, only the trifling memory of a sleepless night. This reading makes sense in terms of the loss of imagination theme. Such an emphasis, of course, is not consistent with House's contention that the theme of "Dejection" is Coleridge's concern for the well-being of Sara; so he is forced to see the "evils, torments, and sorrows" of the wind-as-poet as also threatening Sara. But this will not do. In what conceivable way can the trampings and groans of men in epic struggle and the plaintive cries of a little girl on the heath apply to Sara? Florence Marsh cuts this Gordian knot by simply ignoring the imagination theme of "Dejection" and con-centrating on the love theme of the verse letter. "Early in 'Dejection,'" she argues, "Coleridge had wished for the wind and rain 'Those sounds which oft have raised me, whilst they awed,/ And sent my soul abroad.'" And the vigor of the storm *"has* roused Coleridge and sent his soul abroad in thoughts of Sara." He hopes "the winds may die quickly so that Sara may sleep untroubled." Hence, it is improbable, she concludes, that sounds which "raise" and "awe" should have overtones of "ridiculus mus."

Although Humphry House and Florence Marsh appear to agree that the "mountain-birth" passage constitutes a wish that what seems terrible may be a mere trifle, they are actually talking about two different things: House about the imagination theme developed in "Dejection," Marsh the unrequited love theme in the original verse letter. The apparent confusion points, quite pertinently for any final judgment of the unity of the poem, to a real confusion inherent in the ambiguous reference of the poem.

House may have had this ambiguity in mind when he complains that Coleridge, after honestly analyzing the cause of his deadened creative spirit in stanza 6 of "Dejection," falsely characterizes this analysis as "viper thoughts" that coil around his mind like "reality's dark dream" in stanza 7. More truthful, House contends, is the reference of stanza 7 in the verse letter. There, the "viper thoughts" are Coleridge's fanciful fears that Sara may be unwell. This ambiguity of reference vanishes, I think, when we perceive that House is still reading the verse letter and "Dejection" as one poem and confusing the intention of one with that of the other. Coleridge may have accurately and honestly diagnosed the cause of his creative problem, but the facts of the diagnosis need not, *ipso facto*, be desirable and pleasant. Since Coleridge is not praising honest psychological analysis in "Dejection" but bewailing the mood of dejection accompanying a loss of creativity, it seems quite appropriate then, considering the importance he attributed to the imagination, for him to refer to a passage explaining the failure of his imagination as "viper thoughts" and "reality's dark dream."

An ambiguity of reference in the last strophe of "Dejection," however, is not so easily justified. In the verse letter, the description of the storm occurs when Coleridge is contrasting the strife of his home life with the harmony of the Wordsworth-Hutchinson's. Here the storm functions on a literal plane, descriptive of a cloudburst like the sudden mountain-birth of one that he had experienced in a climb over Kirkstone, when, pelted with rain and buffeted by wind, he had toiled upward, only to find "on turning the mountain, at the first step of descent, [that] all was calm, breathless— . . . as if there was a great fountain of wind and tempest at the summit that rolled down a Niagara of air" on only one side of the mountain (*CL,* II, 911; cf. I, 638 and II, 858). Paralleling, and hence heightening, the human situation, the spring tempest is described as raging around his house in Keswick, while the stars shine in a clear sky over Grasmere and Gallow Hill on the other side of Dunmail Raise.

In "Dejection," the theme of unhappy domestic life and unrequited love is censored; but the storm is retained and combined with the theme of suspended imagination. Now, besides literally depicting an April cloudburst, the storm also symbolizes Coleridge's quickening imagination.

Just as the wind makes evil, tormented, and sorrowful sounds, so Coleridge's mood of dejection creates only thoughts of pain, despair, and unhappiness.

It is hard to believe that Coleridge means the whole complex of ideas evoked by the storm (imagination) image in "Dejection" to apply to Sara exactly as they apply to himself; for nowhere in "Dejection" has he developed the possibility that her experience corresponds to his. The correspondence present in the verse letter—one of unrequited love—disappeared when, in revising the verse letter into "Dejection," he excised the passages expressing concern that Sara might, like him, be awake and unhappy. Coleridge seems to have recognized the *non sequitur,* for he valiantly tries to relate Sara to the imagination theme by adding the wish that sleep may visit her with "wings of healing" and that the shaping spirit of her imagination may have a joyous wholeness which his lacks. But he has suggested no reason in "Dejection" for our believing that Sara might be otherwise than hale and happy. The wish is at best superfluous, and at worst confusing. In the verse letter, Coleridge expresses this sentiment more appropriately in conjunction with a final envious sigh for the domestic bliss found at Dove Cottage and heartfelt thanks that this joyous love which Sara shares fully with the Wordsworth family will assuage the grief and sleeplessness which he has caused her.

In short, we have in stanza 8 of "Dejection" an instance of the difficulty Coleridge faced when he reduced the double theme of his "coarse domestic life" and his deadened spirit to the single theme of dejection over the loss of his creative imagination. He took the description of a storm associated in the verse letter with his domestic problem and combined it in "Dejection" with his imagination crisis. But, in terms of the new personal and symbolical application of the storm image, the lines wishing that the April shower at Keswick may not obscure the skies at Grasmere and Gallow Hill have no meaning. They remain a vestige of the discarded theme of unrequited love. It is no wonder that critics must be nimble if they wish to fit these lines into the context of the poem and the theme of the loss of imagination.

APPENDIX III

Glycine's Song and "Herbstlied"

*T*he unanswered questions prompted by the prose redaction of Tieck's "Herbstlied"—which contains lines translated literally, interspersed with lines not found in the German poem—is an excellent example of the difficulty attending any consideration of Coleridge's working habits. Is Glycine's song, as F. W. Stokoe suggests, a mechanical composite of lines from an early Coleridge effort and lines from "Herbstlied"? Or is Glycine's song an instance of the fecund way that a congenial idea sometimes affected Coleridge's mind?

Stokoe argues that "Coleridge, requiring a song for Glycine in *Zapolya,* had noted down certain lines or ideas for lines before he came across Tieck's 'Herbstlied'; . . . reading it, he was struck by the metrical arrangement, and the theme of the bird that sings farewell at the summer's end, and resolved to blend so much of the 'Herbstlied' with his own previous idea as might be convenient: hence the prose version, in which lines literally translated from the 'Herbstlied' alternate with some drawn from the earlier scheme."[1] According to this hypothesis of how Glycine's song came to be written, Coleridge purloined another person's idea and coolly modified it to suit his own purposes. Such a view of Coleridge accords with the repeated charges of plagiarism that have followed him from De Quincey's hue and cry in his day to Wellek's in ours.

At least two qualifications of, and one alternative to, Stokoe's hypothesis can be advanced. First, Coleridge was not as impressed with the metrical arrangement of "Herbstlied" as Stokoe would have us believe. Certainly in the prose translations, Coleridge retains the strikingly dramatic short lines ending each stanza of "Herbstlied"; but he did not transmit this scheme intact into his finished poem. The stanza of "Herbstlied" consists of two rhymed octosyllabic couplets, plus a coda of two short rhymed lines, while that of Glycine's song is a modified ballad measure. Only in the important concluding stanza does Coleridge reproduce the coda, with its repeated rhymes and short lines, to support metrically the haunting song of the bird about the transiency of time and love.

Second, Stokoe apparently did not know of the prose redaction in Coleridge's notebooks and the probability that these lines were written in Rome when Coleridge first made Tieck's acquaintance. It is too bad because Stokoe would have quickly seen that Redaction 1 (*N*) is clearly an attempt at a faithful translation of the German; and, in addition, that Redaction 2 (*CPW*) is not a heterogeneous compilation of "Herbstlied" and early verses of Coleridge, but most probably a revision of the initial prose translation—in short, that Redaction 2 represents a version midway between Redaction 1 and Glycine's song. Worthy of notice is that each new version of the "sunny shaft" image is an improvement on the previous:

column of sunshine (*N*)
slanting pillar of sun mist [and] slanting sun-shaft (*CPW*)
sunny shaft [and] shaft of sunny mist (Glycine's song)

Third, it does not necessarily follow, because some lines in the prose translations have no verbal parallel in the German original, that Coleridge must have written them first and then, happening opportunely upon "Herbstlied," have resolved to take from it what he needed to complete his fragmentary verses. The new images could just as conceivably have arisen from the well of his memory during the heated moment of translating Tieck's poem, loosened by a train of chance associations suggested by similar thoughts or feelings in "Herbstlied." In question, mainly, are the allusions to the slanting shaft of sunlight and to the openings of blue in a cloudy sky, the only Coleridgean additions to appear in both redactions. Stokoe would have it that these two allusions originally formed a part of an "earlier scheme" principally because as early as 1800 Coleridge had been struck by the "slanting pillars of misty light" that occasionally move across the landscape. But could not the image of sunlight appearing and disappearing through the clouds, as pictured in the phrases, "muntern Sonnenschein" and "Doch rückwärts kam der Sonnenschein," have instantly recalled to Coleridge an effect in nature which so impressed him that he tirelessly recorded instances of it in his notebooks as if struck afresh each time with the wonder of it? The presence of these images in Redaction 1, in the otherwise literal translation of "Herbstlied," would suggest that some such process of thought as I have suggested took place. No doubt the images represent Coleridge's effort to render the German phrases as faithfully, and yet as connotatively, in terms of his own experience as possible. In the process he has expanded conventional description into vivid metaphor. We know from other translations that Coleridge sometimes elaborated a suggestion in the original into a fuller, more concrete, statement. Thus, he renders "Ich habe gelebt und geliebet" from Thekla's song in *The Piccolomini* to

> I've lived and loved, and that was to-day—
> Make ready my grave-clothes to-morrow.

Even more wonderful, he is inspired by Max Piccolomini's defense of astrology (*The Piccolomini*, II, iv, 110–18) to add twenty lines of moving lament for the loss of faith in poetic fable. Glycine's song may well have originated in the same way: "Herbstlied" firing Coleridge's imagination to rephrase anew a universal sentiment. Such an action is consistent with his assertions that truth belongs to no single master but is the common property on which all men erect their edifices. The "old" German poem talks about the mutability of love and life; this sentiment touches a chord in Coleridge's own thoughts about the ideal world which is forever retreating before our outstretched hands; and Glycine's song is the new expression of this knowledge.

In either case, whether a combination of an earlier poem and "Herbstlied," or an inspired translation and expansion of the original idea expressed in "Herbstlied," Glycine's song reveals Coleridge's "coadunating" mind recasting the German version into a new form stamped with the ordering bent and inspired truth of his own imagination and experience. It is an instance of "that synthetic and magical power" (*BL*, II, 12) of Coleridge's imagination "by which one image or feeling is made to modify many others and by a sort of *fusion to force many into one*" (*SC*, I, 212–13).

TEXT REFERENCES

Alison   Archibald Alison. *Essays on the Nature and Principles of Taste.* Edinburgh: Bell and Bradfute, 1790.

Allsop   Thomas Allsop. *Letters, Conversations and Recollections of S. T. Coleridge.* 2 Vols. London: Moxon, 1836.

AP   *Anima Poetae from the Unpublished Note-books of Samuel Taylor Coleridge.* Edited by Ernest Hartley Coleridge. London: William Heinemann, 1895.

Bald   R. C. Bald. "Coleridge and *The Ancient Mariner.*" *Nineteenth-Century Studies.* Edited by Herbert Davis, William C. DeVane, and R. C. Bald. Ithaca, New York: Cornell University Press, 1940.

Beer   J. B. Beer. *Coleridge the Visionary.* London: Chatto & Windus, 1959.

BL   *Biographia Literaria by S. T. Coleridge, with His Aesthetical Essays.* 2 Vols. Edited by J. Shawcross. Oxford: University Press, 1907.

Bonjour   Adrien Bonjour. *Coleridge's "Hymn Before Sunrise," A Study of Facts and Problems Connected with the Poem.* Lausanne: Imprimerie la Concorde, 1942.

CL   *Collected Letters of Samuel Taylor Coleridge.* 4 Vols. Edited by Earl Leslie Griggs. Oxford: at the Clarendon Press, 1956–59.

Coleorton   *Memorials of Coleorton, Being Letters from Coleridge, Wordsworth and His Sister, Southey, and Sir Walter Scott to Sir George and Lady Beaumont of Coleorton, Leicestershire, 1803 to 1834.* 2 Vols. Edited by William Knight. Edinburgh: D. Douglas, 1887.

CPW   *The Complete Poetical Works of Samuel Taylor Coleridge.* 2 Vols. Edited by Ernest Hartley Coleridge. Oxford: at the Clarendon Press, 1912.

Fogle, AM   Richard Harter Fogle. "The Genre of *The Ancient Mariner.*" *Tulane Studies in English,* VII (1957), 111–24.

Fogle, C   ——— "Coleridge's Conversation Poems." *Tulane Studies in English,* V (1955), 103–10.

Fogle, D   ——— "The Dejection of Coleridge's Ode." *Journal of English Literary History,* XVII (1950), 71–77.

Hartley   David Hartley. *Observations on Man, His Frame, His Duty, and His Expectations.* 2 Vols. 5th Ed. London: Wilkie and Robinson, 1810.

House   Humphry House. *Coleridge.* "The Clark Lectures, 1951–52." London: Rupert Hart-Davis, 1953.

L   *Letters of Samuel Taylor Coleridge.* 2 Vols. Edited by Ernest Hartley Coleridge. Boston: Houghton, Mifflin and Co., 1895.

Lowes   John Livingston Lowes. *The Road to Xanadu: A Study in the Ways of the Imagination.* New York: Houghton, Mifflin and Co., 1927.

MC   *Coleridge's Miscellaneous Criticism.* Edited by Thomas M. Raysor. Cambridge, Massachusetts: Harvard University Press, 1936.

N   *The Notebooks of Samuel Taylor Coleridge.* 2 Vols. (4 Parts, 1794–1808). Edited by Kathleen Coburn. New York: For Bollingen Foundation, Inc., by Pantheon Books, Inc., 1957–61.

PW   *The Poetical Works of Samuel Taylor Coleridge.* Edited by James Dykes Campbell. London: Macmillan and Co., 1914.

SC   *Coleridge's Shakespearean Criticism.* 2 Vols. Edited by Thomas M. Raysor. Cambridge, Massachusetts: Harvard University Press, 1930.

Schneider   Elisabeth Schneider. *Coleridge, Opium, and Kubla Khan.* Chicago: The University of Chicago Press, 1953.

Spirit   *Inquiring Spirit: A New Presentation of Coleridge from His Published and Unpublished Prose Writings.* Edited by Kathleen Coburn. New York: Pantheon Books Inc., 1951.

Symons   Arthur Symons. *The Romantic Movement in English Poetry.* New York: E. P. Dutton and Co., 1909.

TT   *Specimens of the Table Talk of the Late Samuel Taylor Coleridge.* 2 Vols. Edited by Henry Nelson Coleridge. London: John Murray, 1835.

UL   *Unpublished Letters of Samuel Taylor Coleridge.* 2 Vols. Edited by Earl Leslie Griggs. New Haven, Connecticut: Yale University Press, 1933.

Warren   Robert Penn Warren. "A Poem of Pure Imagination, an Experiment in Reading." *The Rime of the Ancient Mariner, with an Essay by Robert Penn Warren.* New York: Reynal & Hitchcock, 1946.

Whalley   George Whalley. *Coleridge and Sara Hutchinson and the Asra Poems.* Toronto: University of Toronto Press, 1955.

NOTES

CHAPTER I

1. (Ithaca, N.Y., 1940), p. 37.
2. Two of the most recent and satisfying critics are R. A. Durr, " 'This Lime-tree Bower My Prison' and a Recurrent Action in Coleridge," *Journal of English Literary History*, XXVI (1959), 514–30, and A. Gérard, "The Systolic Rhythm: The Structure of Coleridge's Conversation Poems," *Essays in Criticism*, X (1960), 307–19.
3. A marginal comment by Coleridge on a Southey essay, quoted by I. A. Richards, *Interpretation in Teaching* (New York, 1938), p. 12.
4. *The Letters of John Keats, 1814–1821*, edited by Hyder Edward Rollins (Cambridge, Mass., 1958), I, 279.

CHAPTER II

1. An exception is David V. Erdman, "Coleridge as Nehemiah Higginbottom," *Modern Language Notes*, LXXIII (1958), 569–80, who has examined the satirical context of the three "Sonnets Attempted in the Manner of Contemporary Writers."
2. *Poems* (London, 1791).
3. Donald Davie, *Purity of Diction in English Verse* (Oxford, 1953), pp. 123–28, is the first, to my knowledge, to call attention to the satirical mode of this poem to Lamb. Davie and I part company in the uses to which we put our analyses. Davie is concerned with the poem simply as an illustration of the impure diction and amorphous structure which the Romantic poets frequently used to achieve a natural style. Since he adopts a broad historical perspective, he fails to note that this poem is one of a group written by Coleridge in the 1790's, which share in theme and form a set of conventions distinguishing them from other poems of Coleridge.
4. *The Letters of Charles Lamb*, edited by E. V. Lucas (New Haven, Conn., 1935), I, 72–73.
5. It is questionable if Coleridge had a specific victory in mind. At any rate, the reference has never been satisfactorily identified. For a careful review of the possibilities, see Carl R. Woodring, *Politics in the Poetry of Coleridge* (Madison, 1961), pp. 237–42.
6. That Coleridge wrote "Lines Composed in a Concert-room" in late 1799 is by no means certain. The evidence supports a date prior to his recantation of faith in the French Revolution in April 1798, in "France: An Ode." Dates suggested have been 1791, 1793, 1794, and 1796. Cf. Woodring, *Politics in the Poetry of Coleridge*, pp. 237–42.
7. See Appendix I for a discussion of this variant of the farrago form.

CHAPTER III

1. I use the orthographical distinction between the true Pindaric and the false Pindarick employed by George N. Shuster in *The English Ode from Milton to Keats* (New York, 1940).
2. *Werke* (1899), XXXII, 62, quoted by William K. Wimsatt, Jr., and Cleanth Brooks, *Literary Criticism: A Short History* (New York, 1957), p. 373 n.
3. *The Complete Poetical Works of Robert Southey*, edited by Robert Southey (London, 1837–38), II, 170–74.
4. *The Letters of John Keats*, I, 224.
5. The fertility motif implicit in the image of the April shower appears in other guises. In an earlier time, Coleridge tells us, joy grew around him "like the twining vine, and

fruits, and foliage" not his own, seemed his. His power to experience this joy is also represented as a wedding garment bestowed upon him at birth by nature.

6. This entry is dated by Coleridge 23 December [1804]. Another instance of Coleridge's seeing his opium addiction as an ensnarement by "serpent folds" occurs in a letter to Morgan of 15 May 1814 (*CL*, IV, 927).

7. Harold Bloom, *Shelley's Mythmaking* (New Haven, 1959), p. 12.

8. *The Subtler Language* (Baltimore, 1959), p. 196.

9. *Revaluation: Tradition and Development in English Poetry* (London, 1936), pp. 233–35.

10. Cf. A. P. Rossiter, "Coleridge's 'Hymn Before Sunrise,'" *Times Literary Supplement*, September 28, 1951, p. 613 and October 26, 1951, p. 677 and his note printed in *CL*, II, 865 n. Rossiter argues that Coleridge wrote "Hymn Before Sun-rise" with Bowles's "Coombe Ellen" and Friederike Brun's poem on Mont Blanc lying open before him; that the composition of it occurred *after* his letter to Sotheby of 26 August 1802 (cf. *CL*, II, 858) and not at the time of his sojourn on Scafell as he claims in a subsequent letter to Sotheby of 10 September 1802; and that "the involuntary hymn story was an estecian myth."

11. *Shelley's Mythmaking*, p. 16.

12. See Emerson R. Marks, "Means and Ends in Coleridge's Critical Method," *Journal of English Literary History*, XXVI (1959), 387–401.

13. *The English Ode*, p. 248.

CHAPTER IV

1. Originally published in the *Morning Post* for 21 December 1799, with four introductory and three concluding stanzas, as "Introduction to the Tale of the Dark Ladie."

2. *Samuel Taylor Coleridge* (New York, n.d.).

3. "The Mariner and the Albatross," *University of Toronto Quarterly*, XVI (1946–47), 381–98.

4. *Archetypal Patterns in Poetry: Psychological Studies of Imagination* (Oxford, 1934), pp. 26–89.

5. *Five Poems: 1470–1870* (London, 1948), pp. 66–74.

6. Warren, "A Poem of Pure Imagination."

7. Garrigues, "Coleridge's 'Ancient Mariner,'" *Journal of Speculative Philosophy*, XIV (1880), 327–38; Beer, p. 158.

8. Florence G. Marsh, "The Ocean-Desert: *The Ancient Mariner* and *The Waste Land*," *Essays in Criticism*, IX (1959), 126–33.

9. It should be noted that Beer depends for his illustration of these associations principally on other-literary statements. He does not show in any thoroughgoing way how the poem itself is working to formulate the meaning which he ascribes to it, as Warren, at least in his essay "A Poem of Pure Imagination," is striving to do.

10. "Symbolism in Coleridge," *PMLA*, LXIII (1948), 214–33; and "Kenneth Burke and Robert Penn Warren: Criticism by Obsessive Metaphor," *Journal of English and Germanic Philology*, LIII (1954), 172–77.

11. *Wordsworth: A Re-Interpretation* (London, 1954), p. 14.

12. *The Friend*, Section II, Essay 10, in *The Complete Works of Samuel Taylor Coleridge*, edited by W. G. T. Shedd (New York, 1854), II, 449–50.

13. See Chapter X for a discussion of the hybrid poems, which combine several styles, and the single naked voice which underlies all the inflected voices.

14. "The Poetical Works of S. T. Coleridge," *The Quarterly Review*, LII (1834), 29.

15. [Anon.], "Reminiscences of Coleridge, Biographical, Philosophical, Political, and Critical," *Fraser's Magazine*, X (1834), 393.

16. For a detailed study of the revision, see B. R. McElderry, Jr., "Coleridge's Revision of *The Ancient Mariner*," *Studies in Philology*, XXIX (1932), 68–94.

CHAPTER V

1. *Letters of John Keats*, II, 89.
2. Cf. *TT*, I, 265–66; II, 121, 135–38, and 300–01.
3. See George Whalley, "The Bristol Library Borrowings of Southey and Coleridge, 1793–8," *The Library*, IV (1949), 114–32.
4. Mary Moorman, *William Wordsworth: The Early Years* (Oxford, 1957), p. 270.
5. *Ibid.*, p. 291.
6. "Coleridge's Conversation Poems," *The Quarterly Review*, CCXLIV (1925), 291.
7. Cf. Henry J. W. Milley, who characterizes "The Eolian Harp" as having a "single emotional curve," "Some Notes on Coleridge's 'Eolian Harp,'" *Modern Philology*, XXXVI (1939), 368–69.
8. See my article, "Coleridge Agonistes," *Journal of English and Germanic Philology*, LXI (1962), 268–77, for a psychological explanation of Coleridge's rejection of the bowery retreat.
9. *The Quarterly Review*, CCXLIV (1925), 284–98.
10. "The Systolic Rhythm: The Structure of Coleridge's Conversation Poems," *Essays in Criticism*, X (1960), 307–19.
11. "Oneness and Multeity in Coleridge's Poems," *Tulane Studies in English*, IX (1959), 53–60.
12. *Essays in Criticism*, X (1960), 317.
13. See my note, "Coleridge, Milton, and Lost Paradise," *Notes and Queries*, VI (1959), 143–44.
14. *Ennead*, III, viii, 9, translated by Stephen MacKenna (Boston, n.d.).
15. Robert Mayo, "The Contemporaneity of the *Lyrical Ballads*," *PMLA*, LXIX (1954), 494.
16. The most exhaustive survey of Coleridge's poetry for wind and moon imagery as symbolic of the imagination has been made by Marshall Suther, *The Dark Night of Samuel Taylor Coleridge* (New York, 1960), pp. 67–118. He examines all the poems prior to "Dejection," except "The Ancient Mariner" and "Christabel."
17. *Ennead*, V, i, 2.
18. House, pp. 79–83 and Langbaum, *The Poetry of Experience* (New York, 1957), pp. 45–46.
19. *Complete Works of Samuel Taylor Coleridge*, Edited by Shedd, I, 436.

CHAPTER VI

1. *Samuel Taylor Coleridge* (New York, n.d.).
2. "Is it from any hobby-horsical love of our old writers, . . . or is it a real beauty, the interspersion I mean (in stanza poems) of rhymes from polysyllables—such as eminence, obedience, reverence. To my ear they convey not only a relief from variety, but a sweetness as of repose—and the understanding they gratify by reconciling verse with the whole wide extent of good sense" (*MC*, pp. 237–38).
3. Derek Patmore, *The Life and Times of Coventry Patmore* (Oxford, 1949), p. 98.
4. Critics who have presented variations of this view include E. H. W. Meyerstein, "Completeness of Kubla Khan," *Times Literary Supplement*, October 30, 1937, p. 803; Elisabeth Schneider, "The 'Dream' of Kubla Khan," *PMLA*, LX (1945), 784–801; and Humphry House, *Coleridge*, pp. 114–22.
5. I have expressed my views on the problem of the prefaces to Coleridge's poems in "Coleridge's 'Apologetic' Prefaces," *Tulane Studies in English*, XI (1961), 53–64.

6. See below, pp. 126–127 for an analysis of "Recollections of Love."

7. "Coleridge, Hartley, and the Mystics," *Journal of the History of Ideas*, XX (1959), 477–94.

8. *Ibid.*, 494.

CHAPTER VII

1. From a version of "The Pains of Sleep" sent to Southey in a letter of 11 September 1803 (*CL*, II, 984).

2. How aptly Leigh Hunt, in "Sketches of the Living Poets. No. 4. Mr. Coleridge," in the *Examiner* for 21 October 1821, has put his finger on this introspective habit! "[Coleridge] in the greater part of his minor poems . . . only touches upon the popular creeds . . . and then falls musing upon the nature of things, and analysing his feelings"; reprinted in *Leigh Hunt's Literary Criticism*, edited by Lawrence Huston Houtchens and Carolyn Washburn Houtchens (New York, 1956), p. 171.

3. *The Letters of Sara Hutchinson*, edited by Kathleen Coburn (Toronto, 1954), pp. xxxi, xxxi n, and 262–67.

4. *The Dark Night of Samuel Taylor Coleridge*, pp. 25–64.

5. Reprinted by Warren E. Gibbs, "S. T. Coleridge's 'The Knight's Tomb' and 'Youth and Age,' " *Modern Language Review*, XXVIII (1933), 85.

6. *The Dark Night of Samuel Taylor Coleridge*, pp. 130–34.

7. *Letters of John Keats*, I, 193–94.

8. "Coleridge and Kant's Two Worlds," *Journal of English Literary History*, VII (1940), 350.

9. Cf. "The Day-dream," 13–18; "The Pains of Sleep," 40; "The Blossoming of the Solitary Date-tree," 65–71; "To William Wordsworth," 65–66; "To Two Sisters," 3–5; and "The Pang More Sharp Than All," 11–20.

10. Cf. "Dejection," 79–81; "The Picture," 7–25, 87–102; "The Blossoming of the Solitary Date-tree," 17–21; "Work Without Hope," 9–10; "Youth and Age," 1–3, 18–19; "The Pang More Sharp Than All," 21–22; and "Love's Apparition and Evanishment," 1–6, 10–13.

CHAPTER VIII

1. "The Visionary Hope" and "The Blossoming of the Solitary Date-tree," although confessional in tone and content, incorporate some of the characteristics of the improvisation poem: the guise of the steadfast servant of truth and love ("The Visionary Hope") and an improvisation structure ("The Blossoming of the Solitary Date-tree").

2. *The Life of John Sterling* (London, 1851), p. 46.

3. Cf. also "A Wish: Written in Jesus Wood, Feb. 10, 1792"; "Written after a Walk before Supper"; "To the Rev. W. J. Hort: While Teaching a Young Lady Some Song-tunes on His Flute"; "Lines Composed While Climbing the Left Ascent of Brockley Coomb, Somersetshire, May 1795"; "Sonnet on Receiving a Letter Informing Me of the Birth of a Son"; and "Lines to W. L.: While He Sang a Song to Purcell's Music."

4. Exceptions are the *jeu d'esprit* "An Ode to the Rain: Composed before Daylight, on the Morning Appointed for the Departure of a Very Worthy, But Not Very Pleasant Visitor, Whom It Was Feared, the Rain Might Detain" (1802), and the conversation poem "To William Wordsworth: Composed on the Night after His Recitation of a Poem on the Growth of an Individual Mind" (1807).

5. It was restored to the title when the poem was printed in *Sibylline Leaves* (1817).

6. This is the title as published in an emended version in *Felix Farley's Bristol Journal* for 21 February 1818.

7. *Early Years and Late Recollections* (London, 1856), I, 66.

8. Since it was an early poem in a new mode, Coleridge was evidently unable to resist adding, for good measure, the old formula, "A Dialogue Written on a Blank Page of Butler's Book of the Roman Catholic Church," to the title when he first published it in the *Evening Standard* for 21 May 1827. "The Good, Great Man" (1802) and "The Suicide's Argument" (1811) may also be read as early forecasts of the same kind of poem.

9. Cf. *AP*, p. 304, for a further remark of Coleridge relative to this problem.

10. Cf. also "The Improvisatore," 63–67; "The Visionary Hope," 17–28; "Constancy to an Ideal Object," 7–10; "Love's Apparition and Evanishment," 17–28; and "To Two Sisters," 40–44.

11. Cf. Langbaum, *The Poetry of Experience*, p. 204.

CHAPTER IX

1. "The Poetical Works of S. T. Coleridge," *The Quarterly Review*, LII (1834), 1–38. John Sterling's essay on "Christabel" in the *Athenaeum*, XXXVI (1828), 567–68, is earlier but emphasizes the "thrilling and ghost-ridden feeling which is the proper recipient of the mysterious story." Leigh Hunt's essay, "Sketches of the Living Poets. No. 4. Mr. Coleridge," which appeared in the *Examiner* for 21 October 1821, singles out "The Ancient Mariner," "Christabel," and "Kubla Khan" for mild praise; but not until 1844 in the essay "What is Poetry?" in *Imagination and Fancy* does he stress Coleridge's sweetness of versification as a "prevailing characteristic."

2. T. Hall Caine, *Recollections of Dante Gabriel Rossetti* (Boston, 1883), pp. 147–48.

3. "Essays and Studies," *The Complete Works of Algernon Charles Swinburne*, edited by Sir Edmund Gosse and Thomas James Wise (London, 1926), XV, 143–54.

4. *Appreciations; with an Essay on Style* (London, 1889), pp. 87–88.

5. There is some question about the part played by Tieck's poem in the evolution of Glycine's song; see Appendix III for a discussion of this problem.

6. A report by Christopher Wordsworth, *Memoirs of William Wordsworth* (London, 1851), II, 306, of a conversation in 1836 between Justice Coleridge and William Wordsworth.

CHAPTER X

1. *Politics in the Poetry of Coleridge*, chapter 8.

2. In his nostalgic celebration of conjugal affection and the ordinary routine of family life, Coleridge foreshadowed the Victorian appetite for quiet bourgeois *Gemütlichkeit*. Like a true Biedermeier, he showed a taste, especially as he advanced into the years of the nineteenth century, for the "small world of good sense and good manners, domestic pleasures and the cult of a gentle, well-groomed nature, subservience to sane principles, minute love of the concrete, with, from time to time, a few flights on the wings of a mild and perhaps slightly melancholy dream"—to quote Mario Praz's description of the attitude which flourished in Germany, particularly, from 1815 to 1870, *The Hero in Eclipse in Victorian Fiction* (London, 1956), p. 118 n.

3. *Proust* (London, 1928), p. 67.

4. *The Decline and Fall of the Romantic Ideal* (New York, 1936), p. 174.

5. "On the Logic of Romanticism," *Essays in Criticism*, VII (1957), 266.

6. Neither Earl Leslie Griggs nor Stephen Potter includes more than one dream poem, "Love's Apparition and Evanishment," in their editions, respectively, of *The Best of Coleridge* (New York, 1947) and *Coleridge: Select Poetry & Prose* (London, 1950). The neglect is as thoroughgoing among the standard college anthologies of Romanticism. There is no representation of the dream poem, except of course for the ubiquitous "Kubla Khan," in *Anthology of Romanticism*, edited by Ernest Bernbaum (New York, 1948); nor in *Poetry and Criticism of the Romantic Movement*, edited by Oscar James

Campbell, J. F. A. Pyre, and Bennett Weaver (New York, 1941); nor in *English Romantic Poets*, edited by James Stephens, Edwin L. Peck, and Royall H. Snow (New York, 1935); while only "Love's Apparition and Evanishment" appears in *English Romantic Poetry and Prose*, edited by Russell Nöyes (New York, 1956); and "Phantom or Fact" and "The Garden of Boccaccio" in *English Poetry and Prose of the Romantic Movement*, edited by George Benjamin Wood (New York, 1950).

APPENDIX II

1. "Coleridge: 'A Mountain-Birth,' " *Notes and Queries*, New Series, II (1955), 261–62.

APPENDIX III

1. *German Influence in the English Romantic Period, 1788–1818* (Cambridge, 1926), p. 126.

INDEX

"Addressed to a Young Man of Fortune Who Abandoned Himself to an Indolent and Causeless Melancholy," 31; as farrago poem, 13; analysis of theme and structure, 18–19

Aeolian harp. *See* Imagery, key

Aeschylus: Coleridge on criticism of, 4

"Alice du Clos; or, the Forked Tongue": ventriloquism poem, 51; as Georgian ballad, 67–68; language compared to "The Ancient Mariner," 68–69; clichés of sentiment in, 70

Alison, Archibald: *Principles of Taste,* 29; on mental images,104; associationist psychology of, 107; on mental images, 112

Allsop, Thomas: Coleridge's letter to, 66, 189, 193; on Coleridge's search for principles, 124

Allston, Washington: "The Moonlit Landscape" compared to "An Invocation," 180

"Ancient Ballad of Chevy Chase, The": comparison with "The Ancient Mariner," 57

"Ancient Mariner, The": Lowes' criticism of, 5; compared to "Dejection," 38; as ventriloquism poem, 51, 195; simplicity by assumption, 52; ballad traits of, 52–53; diction of, 53; allegorical readings of, 54–55; as study in abnormal psychology, 55; use of antagonistic dramatic view, 55; analysis of, 55–64; psychological realism of, 56; on killing of albatross, 56–57; on writing of gloss, 57–59; lyricism of, 58–59; mariner's blessing of the water-snakes, 60; judged by Coleridge, 60–61; compared to later ballads, 61; dual structure of, 61; Georgian elements of, 61–64; origin of, 62; use of *deus ex machina,* 62; obtrusive moral in, 62–63; supernatural elements in, 62, 70; narrative ambiguity of, 63, 67; unity of theme and expression in, 64; compared to "Christabel," 64, 65, 66; Lamb's criticism of, 65; compared to "Alice du Clos," "Love," and "The Dark Ladié," 67, 68–69, 70; revisions of, 69–70; reconciliation of opposites in, 69, 191; music of, 171, 172; praise of, 171, 217; colloquial structure of, 184; naked voice of, 186, 189; on theme of one life, 187; mentioned, 1, 6, 22, 60, 101, 102, 134, 161, 193

Andersen, Hans Christian, 156

Anima Poetae: description of the imagination, 5; on passion in poetry, 27; on theme of one life, 128; description of a true poet, 165; Coleridge's self-characterization, 195

Annus Mirabilis, 141; poems prior to, 11, 23

"Apologetic Preface to 'Fire, Famine, and Slaughter' ": analysis of hatred, 60

"Apologia Pro Vita Sua": quoted, 124

Aquinas, Thomas, 108

Armour, Richard W.: *Coleridge the Talker,* 6

Arnold, Matthew: "The Scholar Gipsy," 147–48

Associationist psychology: cause and effect of physical sensations, 104–05; defined by Coleridge, 104–07; memory, 105–06; passivity of, 107; association in Glycine's song, 208

Augustan. *See* Poetics

"Away in a Manger," 20

Bald, Robert Cecil: on "The Ancient Mariner," 6; on Coleridge's definition of reverie, 125

Ballad: in ventriloquism voice, 24, 53, 70, 191; characteristics of, 50, 51, 52–53, 61; "The Three Graves," 55; in *Lyrical Ballads*, 56; world of, 56–57; form transcended in "The Ancient Mariner," 57; Georgian tradition of, 61, 64, 66, 67, 69, 192; contributes to the stanzaic structure of "Youth and Age," 141, 142, 143; contributes to the colloquial structure of Coleridge's poems, 184; combined with new sensibility in Coleridge's poems, 192; Coleridge's achievement in, 194; stanza of Glycine's song, 207; mentioned, 6, 24, 61, 186. *See also* Ventriloquism voice

"Ballad of the Dark Ladié, The": as ventriloquism poem, 51; supernatural and Spenserian elements in, 61; as Georgian ballad, 67, 68; language compared to "The Ancient Mariner," 68–69; abandoned by Coleridge, 70

Barbauld, Mrs. Anna Letitia, 161; on "The Ancient Mariner," 62; tender sensibility of, 192

"Baron Guelph of Adelstan": as ventriloquism poem, 51; as Georgian ballad, 67; abandoned by Coleridge, 70

Bateson, Frederick Wilse: Wordsworth's two voices, 56

Baxter, Andrew: *Inquiry into the Nature of the Human Soul,* 107

Beaumont, Francis: *The Elder Brother,* 162

Beaumont, Sir George: manuscript version of "Hymn Before Sun-rise" sent to, 40

Beddoes, Thomas Lovell: *The Improvisatore,* 156; his exploration of metrical effects, 178; song in *Torrismond,* 178; "Wolfram's Dirge," 178

Beer, John B.: on *Zapolya,* 36; on "The Ancient Mariner," 54–55, 214; on Kubla as commanding genius, 115; on Kubla's palace, 115; on Coleridge as occultist, 124

Bell, Clive: on artistic form, 193

Benevolism: influence on Farrago voice, 18

Biedermeier: characteristics of, in Coleridge, 217

Bijou: early version of "Youth and Age," 143

Biographia Literaria: on reconciliation of spontaneous and formal, 8; "On a Ruined House in a Romantic Country," 12; definition of a poem, 23, 30; on subject and object, 42, 59; on poetic diction, 46, 47, 51, 81, 99; on modifying power of the imagination, 46, 97, 209; on the logic of poetry, 47; on Wordsworth, 47, 80; on ventriloquism, 52; quoted on causes of joy, 60; on success of "The Ancient Mariner," 61; on willing suspension of disbelief, 64, 125; on conversational verse, 72; on Daniel and Massinger's verse, 74; on act of perception, 97; quoted on laws of association, 106; on fragmentation of dreams, 113; reference to palace of ice, 120; on unity of a poem, 149; on form, 157; "On Poesy or Art" quoted, 163; on Coleridge's early verse, 190; on Coleridge's achievements, 195; on meter, 170, 176, 178, 179; mentioned, 30, 38, 81, 193

Blackmur, Richard P.: on acceptance of poetic ideas, 165

Blackwood's Magazine: version of "Youth and Age," 143

Blake, William, 55, 181; his exploration of metrical effects, 178; his literary revolt, 194

Bloom, Harold: on "Hymn Before Sun-rise," 38–39, 41

"Blossoming of the Solitary Date-tree, The": as confession poem, 131; ends with question, 136; as improvisation poem, 144, 216; analyzed, 158–60; origin of, 159–60; on Coleridge's fondness for colloquial address, 185; as an interesting experiment, 196; imagery of, 216, 296

Boccaccio, Giovanni: in "The Garden of Boccaccio," 102, 103

Bodkin, Maud: on "The Ancient Mariner," 54

Bonjour, Adrien: on "Hymn Before Sun-rise," 39

Bowles, William Lisle, 22; letter to, 73; his prosody praised by Coleridge, 177–78

Bowyer, James: on the logic of poetry, 47

Bracy: on his projected journey, in "Christabel," 66

Brooke, Rupert: love of England, 149

Browne, Sir Thomas: quincunx, 194

Browning, Robert: his dramatic verse compared to Coleridge's, 164; "The Bishop Orders His Tomb at Saint Praxed's Church," 167; "My Last Duchess," 167; *The Ring and the Book*, 167; his dramatic monologue compared to improvisation poem, 167; his dramatic monologue, 194–95

Brun, Friederike (Friderike Sophie Christiane Münter), 39, 43, 45

Bürger, Gottfried August: on the verse of *Lenore*, 30

Burney, Charles and Fanny (D'Arblay, Frances): taste of, 61

Burns, Robert: in "To a Friend," 17, 18; Orpheus inspired, 156; "The Jolly Beggars," 172; his exploration of metrical effects, 178

Byron, George Gordon, Lord: Orpheus inspired, 156

Caliban, 172

Campbell, James Dykes: on "The Old Man's Sigh," 143

Carlyle, Thomas: description of Coleridge, 153

Carlyon, Clement: on the composition of "Homesick," 157

Catherine the Great, of Russia, 31

Cellini, Benvenuto, 175

"Character, A": as improvisation poem, 153; characterization of Coleridge, 154

Chatterton, Thomas: treatment of ballad, 67

Chaucer, Geoffrey: love of England, 149

"Chevy Chase." *See* "Ancient Ballad of Chevy Chase, The"

"Christabel": metrics of, 32, 171; imagery of, 35; as ventriloquism poem, 51; Spenserian elements in, 61; supernatural elements in, 61, 64–65, 70; compared to "The Ancient Mariner," 64, 65, 66; analysis of, 64–66; failure of narrative invention in, 64, 65, 67, 70; descriptive of landscape, 65–66; moral sentiments of, 66; projected additions, 66; ending of, 67; on its incompleteness, 69, 70, 191; compared to "Love," 70; alluded to in *The Prelude*, 134; praised, 171, 217; music of, 172; as ghost story, 217; mentioned, 1, 6, 22, 67, 101, 102

"Christmas Carol, A," 19; as farrago poem, 13; analysis of, 20–21; compared to "A Carol," 21; praised by Coleridge, 24

Churchill, Charles, 13

Claude, Lorraine (Gellée, Claude): reflected light, 91

Coburn, Kathleen: on edition of Coleridge's notebooks, 7; quoted on Coleridge, 63; on Andrew Baxter, 107; on redaction of "Herbstlied," 173

Coleridge, Berkeley, 127

Coleridge, Derwent, 127

Coleridge, Ernest Hartley: edition of Coleridge's poems, 1; "Fragment 32," 59; redaction of "Herbstlied," 173

Coleridge, George: Coleridge's letter to, 87, 136–37

Coleridge, Hartley: in "Frost at Midnight," 73, 93, 94, 96; in "The Nightingale," 74, 89, 186

Coleridge, Henry Nelson: appendix to "The Hour When We Shall Meet Again," 22; on "Christabel," 64; Coleridge as poetic musician, 171

Coleridge, Samuel Taylor: colloquial powers of, 1–2, 152, 153–55, 157–58, 165, 183–84, 185; need for re-examination of, 2, 6; on criticism, 4, 10, 13, 75; view of poetry, 5, 7–8, 8–9, 23, 27, 29, 80–82, 107, 123–24, 176; self-criticism, 6–8, 11, 15, 33, 35–38, 44–45, 52, 83, 130, 131, 132, 133, 136–37, 139, 144–46, 147, 186, 214, 215; evolution of his poetry, 8, 31, 51–53, 67–69, 166–67, 172; inhibiting poetic attitudes, 11, 12, 62, 67, 69–71, 191, 192, 194–95; myriad-faceted personality, 12–13, 18, 29, 101, 120–21, 190; compared to other poets, 16, 20, 163, 164, 187; criticism of Della Cruscans, 15; relationship with Lamb, 18; intentions in farrago voice, 18, 21–23, 23–24; craftsmanship in farrago voice, 19; criticism of his society, 20; passion for order, 29–30, 157, 172, 193–94; his odes, 30, 46; as poetic innovator, 32, 178–79, 192, 194–95, 196; on inhibition of visionary insight, 36; conception of "Hymn Before Sun-rise," 39, 40, 41; influence of other poets, 43, 77, 80–82; natural diction of, 45; reconciliation of opposites, 46, 189–90, 192; theme of one life, 47–48, 83–84,

86–90, 187–88; as Blake, 55; psychological subject matter, 55–56; "The Ancient Mariner," 57–59, 60–61, 62–63, 63–64, 69, 191–92; on love, 59–60; on supernatural, 65; on his finishing of "Christabel," 66; nature of the failure of the ventriloquism voice, 70; on poetic diction, 80–82; as renovator of descriptive-meditative poem, 92; on dreams, 103–04, 105, 125–26; on associationist psychology, 104–07; rationalism of, 124, 129; psychoanalytical honesty of, 140; failure of imagination, 141, 147, 148; as S. T. C., 153; as successful playwright, 155, Orpheus inspired, 156, prefaces to his poems, 159, 160, 215; imaginatively tired, 166; reputation in nineteenth century, 171–72; metrical regularity of, 178: on transciency of life, 179–81; poems not examined in this study, 190–91; on his plagiarism, 207, 209

Coleridge, Sara (Coleridge's daughter), 127

Coleridge, Sara Fricker (Coleridge's wife): letter to, 47; in "The Eolian Harp," 120

Coleridge family: dramatis personae of conversation poems, 155

Collected Letters, Coleridge's: his praise of "A Christmas Carol," 24; his comparison of Greek and Hebraic poetry, 28; on Collin's "Ode on the Poetical Character," 29; on sublime poetry, 29; on himself, 29, 139; on Taylor's translation of *Lenore,* 30; on "Hymn Before Sun-rise," 39, 40; on simplicity of poetic style by assumption, 52; his occult reading, 55; on *Faust,* 65; on Southey, 67; Wordsworth's criticism of his scientific studies, 69; on style of *Osorio,* 73; on Cowper, 75; on parentheses, 75; on Wordsworth, 80, 81, 192; on preface to *Lyrical Ballads* (1800), 81; on poetic language, 81, 145; on one life within us and abroad, 86, 87, 95, 124; on "The Nightingale," 89–90; on nature, 91; on Milton, 98, 166; on his dreams, 100, 105; on warmth about his heart, 105; on mystics, 124; on "Lines on a Friend Who Died of a Frenzy Fever Induced by Caluminious Reports," 136–37; on Gessner, 137; on man's excellences and faults, 146; on the unity of a poem, 146; on Bowles' prosody, 177–78; on metrical regularity, 178; on poetic trans-formation of ideas, 181; on a puff of his lectures on Shakespeare and Milton, 183; on newspaper verse, 190; on difficulty of finishing "Christabel," 191; on his shortcomings as a poet, 191–92, 193; as arbiter between the old and the new, 192; describes storm over Kirkstone, 205; quoted, 22, 60, 88, 108, 179; mentioned, 101

Collier, John Payne; Coleridge on "Kubla Khan," 115; Coleridge's lectures, 152

Collins, William: poetic tradition of, 7; "Ode on the Poetical Character," 29; view of ballad, 67

Colman, George, the Elder: editor of Massinger, 80

Confession voice, 131–50 *passim,* 22, 183; naturalness of, 7; "Dejection," defined as, 28; characteristics of, 28, 131–32, 133; "Youth and Age," defined as, 38; organic form of, 48; compared to dream poems, 129; poems listed, 131, compared to conversation voice, 132–34; themes of, 134–35; temporal arrangement of, 135; inconclusiveness of, 135–36, 146–47; as prayer, 136; psychological observation of, 140, 148–49; shortcomings of, 144–50 *passim;* regenerative symbols of, 150; portrait of Coleridge, 154–55; relationship to naked voice, 185, 190; love poems in mode of, 191; achievement of, 195

"Constancy to an Ideal Object," as confession poem, 131, 141; theme of, 134; shortcomings of, 147; psychological accuracy of, 149; naked voice of, 185; formula diction of, 217

"Constantius" (*pseud.*) 154, 161

Conversation voice, 51–71 *passim;* naturalness of, 7; compared to farrago voice, 13, 24; "Dejection" defined as, 28; characteristics of, 28, 73–74, 82–86, 99, 110–11, 131, 184, 185, imagery of, 33, 40, 90–91; organic form of, 48; low-keyed tone of, 51–52, 98, 99; poems of compared to other poems, 58, 71, 73–74, 101, 110–11, 129, 132–34, 155, 166, 167, 179; poems listed, 73; origins of, 74–77, 80, 92; evolution of blank verse of, 74–80; theme of one life, 86–90; 94–96, 97–98, 187, 188, 191; unity of, 88–90; Coleridge's achievement in, 141, 194, 195; Coleridge's low opinion of, 179; naked voice of, 183–85, 186; most characteristic of Coleridge, 185; mentioned, 6, 22, 24, 102, 183

Corbière, Tristan (Edouard Joachim), 165

Cottle, Joseph: Coleridge's criticism of his poetry, 22; *Poems*, 27; Coleridge's advice to on poetizing, 29; Coleridge's letter to, 67

Cowley, Abraham: Coleridge's criticism of, 10; Pindarick excesses of, 27, 30

Cowper, William: blank verse of, 6; *The Task*, influence on conversation voice, 74–77, 98, 99; mentioned, 80

Daniel, Samuel: influence on conversation voice, 74

Dante Alighieri: Coleridge on criticism of, 4; *The Divine Comedy*, 165

Darwin, Erasmus: poetic style of, 22; descriptive verses compared to conversation poems, 74; associationist psychology of, 107

"Darwiniana." *See* "Hour When We Shall Meet Again, The"

David: *Psalms*, 38

Davie, Donald: on amorphous structure in Coleridge's poetry, 23; *Purity of Diction in English Verse*, 213

Davy, Humphry: Coleridge's letter to, 192

"Day-dream, A": mentioned, 69; as dream poem, 102, 107; analyzed, 109–13; dating of, 109–10; as poetic rendition of daydream, 121; compared to "Kubla Khan," 122; psychological realism of, 126, 129; colloquial structure of, 184; theme of one life, 187; naked voice of, 189; reconciliation of spontaneous and formal, 191; as finished example of dream voice, 195

"Day-dream, The": as dream poem, 102, 144; analyzed, 114; as confession poem, 131; theme of, 134; imagery of, 216; mentioned, 126

Defoe, Daniel: *Robinson Crusoe*, 193

"Dejection: An Ode": as prophecy poem, 28–29, 144; as culmination of Coleridge's artistry, 30; analysis of theme and structure, 33–38, 40, 160, 216; relationship with "Ode on Intimations of Immortality," 40; as culmination of prophecy voice, 45; tone and diction of, 45, 184;

unity of, 46, 47, 141, 149–50, 191; projectionist belief expressed, 84; from "Verse Epistle to Sara," 109; as confession poem, 131; camouflaged self-revelation, 140; ambiguity of, 144–45, 204–06; nostalgic, 186; theme of one life, 187, 188; theme of, 134; naked voice of, 189; as finished example of prophecy voice, 195; conclusion to, 201–04; quoted, 137–38, 188; mentioned, 38, 69, 102, 141, 188

"Delinquent Travellers, The": analyzed, 199

Della Cruscan: false diction and amorphous design of, 12; compared with farrago voice, 13–17 *passim;* relationship to farrago voice, 21–23; in "Love, Hope, and Patience in Education," 194; mentioned, 22, 191

Denham, John: "Cooper's Hill," 41

DeQuincy, Thomas: on Coleridge's plagiarism, 207

Descriptive-meditative poems: low-keyed naturalness of, 51; topographical, 73; as conversation poem, 72–73, 92; curve of emotion in, 82–84; compared to songs, 180, 186; combined with new sensibility in Coleridge's poems, 192; mentioned, 6, 84, 90

"Destiny of Nations, The": as prophecy poem, 27; multiple voices of, 191

"Devonshire Roads," 156

"Devil's Thoughts, The," 190

Diction, poetic: natural, 7, 101; extravagance of Coleridge's, 11; of "On a Ruined House in a Romantic Country," 12; of farrago voice, 13; inflated satirical rhetoric of "To a Friend," 17; Coleridge's desire for simplicity of, 51–52; in "The Ancient Mariner," 53; Coleridge's disagreement with Wordsworth on, 80–82

Dodsley, Robert, 46

Donne, John: Coleridge's criticism of, 10; "Go and Catch a Falling Star," 133

Dramatic Monologue: of Browning, 167–68

Dream: as poetry, 104

Dream voice, 48, 183; naturalness of, 7; poems listed, 102; compared to other voices, 101–102, 110–11, 129, 179, 191; defined, 102–03, 112, 131; as reverie, 104; use of associationist principles, 104–07, 107–12; warmth about heart, 105; temporal arrangement of, 110–11, 135;

fragmentariness of, 113–14; use of dreams, 115; hallucination or reality, 123–24, 125–29; as artifact, 126–27; psychological significance of, 127–28; limited objective of, 128–29; inner world of mind and heart of, 132; Coleridge's achievement in, 141, 195; naked voice of, 184, 185, 187; in college anthologies of Romanticism, 217

Drinking songs: lack creative energy, 172

Dryden, John: versification of, 163, 164

"Duty Surviving Self-love": the poet as improviser, 152; as improvisation poem, 153, 161; characterization of Coleridge, 154; as soliloquy, 160; smug tone of, 165; naked voice of, 186; mentioned, 160, 164

"Edward": comparison with "The Ancient Mariner," 57

Effusion: relationship to farrago voice, 190–91

Elegy: with Georgian sentiments, 43

Elijah, 28

Eliot, Thomas Stearns: poetic method of, 20, 195; "The Love Song of J. Alfred Prufrock," 195

"Eolian Harp, The": simple and natural style of, 51; address machinery of, 73; as conversation poem, 73, 195; discursiveness of, 74; shortcomings of, 77–78, 86; curve of emotion in, 82–83; revision of, 83–84, 98–99; theme of one life, 87, 96, 188; imagery of, 91; pantheism of, 96; rejection of daydreams in, 120; as visionary poem, 123, 124; naked voice of, 186, 189; quoted, 47, 116–17; mentioned, 80, 123

Epic: Spenserian, 64

Extempore: creative process as part of poem, 155

Ezekiel, 28

Fall of Robespierre, The, 172

Faraday, Michael, 115

Farrago voice: 11–24 passim; in tradition of sensibility, 7, 51; poems listed, 13; characteristics of, 13; satire of Della Cruscan sentiment in, 17–18; themes of, 18, 24; shortcomings of, 19, 20–23; place in Coleridge's poetic development, 23; diction of compared to ballad's, 69; naked

voice absent in, 190; effusions and juvenilia, 190–91; amorphousness of, 191; failure of, 195; subspecies of, 197–99; mentioned, 31, 73, 101, 183

Fausset, Hugh I'Anson: on "The Ancient Mariner," 54; Coleridge as dreamer, 101

"Fears in Solitude": compared to "The Ancient Mariner," 57; as conversation poem, 73; sermonizes in, 73; return of thought in, 84; depiction of nature in, 87, 97; mixed style of, 98; as prophecy poem, 123

Fletcher, John. See Beaumont, Francis

Fogle, Richard Harter: on "The Ancient Mariner," 69; on "To William Wordsworth" as conversation poem, 132; on the conclusion to "Dejection," 201–02

Ford, Newell F.: on "The Ancient Mariner," 55

"Foster-Mother's Tale, The": colloquial structure of, 183–84

"Fragment 31": quoted on love, 60

"Fragment 32": quoted on love, 59

"France: An Ode": as prophecy poem, 27; on nature, 28; analysis of theme and structure, 32; compared to "Dejection," 33; autobiographical, 186

Franklin, Ben: "Edict by the King of Prussia," 198

Friend, The: on reconciliation of subject and object, 59

Friendship's Offering, 148

Frost, Robert, 7

"Frost at Midnight," 80; simple style of, 51; address machinery of, 74; blank verse of, 78; spontaneity of, 82; return of thought in, 84; theme of one life, 87, 96, 97, 188; imagery of, 88; depiction of nature in, 88, 97; analysis of, 92–94; variant readings of, 97; Cowperian influence on, 98; ending of, 99; motif of hope in, 160; natural diction and syntax of, 184; naked voice of, 186, 189; reconciliation of spontaneous and formal, 191; unity of effect of, 193; as finished example of conversation voice, 195

"Garden of Boccaccio, The": as dream poem, 102; analyzed, 102–03; has sense of fragmentariness, 113; poetic rendition of daydream, 121, 126; depiction of ideal world, 128; psychological realism of, 129; in college anthologies of Romanticism, 218

Garrigues, Gertrude: on "The Ancient Mariner," 54

Gay, John, 167

George III: in "Talleyrand to Lord Grenville," 198

Gérard, Albert: on conversation poems, 84–85; on English Romantic poets' pursuit of the ideal, 194

Gessner, Salomon: pastoral idylls of, 22; "Der feste Vorsatz" compared to "The Picture," 137–39; satirized in "The Picture," 145

Gifford, William: influence on Coleridge, 13

Gillman, James: taste of, 61

Gilpin, William, 66

Glycine's song: as song, 172, 195; as redaction of Tieck's "Herbstlied," 173–75, 207–09; analysis of, 173–76; meter of, 178; structure of, 178; music of, 179

Godwin, William: rationalism of, 18; letter to, 44, 139

Goethe, Johann Wolfgang von: Faust, 65

"Good, Great Man, The": as improvisation poem, 217

Gothicism: in "The Ancient Mariner," 62, 70; in "Kubla Khan," 118; in An Invocation, 180; in ventriloquism voice, 191

Grave-yard poem: "Addressed to a Young Man of Fortune," 19

Gray, Thomas, 145; political odes of, 6; poetic tradition of, 7; "The Bard," 30; "The Progress of Poesy," 30

"Greek Ode on Astronomy": comparison with "Ode on the Departing Year," 30–31

Grenville, William Wyndham: in "Talleyrand to Lord Grenville," 198–99

Hamlet: Coleridge's analysis of, 186

Harper, George McLean: on conversation poems, 84, 132

Hartley, David: on reverie, 104, 105; on laws of association, 106; on fragmentation of dreams, 113

Haven, Richard: Coleridge as reconcilor of old and new, 124

Hebraic: Psalmist despondency, 28

Herder, Johann Gottfried: on the ode, 29

Homer, 4, 103

"Homesick:" as impromptu composition, 157

Hood, Thomas, 7

Hopkins, Gerard Manley: "The Caged Skylark," 36; "The Windhover," 88; "Thou Art Indeed Just, Lord," 148

Horace (Horatius Flaccus, Quintus): Ars Poetica, 204

Hosea, 28

"Hour When We Meet Again, The": as possible satire, 22

House, Humphry, 97; on the variety of poetic styles in Coleridge, 6; on conversation poems, 84; on "Frost at Midnight," 92, 98; on "Kubla Khan," 114, 115, 116, 117, 120, 121; on "Dejection," 201, 204–05; quoted, 55, 87

Howes, Raymond F., See Armour, Richard W.

Hudibrastic verse: in Coleridge's satires, 190; in "Parliamentary Oscillators," 197

Hunt, Leigh: Imagination and Fancy, 141, 196; Examiner, 217; on Coleridge's versification, 217

Hunting Song: (in Zapolya) as song, 172

Hutchinson, Mary: in "Verse Epistle to Sara," 108; in "A Day-dream," 109, 110, 184, 187

Hutchinson, Sara: Coleridge's love for, 60, 137, 140, 159; things Coleridge associated her with, 108; in "A Day-dream," 109–12 passim, 184, 187; in "Verse Epistle to Sara," 205; in "The Day-dream," 114; in "The Pang More Sharp Than All," 146; in "Dejection," 184, 203–06 passim; mentioned, 102, 103, 107

"Hymn Before Sun-rise": as prophecy poem, 27–28, 45; its paean to nature, 28; culmination of Coleridge's artistry, 30; Hebraic, 38; analysis of theme and structure, 38–44; its use of personification, 41, 46–47; act of perception, 42; forced tone of, 44; shortcomings of, 45; structural unity of, 46, 47; sources of, 48, 214; theme of one life, 187, 188; mentioned, 30, 45, 69, 188

"Idoloclastes Satyrane" (pseud.), 154

Imagery, key: storm, 33–38, 46, 201, 204, 205–06; joy, 34–35, 38, 89, 91, 160, 165–66; rain, 34–35, 38, 142, 204; aeolian

harp, 34–35, 82–84, 90–92, 201–04; blossoming plant, 34–35, 142, 150, 216; wind, 34–36, 38, 82–84, 90–92, 100, 142, 204, 205–06, 215; bird, 35–36, 143; reptile, 35–38; light-dark, 39–40, 96; sun, 54, 62, 91; moon, 54, 62, 91, 92, 215; cloud, 91–92; silence-sound, 92–96, 188–89; warmth, 105, 111–112, 114, 126; body, 142, 143; baby, 150, 216
Imagination: Coleridge's description of, 5; defined, 96; creative, 104, theme of, in "Dejection," 201–06 *passim;* defined by Fogle, 202. *See also* Coleridge, Samuel Taylor
"Imitation of One of the Minnesingers of the Thirteenth Century," 159. *See also* "Blossoming of the Solitary Date-tree, The"
Improvisation voice, 153–68 *passim,* 183; naturalness of, 7; form of, 48, 155; poem listed, 153; content and tone of, 153–55; origins of, 155–58; psychological implications of, 158; poems of 1820's analyzed, 158–63; characteristics of, 160, 161, 163; verse analyzed, 163–64; shortcomings of, 164–66, 167–68, 195; compared to other poems, 167–68, 179, 184, 185; reminiscent, 185, 186; naked voice absent from, 190; Coleridge's achievement in, 194–95; poems with impromptu titles, 216
"Improvisatore, The": as improvisation poem, 153; diction of, 160, 217; analyzed as improvisation poem, 161–62; verse analyzed, 163; cant of, 165; naked voice of, 186; as interesting experiment, 196
Inquiring Spirit: Coleridge on his sense of guilt, 139; quoted, 115–116, 124, 189
"Inscription for a Fountain on a Heath": as love poem, 191
"Introduction to the Ballad of the Dark Ladié": failure of ventriloquism voice, 70. *See also* "Love"
Invocation, An (in *Remorse*): as song, 172, 195; analysis of theme and structure, 177–79; Wordsworth's opinion of, 181
Isaiah, 184
Isis: in "The Ancient Mariner," 54

Jacobin, 29
Jean Paul. *See* Richter, Johann Paul Friedrich.
Jeu d'esprit, 172

Jungian criticism: of "The Ancient Mariner," 54

Keats, John, 8; "Ode on a Grecian Urn," 32, 181; on Wordsworth, 33; stroll with Coleridge, 74; "Sleep and Poetry," 83; on Coleridge, 146; stanzaic structure of his odes, 179; his yearning for immutability, 179
"Keepsake, The": as love poem, 191
"Knight's Tomb, The": as song, 172; on transciency of life, 180
"Kubla Khan": Lowe's criticism of, 5; as dream poem, 102, 195; preface to, 113, 159, 160; analyzed as dream poem, 114–24; ideal world of, 128; praised by Swinburne, 171; music of, 172, 179; as miracle of art, 181; naked voice of, 185, 189; as reconciliation of spontaneous and formal, 191; unfinished, 195; critics on its completeness, 215; praised mildly by Leigh Hunt, 217; in college anthologies of Romanticism, 217; mentioned, 1, 6, 123

Laforgue, Jeuls: compared to the *Improvisatore,* 165
Lamb, Charles: in "To a Friend," 16–17; letter to Coleridge, 18; satirized in "To Simplicity," 18; on "The Ancient Mariner," 65; in "This Lime-tree Bower," 74; "Sanity of True Genius," 104; mentioned, 85, 86, 131
Lamb, Mary: first bout of insanity, 18
Landon, Letitia Elizabeth, 7; *The Improvisatore,* 155; *The Golden Violet,* 156
Landor, Walter Savage: Coleridge condemns his artistry, 193
Langbaum, Robert: on "Frost at Midnight," 92
Lawrence, David Herbert: *The Plumed Serpent,* 55
Leavis, Frank Raymond: criticism of "Hymn Before Sun-rise," 38–39
Lewis, C. Day: "A Carol," 20–21
Lewis, Matthew: "Sleep you, or wake you, Lady Bright" in *The Castle Spectre,* 50
"Limbo," 113
Lloyd, Charles, 67; in "To a Young Friend," 13–16, 17
"Lines Composed in a Concert-room": as farrago poem, 13; analysis of theme and

structure, 19–20; later printings of, 22; publication of, 24; date of composition of, 213

"Lines Composed While Climbing the Left Ascent of Brockley Coomb," 216

"Lines on a Friend Who Died of a Frenzy Fevery Induced by Calumnious Reports": Coleridge's self-confession, 136–37, 190

"Lines Suggested by the Last Words of Berengarius ob. Anno. Dom. 1088," 160; as improvisation poem, 153; Coleridge as Berengarius, 154–55; verse analyzed, 164; righteous tone of, 165; naked voice of, 186

"Lines to W. L.: While He Sang a Song to Purcell's Music," 216

"Lines Written at Shurton Bars," 11

"Lines Written in Commonplace Book of Miss Barbour, Daughter of the Minister of the U.S.A. to England," 157

"Lines Written in the Album at Albingerode, in the Hartz Forest," 156

Literary Remains, 22

Literary Souvenir, 143

Locke, John: sensational psychology of, 84

London Philosophical Society, 159

Lorraine, Claude. See Claude Lorraine.

"Love": as ventriloquism poem, 51; as Georgian ballad, 67, 68; compared to "The Ancient Mariner," 68–69; sentimental, 70; naked voice of, 184, 186

"Love, Hope, and Patience in Education": on love, 140; as occasional verse, 157; on revision of, 193–94

Lovejoy, Arthur Oncken: on "Dejection," 150

"Love's Apparition and Evanishment," 126; theme of, 128, 134, 140; as confession poem, 131; as dream poem, 102, 144, 147–48; psychological accuracy of, 149; impromptu composition of envoi, 158; imagery of, 216; formula diction of, 217; in college anthologies of Romanticism, 217, 218

"Love's Sanctuary," 60

Lowes, John Livingston, 115; influence on Coleridgean studies, 1; influence of The Road to Xanadu, 5–6; on "The Ancient Mariner," 52, 62

Lucas, Frank Laurence: on Coleridge's striving for unity, 194

Lyrical Ballads: as studies in psychological abnormality, 56; writing of the preface, 81; mentioned, 90, 99, 157, 183

"Madman and the Lethargist, The": as satire, 190

Manning, Thomas; Lamb's letter to, 65

Marsh, Florence: on "Dejection," 204

Mason, William: his political odes, 6; influence on Coleridge, 13

Massinger, Philip: influence on Coleridge, 74, 80

Matilda, Anna, 21–22

Merry, Robert, 21

Mickiewicz, Adam: Forefathers' Eve, 156; as improviser, 157

Milton, John: Coleridge's marginalia on Poems Upon Several Occasions (1791), 4; "Il Penseroso," 19; "On the Morning of Christ's Nativity," 20, 21; influence on Coleridge, 22, 51, 71, 74–76, 145; elegiac sentiments of, 23; Paradise Lost, 23, 75–76; influence on eighteenth-century poets, 69; style of, 98; on paradise, 116; his definition of poetry, 166; on puff of Coleridge's lectures on, 183; on melancholy song of nightingale, 203

Miscellaneous Criticism, Coleridge's: on need for poetic method and unity, 23, 193; on Cowper's verse, 74; on Massinger's verse, 80; on Pope's meter, 80; on the logic of verse, 176; praise of Defoe's artistry, 193; on rhyme, 215

Mock-heroic: in Coleridge's satires, 190; in "Parliamentary Oscillators," 197

Modigliani, Amedeo, 29

"Monody on the Death of Chatterton": comparison with "Hymn Before Sun-rise," 23, as prophecy poem, 27; on nature, 28; gaudy diction of, 51; quoted, 45, 102

Mont Blanc: see "Hymn Before Sun-rise"

Monthly Magazine, 81

Moore, Thomas: as society poet, 156, 164; Irish Melodies, 162; his exploration of metrical effects, 178

Morning Post: publication of "Lines Composed in a Concert-room" and "A Christmas Carol," 24; preface to "Hymn Before Sun-rise," 39; publication of 'Hymn Before Sun-rise," 40; mentioned, 137, 190, 198

Murray, John: Coleridge's letter to, 65

Naked voice, 71, 183–90 *passim*, in "The Ancient Mariner," 59; characteristics of, 183; conversational, 183–85, 192; naked voice of, 185–86, 192; theme of one life, 187–88; defined, 189–90

Napoleon Bonaparte: era of, 21, 192; in "Talleyrand to Lord Grenville," 198, 199

Nature, 28, 32, 33–43 *passim*, 46–48, 58, 85–89, 90, 92–96, 97, 112, 131, 133–34, 142, 166, 174–75, 176, 180–81, 186

New Times, London, 159, 160

"Nightingale, The": as conversation poem, 73; characteristics of, 74; blank verse of, 78–80; spontaneity of, 82; theme of one life, 87; analyzed, 89–90; imagery of, 91–92; depiction of nature in, 97; Cowperian influence on, 99; subtitle of, 157; naked voice of, 186; quoted, 123, 203

Notebooks, Coleridge's: on opium taking, 36; on variety in unity, 48; on Erasmus Darwin's poetry, 74; moonscape, 95; on dreams, 100, 103, 105, 112, 125–26, 127; on the unconscious, 103; on Sara Hutchinson, 103; on memory, 106; on free association of images, 106–107, 108, 112; on the poem as artifact, 107; on thought and reality, 127–28; redaction of "Herbstlied," 173–74; pillar of sunlight, 174, 208; quoted, 102; mentioned, 63, 101

Ode, 98; in manner of Gray/Mason, 6; prophetic nature of, 26, 30; passionate expression of, 27; "Dejection" as, 28, 184; definition of, 29; Georgian form of, 38; tradition of combined with new sensibility in Coleridge's poems, 192

"Ode on the Departing Year": dedicatory letter to, 26; as prophecy poem, 27; apocalyptic vision of, 28; compared to other poems, 30–31, 33, 123, 148; analysis of, 31–32; as impromptu composition, 156; preface to, 159; cumulative phrasal sentence structure of, 184; naked voice of, 185

"Ode to Georgiana, Duchess of Devonshire": as prophecy poem, 27; analysis of, 32

"Ode to the Rain, An": Coleridge's opinion of, 190; as improvisation, 216

"Ode to Tranquillity": as prophecy poem, 27; analysis of, 32–33; compared to "Dejection," 33

"Old Man's Sigh, The": incorporation with "Youth and Age," 143

"On a Ruined House in a Romantic Country": analysis of, 12; as interesting experiment, 196

One life, theme of, 47–48, 59–60, 73, 82–84, 85–88, 90–91, 96–97, 124, 131, 133–34, 179, 183, 187–89, 192

"On Revisiting the Seashore": as love poem, 191

Organic unity, 23; in prophecy voice, 30, 157; in "The Nightingale," 90; in conversation, dream, and improvisation voices, 179; of whole and parts, 193, 194

Osiris: in "The Ancient Mariner," 54

Osorio, 73, 183. *See also Remorse.*

Otway, Thomas: in "Dejection," 202

Ovid, 103

"Pains of Sleep, The": on nightmare, 126, 141, 148; as confession poem, 131; theme of, 134; analyzed, 135–36; ends with question, 136; its pathos, 165; imagery of, 216; quoted, 146

"Pang More Sharp Than All, The": as confession poem, 131; reference to Sara Hutchinson, 140; vagueness analyzed, 146–47; Coleridge as object of pity, 149; Coleridge on his failures, 153; imagery of, 216

Pantheism: in "Hymn Before Sun-rise," 41–42; in "The Eolian Harp," 96

"Parliamentary Oscillators": analyzed, 197–98

Pater, Walter: on sudden blossoming of Coleridge as poet, 172

Patmore, Coventry: on "Kubla Khan" as finished poem, 114

Pecksniff: Coleridge as, 153

Percy, Thomas, Bishop of Dromore: "The Hermit of Warkworth," 64

Petrarchan sonnet: in "France: An Ode," 32; in Glycine's song, 178

"Phantom or Fact": as dream poem, 102; psychological significance of its vision,

128; in college anthologies of Romanticism, 218

Piccolomini, The, 172; Coleridge's translation of, 209

"Picture, The": as farrago poem, 22, 144; lines quoted in preface to "Kubla Khan," 118–19; Coleridge's faith in recurrence of daydream, 120–21; as confession poem, 131; analysis of, 137–39; psychological realism of, 138–39; camouflaged self-revelation, 140; lack of focus in, 145–46; naked voice of, 185; imagery of, 216

Picturesque: Della Cruscan, 21; in "Christabel," 66

Pindar, 38; as poet-prophet, 27; translated by West, 30

"Pindar, Peter" (*pseud.*): influence on Coleridge, 13

Pindarick ode: prosopopoeia of, 28; lawlessness of, 29, 40; Coleridge in tradition of, 31; emotional versatility of, 32; "Kubla Khan" and "The Eolian Harp" in the visionary tradition of, 123

Pitt, William: in "Parliamentary Oscillators," 197

Platonism: in "Greek Ode on Astronomy," 31; light-dark symbolism, 40

Plotinus: reflected light, 91; quoted, 86

Poems (1797), 81; preface to, 51

Poetical Register, 97

Poetical Works, 143

Poetics, Augustan: on desire for sublimity, 29; on means and end, 46; Wordsworth's voice, 56

Poole, Thomas, 57; letter to, 100, 105

Pope, Alexander: Coleridge's rejection of, 13; meter of, 80; Horatian satires of, 164

Pound, Ezra: as poetic innovator, 20, 195

Praed, Winthrop Mackworth: *The Troubadour,* 155

Prior, Matthew, 167

Prophecy voice, 27–48 *passim;* in sublime tradition, 7, 51, 191; poems listed, 27–28; tone and theme of, 28; evolution of form of, 30–42; organic unity of, 30, 46–47; imagery of, 40; uncongeniality of for Coleridge, 45; structure of, 47; diction of, 69; naked voice of, 185–86; achievement of, 195; mentioned, 24, 73, 101, 123, 183

Psalms: "Hymn Before Sun-rise" in tradition of, 39

Psychology. *See* Associationist psychology

Pushkin, Alexander Sergeyevich: *The Egyptian Nights,* 156; as improviser, 157

Quickly, Mistress: discursiveness of, 13, 23, 74

Ransom, John Crowe: "The Equilibrists," 146

"Raven, The," 190

"Recantation Illustrated in the Story of the Mad Ox," 190

"Recollections of Love": as dream poem, 102, 195; analyzed, 112, 126–27; as poetic rendition of daydream, 121; confusion of fantasy and reality in, 121, 126; fusion of past and present in, 128; psychological realism of, 129; naked voice of, 184–85, 189; theme of one life, 187, 188; reconciliation of spontaneous and formal, 191; quoted, 189

Reconciliation of opposites, 94, 96; of nature and art, 8; in Coleridge's poems, 69, 116–17, 141–42, 143–44, 149–50, 180–81, 190, 191, 202–03; in Coleridge, 259–60

"Reflections on Having Left a Place of Retirement," 80; language of, 22, 51, 77, 98; as conversation voice, 73; address machinery of, 73; discursive, 74; blank verse of, 78; on subtitle and motto of, 81; spontaneity of, 82; theme of, 83, 87; return of thought in, 84; ambivalence of, 86; naked voice of, 186; quoted, 74–75, 95–96

"Religious Musings": as prophecy poem, 27; gaudy diction of, 51; as impromptu composition, 156; multiple voices of, 191; quoted, 116, 123, 191

Remorse, 172, 177. *See also Osorio.*

"Reproof and Reply, The": as improvisation poem, 153, 160–61; versification of, 164

Richter, Johann Paul Friedrich, 23

Robinson, Edwin Arlington: "Mr. Flood's Party," 133

Robinson, Henry Crabb: on Coleridge's subjectivity, 132; Coleridge's letter to, 183

Robinson, Mrs. Mary ("Perdita"), 21; "Ode to the Muse," 15–16; tender sensibility of, 192

Romanticism: reconciliation of opposites, 8; organicism, 46; fusion of subject and object, 47–48

Romantic poem: "Hymn Before Sun-rise," 42

Romantic poets: search for new poetic forms, 32; Wordsworth's voice, 56; ego of, 84–85, 136; European, 128; as dramatists, 155; impromptu powers of, 156; natural style of, 213; college anthologies of, 217

Rossetti, Dante Gabriel: on Coleridge as poet, 171

Rossiter, A. P.: sources of "Hymn Before Sun-rise," 214

deSallez, Francesco: definition of the beautiful, 194

"Sancti Dominici Pallium": as improvisation poem, 153; dramatic form of, 160; compared to Pope's verse, 164

Schelling, Friedrich Wilhelm Joseph von, 41

Schiller, Johann Christoph Friedrich von, 29

Schlegel, August Wilhelm von, 125

Schneider, Elisabeth: Coleridge, Opium, and Kubla Khan, 6; quoted on Collier, 115; on "Kubla Khan," 119; on Coleridge's definition of reverie, 125

Schubert, G. H.: Allgemeine Naturgeschichte, 115, 139

Scott, Sir Walter: Spenserian influence on, 61, 64; Coleridge on his poetry, 66; influenced by "Christabel," 171; metrics of, 178

Selden, John: Table Talk, 176

Sensibility: poetry of, 18; farrago voice in tradition of, 51; of Coleridge-Wordsworth coterie, 57; of Burneys and Gillmans, 61; Georgian, 64; in "Christabel," 66; in Georgian ballad, 67, 68–69. See also Farrago voice

"Separation": as love poem, 191

Shakespeare Criticism, Coleridge's: Coleridge's criticism of Shakespeare, 4, 29, 67; on organic unity, 23; on organic form, 46; on dramatic poetry, 67; on dreams, 115, 125–26; quotes Crabb Robinson, 132; on extemporaneity of Coleridge's Shakespeare lectures, 183; analysis of Hamlet, 186; on modifying power of the imagination, 209

Shakespeare, William: his sonnet form in "France: An Ode," 32; The Tempest, 164; Antony and Cleopatra, 164; Coleridge's lectures on, 183; mentioned, 171

Sheet of Sonnets, A: introduction to, 157

Shelley, Percy Bysshe, 171; "Mont Blanc," 38–39, 41, 43; "Julian and Maddalo," 180

Shuster, George: dislike of pathetic fallacy in "Hymn Before Sun-rise," 46–47

Sibylline Leaves, 19, 84, 159, 188

"Silver Thimble, The," 190

"Sir Patrick Spens": narrative starkness of, 61; compared to "Love," 67; in "Dejection," 184

"Snow-drop, The," 157, 190

Song voice, 171–81 passim; poems listed, 172; fusion of sound and sense in, 172, 173; metrics of, 178, 179; theme of, 179–81, 208, 209; achievement of, 195

Sonnet: Coleridge's use of in song voice, 178–79

"Sonnet on Receiving a Letter Informing Me of the Birth of a Son," 216

"Sonnets Attempted in the Manner of Contemporary Writers": Coleridge on himself, 11; as farrago poem, 13; foreshadows end of farrago voice, 23; satire of low diction, 99

Sotheby, William: Coleridge's letter to, 40, 81, 95, 194

Southey, Robert, 167; thin-skinned, 18; Annual Anthology, 24; translation of "Greek Ode on Astronomy," 30; poetic characteristics of, 67; Coleridge's letter to, 81, 105, 130, 136, 146, 192; Orpheus inspired, 156; pleased with his writing, 193

Spenser, Edmund: Coleridge's criticism of, 4; influence on the diction of Coleridge's poems, 12, 17, 147; The Faerie Queene, 61, 68, 115; influence on eighteenth-century poets, 67, 69; mentioned, 113, 192

Spontaneity: poetic problem for Coleridge, 1, 7, 11, 51, 71, 191; aim of Coleridge's poetry, 7, 23; of sublime poetry, 29; in the structure of "Hymn Before Sun-rise," 42; of ventriloquism poems, 51; of conversation voice, 74, 82; of dream voice, 112; of improvisation voice, 144, 155–56, 158, 162, 166; of Coleridge's poetry, 190, 191, 192; of "Parliamentary Oscillators,"

197; of "Talleyrand to Lord Grenville," 199

Statesman's Manual, The: on the imagination, 96

Sterling, John: on "Christabel," 217

Sterne, Laurence: *Sentimental Journey,* 192

Stokoe, Frank Woodyer: on Glycine's song and Tieck's "Herbstlied," 207–08

Stoll, Elmer Edward: on "The Ancient Mariner," 55

Stuart, Daniel, 193

Sublime poetry. *See* Prophecy voice

"Suicide's Argument, The": as improvisation poem, 217

Supernatural: in "The Ancient Mariner," 61, 63–64; in "Christabel," 64–65; Coleridge on *Faust,* 65; in ventriloquism poems, 70

Suther, Marshall: on Coleridge's loss of creativity, 141; on Coleridge's domestic difficulties, 144–45

Swinburne, Algernon Charles: praise of Coleridge, 171

Symons, Arthur: on Coleridge's poetic technique, 101; praise of Coleridge, 171

Table Talk, 22; on poetic unity, 31–32, 193; on the obtrusive moral of "The Ancient Mariner," 62–63; on Landor's lack of unity, 193; quoted, 150

"Talleyrand to Lord Grenville," 24; analyzed, 198–99

Taylor, Thomas: read by Coleridge, 55

Taylor, William: letter to about *Lenore,* 30

"Tell me, on what holy ground" (*The Fall of Robespierre*): as song, 172

Tennemann, Wilhelm Gottlieb: *Geschichte der Philosophie,* 113

Thella's song (*The Piccolomini*): as song, 172; theme of, 180; translation of, 209

Thelwall, John: criticism of Coleridge's poems, 15; letter to, 28, 29, 55, 80, 91, 146, 177

Theocritus, 137

"This Lime-tree Bower My Prison," 80; poetic maturity of, 24, 92; address machinery of, 73–74; as conversation poem, 73, 195; informality of, 77; blank verse of, 78; analysis of, 84–85; theme of one life, 87; depiction of nature, 87–88, 97–98; imagery of, 91; compared to "Frost

at Midnight," 93; naked voice of, 186, 189; reconcilliation of spontaneous and formal, 191; quoted, 76–77

Thomson, James: blank verse of, 73

"Three Graves, The": as ventriloquism poem, 51; psychological theme of, 55; supernatural devices of, 70; hallucinatory, 125; preface to, 159, 160; naked voice of, 184, 186

"Three Ravens, The," 57

Tieck, Ludwig: "Herbstlied," 173–76 *passim,* 207–09 *passim*

Tillyard, E. M. W.: on "The Ancient Mariner," 54

"To a Friend Who Had Declared His Intentions of Writing No More Poetry," 31; as farrago poem, 13; analysis of, 16–17; Lamb's permission to publish, 18; as interesting experiment, 195–96

"To Asra," 191

"To a Young Friend on His Proposing to Domesticate with the Author": diction of, 13–15, 51; comparison with "Dejection," 34, 35

"To a Young Lady with a Poem on the French Revolution," 190

Tobin, James: Coleridge's letter to, 191

"To Fortune Composed During a Walk to and from the Queen's Head, Gray's Inn Lane, Holborn, and Hornsky's & Co., Cornhill," 156

"To Mary Pridham," 157

"To Matilda Betham from a Stranger," 157; comparison with "Dejection," 34–35; quoted, 182

"Tombless Eptaph, A": as improvisation poem, 153; characterization of Coleridge, 154

Topographical: *See* descriptive-meditative

"To Simplicity," 18

"To the Author of Poems Published Anonymously at Bristol": as farrago poem, 22; on sublime poetry, 27, 29, 191; comparison with "Dejection," 34

"To the Rev. George Coleridge," 34

"To the Rev. W. J. Hort: While Teaching a Young Lady some Song-tunes on His Flute," 216

"To Two Sisters," 157; as confession poem, 131; theme of, 132, 134; imagery of, 216; formula diction of, 217; quoted, 142

"To William Wordsworth," 69; as conversation poem, 73; theme of one life, 87, 188; imagery of, 91, 216, as confession poem, 132–34; prayerful ending of, 136; on Coleridge's failures, 148, 153; naked voice of, 186; as impromptu, 216; quoted, 45, 135

Transcendentalism: not in songs, 179

Translations, German: Coleridge's lack creative energy, 172

"Two Founts: Stanzas Addressed to a Lady on Her Recovery with Unblemished Looks, from a Severe Attack of Pain, The," 157

"Two Round Spaces on the Tombstone, The," 190

Valery, Paul: on poetic convention, 160

Ventriloquism voice, 51–71 *passim;* in ballad tradition, 7; literary conventions of, 48, 53; poems listed, 51; derivation of term, 52; Spenserian influence on, 64; unfinished poems, 69–71; compared to conversation voice, 71; naked voice of, 185, 186; effect on Coleridge's poetic goals, 191–92; achievement of, 195; mentioned, 24, 73, 101, 183

"Verse Epistle to Sara," 107; as original of "Dejection," 28; analyzed, 108–09; as original of "A Day-dream," 109; as confession voice, 131; self-revelation of Coleridge, 140; on Coleridge's family life, 144–45; love theme of, 204–06

Victorian: viewpoint in Coleridge's poetry, 192

"Visionary Hope, The": as improvisation poem, 216; diction of, 217

"Wanderings of Cain, The": imagery of, 35; psychological theme of, 55–56; preface to, 58, 159; as impromptu composition, 156; publication of, 160

Warren, Robert Penn: on "The Ancient Mariner," 6, 54, 187

Wartons, Joseph and Thomas, 145; sentiment of, 22; use of abstract personification, 46

Wasserman, Earl R.: on Shelley's "Mont Blanc," 39

Watchman, The, 22; "On National Fasts," 184

Wedgewood, Thomas: Coleridge's letter to, 86, 190, 261

Wellek, René: on Coleridge's plagiarism, 207

West, Richard: translation of Pindar, 30

Whalley, George: on "The Ancient Mariner," 54; dating of "A Day-dream," 109–110; quoted, 140

Whately, Thomas: *Observations upon Modern Gardening,* 29

Winters, Yvor: on poetic pseudo-reference, 147

"Wish: Written in Jesus Wood, Feb. 10, 1792, A," 216

Wolcot, John. *See* "Pindar, Peter"

Woodring, Carl R.: Coleridge's political poems, 190

Wordsworth, Dorothy, 109, 153

Wordsworth, William: association with Coleridge, 24, 131, 153; on Taylor's translation of *Lenore,* 30; characteristics of his poetry, 33, 47, 55–56, 192; on poetic language, 45, 80–82, 195; imaginative power of, 47; influence on Coleridge, 47, 52, 69, 80–82, 145–46; Coleridge's letter to, 50, 52, 89–90; contribution to "The Ancient Mariner," 62; on "The Ancient Mariner," 65, 69; in "To William Wordsworth," 132, 133–34 *passim,* 186; Orpheus inspired, 156; ego compared to the *Improvisatore's,* 164–65; on Coleridge as a poet, 179, 181; compared to Coleridge, 187; Coleridge less a poet than, 191–92; harmonious household of, 205; mentioned, 7, 41, 58, 85, 99, 109, 206

—"The Brothers," 192; "Elegiac Stanzas," 124; "Goody Blake and Harry Gill," 56; "The Idiot Boy," 56; "Lucy Gray," 202; "The Mad Mother," 56; "Michael," 192

—"Ode on Intimations of Immortality," imagery of, 40; tone and diction of, 45

—"The Old Cumberland Beggar," 57; return of thought in, 84

—*The Prelude,* Simplon Pass Lines, 43–44; in "To William Wordsworth," 133–34; on Romantic ego in, 136–37; mentioned, 38–39, 46, 47, 188

—"Resolution and Independence," 47; *Salisbury Plain,* 80; "Ruth," 81; "There was a Boy," 88; "The Thorn," 56

—"Tintern Abbey," 194; imagery of, 40; compared to "The Ancient Mariner," 57; return of thought in, 84; on nature as moral teacher, 87

Wordsworths, Dorothy and William: addressed in "The Nightingale," 74; as dramatis personae of conversation poems, 155

"Work Without Hope," 148–49; as confession poem, 131; theme of, 134; imagery of, 216

"Written after a Walk before Supper," 216

"Written in a Blank Leaf of Faulkner's *Shipwreck*, Presented by a Friend to Miss K," 157

Yeats, William Butler: "Adam's Curse," 7; "Sailing to Byzantium," 116, 175

Young, Edward: Coleridge on criticism of, 4

"Youth and Age": imagery of, 36, 216; voices of, 38, 131, 144, 157–58, 185, 189, 195; theme of, 134; analysis of, 141–44; revisions of, 143; note of isolation, 144; artistic success of, 146, 193; reconciliation of opposites, 149–50, 191; theme of one life, 188

Zapolya: imagery of, 36–38; mentioned, 172, 173, 207

This manuscript was edited by Alexander Brede. The book was designed by S. R. Tenenbaum. The type face for the text is Linotype Granjon designed by George W. Jones in 1924 and based on a design originally executed by Claude Garamond in the sixteenth century. The display face is Century Schoolbook, the expanded version of Century cut by Linn B. Benton in the late nineteenth century.

The book is printed on Warren's Olde Style Antique White wove and bound in Schlosser Multicolor Endleaf and Holliston's Sharon cloth. Manufactured in the United States of America.